CHASING RUMOR
A Season Fly Fishing in Patagonia

A Season Fly Fishing in Patagonia

CHASING

patagonia® Ventura, California

RUMOR

CAMERON CHAMBERS

CHASING RUMOR A Season Fly Fishing in Patagonia

Patagonia publishes a select list of titles on wilderness, wildlife, and outdoor sports that inspire and restore a connection to the natural world.

Copyright 2015 Patagonia Works
Text © Cameron Chambers

Illustrations – Andrew Holder
Design – Haruna Madono
Editor – John Dutton
Production – Rafael Dunn and Jordan Damron
Publisher – Karla Olson

First Edition

ISBN 978-1-938340-40-6
E-Book ISBN 978-1-938340-41-3
Library of Congress Control Number 2015937490

One percent of the sales from this book go to the preservation and restoration of the natural environment.
Printed in Canada on 30% recycled paper

Contents

Introduction 6

1 A Place to Start 12

2 American Trout 36

3 Boca Fever 48

4 Richard Ameijeiras 58

5 Great Expectations 72

6 The Prophet 82

7 Río Malleo 94

8 Redemption on the Río Aluminé 108

9 Guides, Shuttles, and Good Fortune 116

10 Río Chimehuín 126

11 Río Chimehuín Part II 138

12 Streams, Rivers, and Conservation 152

13 Back to Chile 166

14 The Carretera Austral 178

15 The De Facto Lodge 192

16 No-Man's-Land 204

17 Patagonia River Guides 212

18 A Modern-Day Thoreau 226

19 Ten-Pound Trout 244

Epilogue 254

INTRODUCTION

If our lives are dominated by a search for happiness, then perhaps few activities reveal as much about the dynamics of the quest— in all its ardour and paradoxes—than our travels. They express however inarticulately, an understanding of what life might be about, outside the constraints of work and the struggle to survive.

Alain de Botton, *The Art of Travel*

T his is a book about Patagonia. Not just the fishing in Patagonia, for if it was that sort of book, far more might be accomplished with bright pictures. As it stands, this is a book about Patagonia experienced by an angler, but by no means limited to the recounting of fish yarns. Trout are newcomers to the Patagonian landscape and are as much a story in themselves of pioneers, nation building, ecosystems, industry, the goddess *Fortuna*, and more than any of these—personalities. Following these story lines, these pages are an exercise in experience and storytelling and, by way of necessity, rooted in rumor. And I can think of no better place for a story of a land and its fish to be rooted, because rumor is the medium of all good fish stories.

In keeping with this theme, this story of Patagonia does not begin on the arid steppe and a desolate Southern Hemisphere river, but in Montana, where, as the heart of my fly-fishing universe, rumors collect themselves, especially in winter. The story soon makes its way to a tent, a puke bucket, and a desolate river on the edge of Patagonia, but skipping the rumors that landed me there would degrade the story from that of a fish story to just a story.

And so I found myself at the beginning of an adventure by staring out the kitchen window at the brown grass and changing leaves of a Montana fall. That is as wonderful a time for a fly fisherman as one could hope for—except for the knowledge that the next big cold front from Canada could start the forces of winter at work piling snow and ice on the riverbanks. With the ice and snow come the numbness of frozen fingers, the frustration of frozen rod guides, and the bone-chilling cold of winter wading. These conditions are manageable, and even on the coldest days a person finds willing fish. But doable and optimal are not the same when speaking of winter fly fishing. It's for this reason that rumors find their way to Montana in the fall, where they are appreciated and nurtured by those uncomfortable with the knowledge of looming ice and snow.

The rumors we pay attention to this time of year split into two categories: New Zealand and Patagonia. New Zealand is said to have trout—big, smart, picky trout. As a utopian escape, a location with big, dumb, aggressive trout seems better. Patagonia is a region; its borders are not hard-and-fast political boundaries, rather rough outlines shaped by individual perception. Its variable boundaries are similar to the wide strip of land stretching from the Pacific Ocean to some amorphous inland line of the United States and Canada that we call the West Coast. Patagonia encompasses the southern third of Argentina and Chile, capturing the eastern and western watersheds of the tail of the great Andes mountain range. Like the West Coast, Patagonia encompasses an immense geographical area holding a variety of landscapes, cultures, lifestyles, and more rivers than a person can hope to fish in a lifetime. Rivers with big, dumb, aggressive trout.

And like Don Quixote I traveled around speaking Spanish
and engaging in a series of follies notable for the
experience much more than the results they produced.

These rivers provide the rumors, my favorite: that Patagonia is like a bygone Montana of seventy years ago. Having no firsthand knowledge of this ancient Montana, I'm left to my imagination and the works of fishing legends such as Joe Brooks and Norman Maclean to form impressions of this untrammeled and fish-laden landscape. Seasoned with a heavy dose of bias for my home waters, such images are grandiose at the least. Imposing the rumored past of Montana on a modern-day Patagonia might cause a conscientious man to take pause. Then, there are few conscientious men who stare out windows at brown grass and changing leaves thinking of ways to escape the snow and ice of winter fishing.

For dreamers like me there's concrete proof available to add credence to grandiose notions. Every November, fishing magazines plaster huge Patagonian browns on the cover. Fishing bums post videos of themselves on the Internet in the depths of an untouched Patagonia heaving bulbous browns out of tiny spring creeks. One might dream up the most fantastic world of trout fishing and have no trouble placing it back in the world of reality after an Internet search of Patagonian lodges. There are huge fish in Patagonia. Fish that North American anglers search for their entire lives. These fish are the reason for the rumors.

Staring out my kitchen window at brown grass and changing leaves, I latched on to the passing wisp of a rumor. A thing not so difficult as one might guess for a man in my shoes. The dark smoke of my summer fighting wildfires for the US Forest Service was but a light haze in the morning sky. Within a month the hard dew of morning would turn to ice and signify the end of fire season and the beginning of unemployment. In winters past I'd traveled, worn the white cross of the ski patroller, and otherwise tried my best to avoid a return to restaurant work. So with a meager sum in my bank account and the prospects of a furlough spent under the economic benefits of a strong exchange rate, the dreamer's part of my brain ran wild with rumor.

I conjured an image of Patagonia based on the best rivers and best fishing moments I could recall from my Montana past. I unconsciously omitted the countless times of winded-out frustration, high-water blowouts, or just slow fishing. When by omission or commission, the magazine writers did as well, I was left to assume, as any hapless angler might, that natural deficiencies were not a burden for the Patagonian angler to combat. In short, I settled Patagonia in my mind as a fishing utopia.

This is the story of my attempt to experience the utopia I created in my mind. I say "attempt" because quite often it fell short of expectations, and at times failed to even make the measuring stick. At other times the Montana highlight reel I used to create my utopia fell short in preparing my mind for Patagonia.

Yet, the ten-pound trout mark became a sort of Holy Grail providing a convenient excuse for the journey. And like Don Quixote I traveled around speaking Spanish and engaging in a series of follies notable for the experience much more than the results they produced. What I ended up chasing was the culture of fishing in Patagonia, a culture still being carved out by both the physical forces of nature and the socioeconomic forces of man. A culture in its infancy and obsessed in its own right with the ten-pound fish.

When asked, "How is the fishing in Patagonia?" these pages are the best answer I can give. Like fishing everywhere, it's a combination of the location, the season, the weather, a person's own skill, and luck. More than anything in Patagonia the fishing depends on the people involved. People like John Titcomb, who introduced the fish to the area at the turn of the nineteenth century; to the business professionals, turned guides, turned business professionals, who dictate where and when we fish; to ourselves and the myriad expectations we bring to each fishing trip, especially places with such mythical names as Patagonia. So, in the course of describing the fishing in Patagonia, the path takes a circuitous route through the lives of people via history and story, and only halfway finds its way back to a fish.

My fact-checking is shoddy when present at all. What I know, I found on the end of a rod, as well as through my eyes and ears. For this reason I assure you this story will remain where it belongs, in the world of rumor.

1
A PLACE TO START

---

*Therefore, bow your back
and fish when you can.*

Thomas McGuane, *The Longest Silence*

That this story begins at all is a function of three important factors. The first two, ice and rumor, played respective roles as whip and carrot. The third factor, and the one of most importance to a broke fishing bum, was the Chilean fisheries legal code, which is as lax a set of laws as a person is likely to find in a developed country. Anyone and everyone may throw a sign above their door announcing themselves a fishing guide, and with that limited effort, establish themselves with every qualification required of the guiding profession in that country. As a no-experience twenty-something desperate for nothing more than an escape from ice and the fulfillment of rumor, I arrived in Chile fully meeting the strict minimum requirements for a Chilean fishing guide: I was alive. And with that I started my new career as a fishing guide.

Though in the end there was a fourth factor: a man in a pink Speedo. At the time I entered Chile I was unaware of the Speedo and having saved a mention of it for the last is a good sign that

I've suppressed much of what needs suppressing. But the man in the pink Speedo deserves some responsibility for my ending up in Chile to take advantage of the lax legal code and ultimately for the Patagonian adventure as a whole.

The man was Chris Spelius. A whitewater kayaker and Olympian, Spelius found his way to Chile after a disappointing 1984 Olympics. As a consolation he flew his kayak to South America and began paddling his way southward along the slivered spine of the Andes. With nonexistent Spanish skills he managed his way around the mountain valleys, racking up a string of first descents on rivers unknown to the wider world of whitewater paddling.

Near the town of Puerto Montt in central Chile he caught a ride up a winding mountain valley with a huge blue river cut through black cliff walls. He followed the river through the mountains to the Argentine border and launched into the massive channel of chalky blue water. For miles he paddled downriver, encountering some of the world's toughest rapids. Halfway through the float the small tributary of the Río Azul entered the river, creating a thin spit of sandy beach. Having just paddled one of the most intense whitewater rivers of his life, he sat down to savor this accomplishment and decided he would build a lodge on the spot and call his operation Expediciones Chile.

Twenty-some years later Spelius is a fixture in the small hamlet of Futaleufú where his decision spawned the beginnings of a commercial whitewater industry. In addition to the Swiss Family Robinson–style lodge he built above the small spit of sand at the confluence of the Río Azul, he runs his company fifteen miles upstream in the town of Futaleufú from a hodgepodge collection of houses and a two-story *hosteria* where there's a hint of civilization and an Internet connection.

I ended up at the hosteria after three days of travel from Montana, across Argentina, and through a tight Andean pass into the narrow slot of land of the Futaleufú River valley. The journey takes a day and a half of plane travel to traverse the eastern seaboard of the United States, make a slow arc from Florida across the Gulf of Mexico to the broad Amazonian delta, then coast downward into the flat, dry pampas of Northern Argentina.

It's another half-day making the airport change in Buenos Aires on a minibus from the outskirts of the capital city with its soccer fields, polo grounds, and parks, through the coral pink and faded yellow of barrio apartment complexes to the domestic airport in the downtown heart of the city. Nearing Ministro Pistarini International Airport, the bronze statues and state buildings hint at the former prosperity of the country.

It's a short flight over the tall grass of the pampas from the inner-city hub westward to the mountains. The mountains are the Andes this time, but following their path on a globe it's not hard to track their rigid line north to the continental divide of the Rocky Mountains I see from my Montana kitchen window. And after an overnight stay in the mountain town of San Carlos de Bariloche, it's a full-day bus ride over mountain passes and up long, broad valleys to a spot low enough that a road can make it through the dark mass of mountains to Chile and the Pacific.

Three days from Montana, the loping diesel engine of the antiquated passenger bus deposits me at the concrete pillbox-looking structure that serves as the international border. I walk across, fill out the paperwork, receive the red-and-blue inked stamp of the Chilean government, and flop myself and my bags into the back of a pickup.

The road from the border follows the tight canyon cut by the Futaleufú River. On both sides dark gray cliffs rise into the low clouds of the ocean moisture trying to escape eastward. When the sun burns a hole through this humid blanket it reveals a jagged landscape of cliff and snow. The valley floor is a thick carpet of green interrupted only by the winding band of the river running milky brown with spring runoff. It flows for several miles before it and the canyon it has carved turn south and bend out of view leaving a stunning mountain vista in its place.

Cresting a small knoll I have my first look at the town of Futaleufú. It's a dot of a town laid out on a precise Roman grid. The south side butts against a corner of the river, the north side runs to the base of steep cliffs that climb into snow thousands of feet above. It's only four blocks from the river to the cliffs and about twice as many wide. The town starts at a lagoon on the eastern side and runs west till the hillside drops off into a steep ravine cut by the Río Espolón, a tributary of the Futaleufú. Farther west out on the horizon the valley opens up into the Espolón valley and the squared-off corners of fields and farmers' homes.

The main road provides a sufficient tour. It enters town along the barbed wire fence of the municipal airport, a grass strip just long enough to get a small single-engine plane on and off the ground. From there the road passes the lagoon and the soccer pitch before the little single-story houses painted in Easter pastels begin. Some are homes, others are posted with hand-lettered signs announcing themselves as a *panaderia*, mini-*mercado*, or whitewater river outfitter. At the corner of Avenida de Manuel Rodríguez and Avenida O'Higgins there are two buildings that differ from the rest only in that they are of concrete construction instead of wood. The first, a pink building with heavy bars on the window, is the bank, Banco Banelco. Kitty-corner to the bank is a whitewashed building with a plaque on the door: "*Policia.*" Both buildings look on to the *Centro Cívico*, a square-block city park with a few trees, some bronze busts of Chilean generals, and a Chilean flag flying in the middle of the park where the crisscrossing sidewalks meet.

Driving past the Centro Cívico is another row of houses that function as mercados, cafes, and a *gomeria* (mechanic). After another block the road bends south on its route through the mountains to the port town of Chaitén. From the bend in the road a person can look up the block to the brand-new school, a three-story, stained-wood structure that fills its own block. Closer to the corner are the Expediciones Chile offices and the hosteria where their guests board and relax after long days on the river.

It's at the foot of the hosteria that I have my first glimpse of the Montana of the 1940s. The bygone Montana may have been a Valhalla of trout, but it was also a place not yet brought to heel by the efforts of man. And here in Chile was a contemporary battle between the desires of man and the tractable but never-tamed forces of the wild. The town had a feeling of decrepitude about it that suggested Mother Nature played an active role taking back land from the advance of man. A collapsed roof

---

and a rusted-out truck were proof of her intent. Throughout town the abuse of a coastal mountain winter showed: black mildew stretched up the sides of buildings, potholes had filled with murky brown water on the dirt streets where horses outnumber cars, and wood fences and window trim were soft with rot.

This small Chilean hamlet tucked deep into the mountain valley is a far cry from the established tourist towns across the border in Argentina, with their immaculate lawns and intricate woodwork. This is a town thrown up to buffer the soul against the onslaught of a cold, wet climate. This is the way with frontier towns across the globe and across history. Like Montana towns of the past, this is a town on the edge of civilization.

I met the rest of the guides at the local soccer field where they gathered to watch the local kids battle on a muddy pitch. The other company guides were young like myself, and most, like me, down for their first season with the company. The group looked like the characteristic river crew. Lounged out on the wooden bleachers, they sported Chaco sandals, visors from prominent whitewater companies, and T-shirts with quirky, offbeat cultural references. They were disenchanted with the modern definition of success enough to disregard their college education and follow a break-even vagabond guiding lifestyle. They were highly competent to the degree that they'd managed good reputations as guides on dangerous rivers around the world and navigated Spelius's twelve-essay application process. They were everything a company owner looks for in a guide, laid-back and dialed-in.

The seven guides were a multinational crew. Mauricio grew up in Futaleufú on about the same time frame as the whitewater industry itself. More than once Spelius uses Mauricio as an example of the opportunities the tourism industry creates in the small town. The other returning guides are Sharon, a stout blond from Australia; and Ferguson, a tall, lanky Brit who runs the kayaking program. The new faces like myself are mostly Americans. Jason, Johnny, and Alex are all accomplished kayakers and boaters who'd spent the last several seasons chasing whitewater from Virginia to California following the spring rains and runoff to piece together a nearly year-long job out of singular river gigs that might last just a week or two. The other new addition is a tall Canadian named Bob, who's coming off a kayaking expedition in Asia.

Group dynamics for guides usually starts as a pissing match. Like dogs circling each other, they throw out whitewater resumes to establish the pecking order. Maybe because they've all spent enough time on big water, nobody emerges as king paddler. Instead, a collaborative dynamic starts to take hold ... most likely because the river itself scares the shit out of them. To a person, it's going to be the biggest, most dangerous river they've ever worked. The rapids are huge and dangerous singularly, but they are also one after another so tight that a mistake in one can mean there's not enough time for a rescue before the victim gets sucked into the next rapid. Swimming a Futaleufú rapid is almost certain death. In the case of a serious injury there's no hospital for hundreds of miles, no Life Flight, no trauma surgeon. If they're lucky, a coworker may be a lapsed Emergency Medical Technician and know the right way to do CPR until the victim dies from other injuries. This fear and respect for the river keeps relations cordial. They need each other—and they know it.

As a fishing guide I was an anomaly. We shared no common thread on the topic of fish so each conversation ended up as an evaluation of my ability to row a whitewater raft. With no harrowing stories about pulling clients from the jaws of a Class V death, they settled on me as a liability and moved on to more fertile conversations. They ultimately turned their attention to the Futaleufú, spinning themselves into such a fervor I've no doubt they all had difficulty sleeping that night with thoughts of wild river waves splashing through their agitated subconscious. I'd have played the same game in a gathering of fishing bums. Instead, alone, I lay in bed wondering when I'd find out about the new fishing program and how I'd fit into this whitewater company.

The next morning I borrowed a bike from the company and set out on the dirt road west of town with a hand-drawn map from Mauricio to find my first Patagonian trout. I rode out of town a mile and turned across a bridge where the canyon constricted the river into a cascade of waterfalls and rapids. The bridge marked the transition of the river from calm and flat to churning whitewater. Below this lay another set of rapids and then another in a continuous chain for the next thirty kilometers. The relentlessness of these big rapids gave the river its reputation and status as a whitewater destination.

I continued past the bridge, turning up a small dirt lane with a heavy wooden gate cracked open. I wound along a green hillside through rough pastureland until I came around a bend and saw the river below in a tight arch. I found a trail to the water through a maze of thick, thorn-covered underbrush and emerged on a narrow cobbled rock bank of the river.

According to the map, I'd arrived at one of the river's prime fishing locations—as indicated by an X and the words "good fishing" scrawled on my scrap-paper map. The scene didn't look like any of the "good fishing locations" I had seen before. The river was high and fast with a brown tint. Sticks and debris whizzed past. Behind me a thick wall of brush shot up thirty feet. A little farther upriver the vegetation gave way to a raw, thirty-foot cutbank that looked likely to crash another few tons of dirt into the river. Despite the tough conditions, the years of accumulated rumors and months of anticipation for my first Patagonian cast negated any doubt. I rigged up a huge yellow stimulator on six-pound tippet with every confidence I'd hook into a monster brown on my first cast.

My first cast in Patagonia was an awkward steeple cast that landed about fifteen feet out in the current and immediately found itself sucked downriver. No fish. Casts two through one hundred were similar in awkwardness and outcome. I varied the cast from steeple to sidearm and still found myself wading into the thicket of thorns to dislodge my fly and untangle the accumulated bird's nest of line at regular intervals. A few hours into the unproductive fishing it started to rain, so I packed up and rode the muddy trails back to Futaleufú, where I found myself less discouraged than dumbfounded. This was supposed to be the Montana of the 1940s. I'd never heard accounts of a fishless Montana of yore.

Back in town Spelius had just arrived from the States and planned a guides' meeting for the evening. We gathered in the four-room, whitewashed corner house that served as the company headquarters. Spelius stood in the small, cramped living room area and welcomed us to Chile and the company. At six feet, four inches and with the build of an Olympian he cut an imposing figure, yet it was hard to take him 100 percent seriously with his Frankenstein haircut, high-water blue jeans, and bright orange clogs. He spoke passionately for half an hour about the river and his stake in the whitewater adventure it provided. He labored the point of river safety and outlined the next few weeks of a training regime to bring the new guides up to speed before clients began arriving.

For the next month, fishing sat on the back burner. The company priority for everyone was getting the whitewater guides comfortable with the river and competent executing the myriad complex safety procedures that make the river a viable commercial pursuit. Instead of setting out across the Patagonian landscape in a company truck to find the next great fishing destination and dazzle clients with epic battles with oversized trout, I put on an old, foul-smelling wetsuit and helped load trailers with stacks of inflatable boats. I played the role of customer, adding weight and paddling muscle to the front of the huge eighteen-foot rafts while the whitewater guys learned the river.

>>>>

On the river I sit in the front of the boat, eddied out to scout the next huge rapid, my hands are clenched white-knuckled around my paddle and helmet strapped tight against my neck. I overhear conversations. "Do you see the surger past the big rock?" the trainer asks the new guide.

"Yep," says new guide.

"Okay, you have to make your move in the trough before that rock. If you don't you'll get pushed either into the rock or around it. Either way you'll lose the boat and you'll swim the rest of the rapid. If you lose the boat, you're fucked. It would be almost impossible for the rescue boater to get in there. You can't miss the move," says the training guide.

"Which trough are we talking about?" asks the new guide with less confidence in his voice.

"There ... ahead of the rock. You can just see it when that wave collapses," replies the trainer. They are both looking at a hundred-yard-wide river full of rock outcroppings and crashing wave fronts. To me it all looks like one violent white battlefield.

"I think I see it," says the new guide.

"You'll find it once you're out there," the trainer tells him.

So off we launched into a train of Class V rapids with the idea that we'd figure it out as we went along. Brilliant. I managed not to die. I credit this to the guides' excellent skills and aid from my paddling just exactly as if my life depended upon it.

>>>>

The temperature outside is in the fifties and most days a cold spring rain falls all day. By the end of the day everyone is exhausted from the stress and physical exertion of paddling big water, but more from the fight to stay warm. Some days I shiver uncontrollably at the takeout and have trouble moving my hands enough to undo the boat straps.

After long days on the river we find our way back to the guides' house next door to the whitewashed main office. The house is a ramshackle two-bedroom shanty abandoned and stripped by its previous tenants. Inside the rotting wooden main door the flowered wallpaper pulls from the walls yellowed and grimy. Round holes poke through the walls where kitchen and heating stoves once warmed the drafty space. The bathroom sits down a short hallway, its porcelain appliances, a white toilet and a pink bathtub, are black with mildew among the rubble of drywall and broken floor tile. Water flows through the pipes, coming straight from the mountains, so cold that our hands can only bear a quick splash for a wash.

Guides are shoehorned into every corner of space, avoiding only the spots where coffee cans are set out to catch the water leaking through the roof. There are no beds, just rolled-out inflatable pads with sleeping bags. We ball up fleece coats to use as pillows and snug the drawstrings of our sleeping bags down tight to ward off the cold that seeps through the loose construction and broken windows. Waking in the half-light of dawn the first look from the cinched-down face hole is the thick fog of breath escaping from the sleeping cocoons. I keep my perpetually damp clothes at the head of my sleeping mat and slip them into the bag, one piece at a time, using the struggle to dress in the confined space as a way to warm up before the shock of emerging. Without any heat in the house it's a challenge to convince myself to get out of the warm sleeping bag.

Each morning I rise to this same frigid routine to stumble through the wet or frozen dew across the back lawn to the waiting equipment. Most mornings the life jackets and wet suits we hung up to dry are frozen with a thin sheet of ice. The guides eat a hurried breakfast at the hosteria before cramming into the vehicles, loaded down with our icy gear, and heading west to meet the river.

Spelius spent most days in the back room of the office splitting time between his keyboard and nonstop phone calls. Midway through the whitewater training he joined the guides on the river. He paddled up to the group in an old orange kayak. His massive upper body and Olympic-grade technique pulled him through the water with stealthy grace. Most of the guides were kayakers themselves and stopped in unison to watch the legend of the sport glide his boat onto the grassy bank. On land he pulled the spray skirt off the kayak's deck and stepped out. Stepping from the kayak, the only thing covering his lower body was a tiny pink Speedo.

As he stood in front of the group with his paddle outstretched like a staff, he gave an assessment of our progress. He was the only one unaware of his outfit's comic value. Everyone struggled to keep a straight face. By the time he got back in his kayak and paddled downstream, no one quite remembered what he'd said. The image of those white legs and the skin-tight, barely-there swimsuit were all that any of us remembered.

In time I saw that the pink Speedo was just an outward expression of a man disconnected from those around him. He failed to register the consequences of his actions on either his employees or his own image. From undermining his own safety talk with a tiny Speedo to the working conditions and decrepit accommodations he devised, he was forever losing respect in the eyes of his employees.

Social awkwardness became a trademark for conversations with Spelius.

>>>>

"Hey, Chris. We're all freezing when we get back from the river. Can we get hot water at the guide house?" I ask.

"There's a shower in the house, right?" he says in a tone that suggests showers don't come without hot water.

"Yeah, it's covered in mold, but there's a shower," I answer.

"Did you try the water?" he asks.

"The pipe for the showerhead runs out the wall and ends. It doesn't go anywhere except the backyard," I say.

"So there's no water?" he asks.

"No. Maybe if it rained real hard some might drip in," I joke.

"So you have water?" he asks in earnest.

"That was a joke, Chris. The pipe is disconnected. As in, you could pull the showerhead off the wall because the piping is cut," I reply in earnest.

"If you pulled the head off the shower that's probably why it doesn't work," he says.

"We didn't pull the showerhead off," I respond.

"So what seems to be the problem?" he asks.

"Maybe you should just come take a look," I say.

The logical breakdowns in conversation didn't help my attempts to fish, either.

"Chris, I came down here to fish and help people fish. All I've done is sit in a whitewater boat and freeze," I tell him.

"Isn't it great? You're lucky to be getting so much time on the river," he replies.

"I haven't fished at all," I say.

"Didn't you float terminator rapid today? Wow, what a rapid! What did you think of the wave train? Incredible, right?" he asks.

He didn't understand a desire to do anything other than crash into whitewater waves. My waders sat dry and my wetsuit got damper and funkier smelling.

>>>>

I scavenged fishing time anywhere I could. The path westward out of town led me to the Río Espolón, a small tributary river that cut along the edge of town before veering south and meeting the much larger Futaleufú. The Espolón flows fast along the flat bottom of an offshoot valley. It's a short river, ten kilometers long that flows from a deep, beautifully blue mountain lake set amongst a ring of snowy Andean peaks like a gem in a silver crown. The water comes from the lake with the same blue tint, clean and cold. Even under the hottest sun the coldness of the river shocks the system like an ice bath. Structurally it contains the proper elements to make anglers drool. Unlike most Chilean rivers it takes its time to meander in places for meandering's sake and not at the whim of stalwart cliff faces. It's fast and slow, deep and shallow, and in such proportions as to appear designed for fish.

I convinced my tired body to pedal the dirt farm road up the valley after a long day of rafting to squeeze a few casts into the last remnants of sunlight. Town rumors took me upstream until I reached the whispers of a roar. I left the bike and picked a route along the cow trails toward the source of the sound. Coming through a thick cluster of brush to a steep embankment I saw the river boiling white, and across it the Garganta del Diablo, "the Devil's Tongue," a nearly two hundred-foot fall of whitewater violently escaping the confines of Lago Espolón. The power of the falls came in gusts of frigid mist. For a hundred yards below the falls, the river roiled in pockets of swirled air and water as the two sought to separate again into their respective mediums.

The lake above, the crashing falls, the calm spot below—
I suspected the eddy held the massive browns I'd read about:
huge carnivorous beasts that held in the easy water waiting
for the chum to float down after a violent death over the falls.

I backed off from the turmoil to the first bend where the river calmed itself in a huge back swirl of an eddy. I saw the coming-together of my fishing knowledge of Patagonia at this spot. The lake above, the crashing falls, the calm spot below— I suspected the eddy held the massive browns I'd read about: huge carnivorous beasts that held in the easy water waiting for the chum to float down after a violent death over the falls. I strung my rod with a heavy sinking line and a six-inch olive bunny leach with silver and red tied along the body to make it shimmer like a blood-spattered baitfish. I waded into the strong current feeling the power of the falls against my legs and lunged to an outstretched rock. I climbed atop this boulder and let loops of line spool off my reel into a pile at my feet.

After several false casts I let the line shoot through the guides across the river in a line along the submerged reef. The fly lit with a small splash. I inched the slack out of the line expecting the huge smash of brown. I waited as the line sank and pulled downriver in a slow arch. With a subtle tug-tug of the line I sent movement to the fly and a message to the fish, "I'm crippled, easy meal here." Near the end of the retrieve I got a small bump and set the hook. The fly peeled out of the water past my head and skimmed under the bankside foliage. Blew it, I thought, and prepared the line for another cast.

On the second cast the strike came quick. Two or three tugs and the fish mouthed the fly and turned to run. I felt the motion and struck with the rod tip to sink the hook. The fight began. The fish turned hard downstream to catch a stronger current and peeled line through the reel. I adjusted the drag tighter, slowing the run, and pushed the rod tip toward the shore to turn the fish's head out of the downstream run. It worked for an instant until the fish swung his tail around and pushed again into the heart of the current.

The river rushed swiftly by the sides of my casting rock. I knew I'd have to make it back to shore to land the fish. I slipped off the rock to find a foothold below the rushing water and then inched downstream. A few feet away a solid line of rock gave safe haven. Reaching the stones, the green fly line sagged across the river strung through a boulder patch. I walked downstream reeling line in. Inches at a time, I worked the line back onto the reel. Applying different angles to the line I pulled the fish one-by-one through the dark midstream rocks. Inches at a time my first Chilean brown trout came to hand.

The fish reminded me of browns taken from Ten Mile Creek near my Montana home: a dark mahogany back that tapered into golden sides and a silver-white belly, red spots with brown outlines dotted the sides. The roar and icy mist of the falls found me as I looked from the fish to my surroundings. The pastoral setting of rural Chile hit me with a glance to the west across crudely hewn fences, rough-edged fields, and a graying wooden oxcart alone on a hill at the base of the Andes. Magic in the scene hinted at possibility.

The feeling that draws an angler ever further upriver under the spell of anticipation swept over me. Kneeling in the Río Espolón, gently nursing water and its attendant oxygen across the gills of my first Chilean trout to revive it, I got the sense that the spell of anticipation in Patagonia is not a bend-by-bend magic, but a river-by-river, valley-by-valley magic. Maybe the same magic that Joe Brooks felt in Montana and later in Patagonia. The feeling that beyond the next mountain there might lie not just an unspoiled fishing hole, but a whole unspoiled rivershed.

I loosened my grip, letting the fish slide back into the cold current. After the hard-fought battle my thirteen-inch brown flicked its tail two quick times and passed its camouflaged skin back into the anonymous colors illuminated in the broken light of the riverbed.

>>>>

A month into training, the whitewater guides looked confident on the river. They had safe lines through the rapids memorized and worked the complex safety schemes without flaw. They were ready to start running clients with no whitewater experience down one of the world's most dangerous rivers.

Clients started arriving shortly after. I rose in the morning to help load the frozen equipment before heading to the hosteria to watch the giddy guides preparing their first clients. As they left for the river I waved good-bye to the full complement of company vehicles and boats. The plan to explore the area's rivers and lakes evaporated into the dust left behind the clamoring trailer.

I saw the clients again in the evenings after dinner at the hosteria. Our conversations were short.

"I didn't see you this afternoon. Are you a guide?" asks the client.

"I'm a fishing guide," I say.

"Oh, really, is there good fishing here?" they ask.

"Some of the best," I say, to convince myself as much as them.

"I had no idea," they say.

Clearly, I'd think.

They would return to their rafting guide to relive their heroic whitewater experiences, leaving me as a curiosity. I admit my stories of thirteen-inch brown trout didn't have the captivating power of the kayak guides' story of a first descent through the new Class VI rapid.

"What's class six?" I hear a middle-aged woman ask.

"It means you're almost certain to die if you fall out of your boat," replies the guide.

"Oh, goodness," says the client.

"And you're likely to fall out of your boat," the guide always adds.

>>>>

The first of the year passed without the company booking a fly-fishing trip. I had been in Chile over two months and had fished from company boats less than five times. One of the five was a disaster of trying to fish between whitewater sections on a guide-training trip. I'd assemble my rod at the tailout of one rapid and try to have it stowed again by the beginning of the next. After going through two Class IV rapids with my rod still together, the whitewater guide and I decided fishing constituted a safety risk. Spelius fed me rumors of multisport clients interested in a day of fly fishing and a large group on the verge of confirming a fishing-only trip in January. Mostly they were empty words, and without clients I dropped to dead last on the priority list, including the one for company resources. Whitewater trips owned the fleet of boats and monopolized the company's two vehicles to run shuttles all day between rapids. Some days I couldn't even snag a bicycle because the three company bikes were out on sightseeing tours of the upper valley. I practiced casting in the large park at the Centro Cívico using benches and statues of Chilean generals to mark my accuracy. The only interest I generated came from local children who were out walking with their mothers.

My utopian dreams faded under a severe attack of reality. I'd fished a limited number of days, meeting success at the briefest of intervals. The largest fish I recorded was eighteen inches, a snaky rainbow that came to hand with minimal protest. Besides the uncooperative nature of the local fish, the decrepit living conditions, and frequent rains, oppression laid over my life.

This Montana of the 1940s was a tough place to live. I couldn't help but imagine I was living in a parallel universe. Spread up a long, tight valley from a dreary remote port, the town of Futaleufú was an outpost of civilization. The fruits and vegetables at the local mercados came off the rumbling transport truck brown with age and mushy with abuse. The market shelves themselves were riddled with empty spaces as a sign of ever-shrinking variety. The paltry meals of thin soup and white bread buns from the hosteria burned off too quickly in the cold, damp atmosphere of Chile, and I wandered the aisles for supplement. I passed the counter of gray, room-temperature meat. Coca-Cola and Mirinda orange soda found spots in a small refrigerator while Tetra Pak milk and dozen-count eggs sat on a warm shelf.

I didn't even have a fishing license. I stopped by the tourist office on the muddy main street on a weekly basis. They were the only vendors of the fifteen-dollar season pass and hadn't received their allotment of carbon-copy licenses. It was now two months after the official opening of the fishing season. I asked the attendant if I could fish anyway.

"Sure. Why not?" she said.

"What if the game warden catches me without a license?" I asked.

She shrugged. "We have no licenses."

I suppose I shouldn't have expected more from a country that allowed me to become a guide simply because I could breathe. However, my fears were unfounded; Futaleufú didn't have a fish warden. I'm not sure Chile had a fish warden either.

A year later I was fishing south of Futaleufú and asked a local guide if I needed a license. His answer summed up the legal code of Chilean fishing: "Why?"

While depressing, the difficulties I experienced made a fine introduction to the international fishing scene. An hour from the river in your hometown, a nasty wind or murky water is an inconvenience and a drive home. In my grandiose vision of Chile I didn't take into account the inevitable facts of fishing: the weather sometimes sucks, the fish don't bite, and the place you thought was going to rock doesn't. I came to Chile during runoff conditions to a river with low fish counts.

Big fish did exist. I found proof on a wall. On one of the dirt-packed streets in town a local fisherman runs a fishing shop in his front room. He is an old man with weathered hands and thin, gray hair. He has two old fiberglass fly rods on the wall for show, but he's a spoon fisherman. Long chains of bright silver spoons and swivels hang off one wall, interspersed with red roe-colored beads. His rods are in the corner, stout poles with big spinning reels and thick line. There are only a few items for sale: a spool of fifteen-pound test, a few boxed-up lures. More than anything, the room is a tribute to his fish.

On the north wall, among a few faded pictures, was the largest trout I've ever seen. It's a gruesome stuffed brown trout with flecks of skin peeling off in places and gums receded to show a row of grisly teeth. It's a grim specimen of taxidermy, but you can't take your eyes off it. The size is unimaginable.

Ten-pound trout are looked on as an achievement of a lifetime in Montana; I wondered if this fish could eat a ten-pound trout in one bite or two. A bronze tag on the wooden backdrop read eighteen and a half kilos (forty-one pounds). It was the third-largest fish ever taken in Chile.

On the rare days I'd have fishing clients, I tried to find one of these leviathans. Most of the clients were novice fishers simply looking for a way to escape the icy water and adrenaline overload of another day of whitewater rafting. Dredging the bottom of long, deep runs with two-handed Spey rods that threw heavy ultraweighted lines was the best way to connect to a huge brown, but most of the clients were limited by skill to light dry flies on five-weight floating lines.

The go-to fly-fishing section, known as El Límite, started at the Argentine border and ran till a twenty-foot waterfall marked the beginning of the whitewater. The other fishing operations in the valley all fished the same stretch, stacking up pressure on the short section. Everyone focused on a handful of big eddies where fish hovered close to the surface and took dry flies indiscriminate of the pattern or the quality of presentation. Within a few weeks clients caught fish with hook sores, maligned mandibles, or still adorned with last week's Royal Wulff. Even in a remote valley of Chile, the fish showed signs of fishing pressure.

After only a handful of trips down the El Límite section, the float began to feel routine. This is a common curse of guides everywhere who spend day after day pounding the same waters gaining an intimate knowledge of its flows and its fish. While it takes some of the chance out of catching fish, a good thing for business, it also takes the mystery out of the river, a bad thing for interest. Between this sense of monotony and a growing guilt about targeting the same pods of fish, it was easy for me to daydream about anywhere else.

The main ingredient of these dreams came from thousands of miles of river rumors that found their way to my ears. Backpacking tourists would stop by the office to book rafting trips, and the rod tubes hanging off their backpacks started conversations about fish scattered in waterways in every direction.

Guides from other lodges told animated stories about their secret lakes where twenty-eight-inch fish leapt clean out of the water to take flies in midair. I heard of a small spring creek where thirty-inch browns sipped beetle patterns in a foot of water. Every week my eyes grew wider at these rumors of back-road fisheries and new adventures.

In the evenings I walked across town to Martín Pescador, the Kingfisher, a restaurant-bar and the only place in town to establish an atmosphere that separated itself from the weathered gloom that hung in the valley. The warm lights bouncing off the light rough-hewn *coihue* lumber pulled from the hills above town gave the space a welcome feeling. Fishing décor spread sparsely around the dining area added to my sense of security. The other fishing guides in the area must have felt the same because it's here that we'd bump into each other. We distinguished ourselves as such by our button-up, long-sleeved fishing shirts embroidered with Sage, Simms, or Orvis logos.

Our relationships developed on a slow track inhibited by envisioned boundaries of competition. Then, after months, commiseration outweighed the false notions of competing interests. Chile has no walk-in fishing business to compete for anyway. No one travels around the world to a tiny slot of land in the heart of the Andes in search of a fishing guide. They come with a booking or they don't come at all. So without the worry that we were divulging too much information to the enemy, we drank local beer with a German name and realized we all had the same issues. Namely, fishing in the valley didn't fulfill our utopian dreams.

In conversations with the other guides, I began to give up the idea the area held unlimited numbers of large fish. Some were out there; we all knew about the fish on the wall. But, in speaking with others who pounded the water with regularity, these fish didn't exist with the frequency we envisioned. Alone, I held the suspicion of my ineptitude. Alone, you always convince yourself it's your fault. In company, we were better able to see what we as experienced anglers knew all along.

At a long, skinny bar table ten inches thick made from the trunk of a single tree, I sat with two older guides from Idaho and discussed how different the Futa was from our home fisheries. In the corner of the bar an older guide with thinning gray hair from Superior, Montana, picked flamenco guitar riffs with inch-long fingernails. We were a valley of Americans, collected from our continent's finest fishing waters and disenchanted with the differences we found in our new home.

Between the snappy, energetic melodies, we surmised that the largest fish in the area were likely sea-run fish that came up the river to spawn. A forty-one-pound fish does not grow to that size in a Chilean whitewater river with gradient too steep to support aquatic vegetation. But, maybe we needed an excuse to cover for our lack of success.

As fisherman our conversations never bogged down on frustrations for too long before we bolstered our spirits with rumor. We came to Chile based on rumor, and we relied on rumor to keep us going. Inevitably someone had heard of a huge fish taken here or there, and the conversation turned toward towns and rivers we knew little about to prevent fact from interfering with our dreams.

I savored these piscatorial rumors, cherishing each bit of information I could glean from them. When I arrived home at night I would open my little brown-leather journal to scribble out the grains of knowledge. The tan pages filled with Spanish names like Lago Verde, Río Rivadavia, and Lago Misterioso. The names meant possibility to me. I collected roughshod directions from nowhere towns, over roads with no names, to nowhere fisheries with hidden fish. My journal turned into a coded and confusing jumble of hand-drawn maps—treasure maps with red Xs and little else.

At night I'd lie in my sleeping bag and read over the notes by headlamp. I revered the stories I'd heard and weaved their words into intricate images of places and fish. I pictured myself stalking the quiet banks of a slow spring creek dropping beetle patterns to huge fish. As I drifted off to sleep I cast flies across the brown grass of the steppe. My fly drifted on the smooth water for a few seconds before an eruption at the surface and the whine of line running off the reel.

My journal turned into a coded and confusing jumble of hand-drawn maps—treasure maps with red Xs and little else.

Out across the Argentine border and south into the flatter country of Chile were rivers with fish. Because they were rumors, the fish were large and did not bear the marks of several parties' worth of anglers. I knew I needed to see these places for myself, to travel these dusty, no-name roads with no other responsibility than to find the trout of my dreams.

By February the stream of clients began to taper off. Four or five groups a week reduced to two, and in the not-too-distant future, to one. After running hard for the past month and a half, the guides all battled fatigue. Red eyes met the sun every morning glazed over from late nights entertaining at the hosteria bar and early mornings prepping for the day's trip. Tension was high in the small crew, who worked every day under dangerous conditions and tight time frames. One of the favorites among the guides had already been fired after a prolonged confrontation with Spelius over his low pay. Everyone had the same gripe and varying degrees of the same argument with our employer at some time during the season.

After four months with Expediciones Chile I decided to call it quits. The poor living conditions, low pay, and thin diet made the decision to leave easier. But the catalyst was the idea that the longer I stayed in Futaleufú, the longer it would be until I caught my dream fish.

I walked into Spelius's office on a sunny afternoon, told him I was leaving, and thanked him for the opportunity to guide in Chile. It was far from our first conversation about my concerns working for him; my announcement didn't seem to surprise him. We shook hands and I walked out the back door of the office toward the guide house. In the morning I was on the white shuttle bus to the border, en route to Argentina—and possibility.

I stayed in Argentina for the next six weeks, living with several other Expediciones Chile guides who had either quit or been fired around the same time as myself. Without a car or boat my fishing remained limited. Guiding was not an option. Argentine guides had, several years earlier, gained the political clout to ban foreigners from guiding in the country. So instead of fishing,

I took Spanish lessons at a local school and bought a book about the best fishing locations in Northern Patagonia. The list of places in my journal kept growing, and I knew that quenching the rumor mill in my brain would require a 4x4, a whitewater boat, and a full Patagonian fishing season.

The time I spent working for Expediciones Chile set me on a course to chase rumor in Patagonia. It grounded my lofty expectations of international fishing while inflating my sense of possibility. Leaving Chile, I couldn't have imagined how much more I had to learn or how far I had to go before my dreams of Patagonian trout would come to fruition. If they would have come easy then, fishing Patagonia would never have become half the adventure it did. I can say now that I'm grateful for my time in Chile; without it I may have never had the experience of a season fly-fishing Patagonia.

2
AMERICAN TROUT

---

*My Elysian Fields lie in Argentina,
where a seemingly endless succession
of clear rivers flow cold from the Andes
eastward into the steppes, each with
a unique set of characteristics,
each sustaining superb populations
of enthusiastic trout ...*

William Leitch, *Argentine Trout Fishing*

The rain came in sheets that pushed the orange nylon walls of the tent in on the condensed space. In and out the thin walls reverberated between the pounding of rain and blasts of cold air. I looked out the small opening in my zipped sleeping bag through the orange half-light at the erratic movement. Then, eyes closed, my ears took me beyond the wild orange confines. Past the rustling flaps of tent material I heard the low roar of the trees standing their ground against the assault. As another gust lashed a sheet of rain into the tent, the noise flared with violence as the world braced. Then, as the gust raged past, came a calm pause and the soft lapping sound of the river.

For three days the storm crashed down in waves on the nylon walls. Inside the tent I lay zipped against the cold. Stuffed into the down bag, I shivered in a fetal ball sweating until my clothes dripped. Like the storm outside, my stomach churned in turmoil. Painful cramps shot through my core in waves of agony. Then, like the many climaxes of rain battering the tent, I vomited. I vomited nothing. A thick sludge of bile was all that remained. Whatever disease plagued my intestines refused to subside. I had no tears to cry, and no one to cry them to.

The lapping of the Río Ñorquincó reminded me of my desolation. I was camped along the small tributary of the Río Aluminé that fingered northwest across the steppe rising to its headwaters at the lake along the Chilean border. The clinic at Junín de los Andes was a full day's drive south across rough roads. I used my remaining energy to climb out of the nylon flap and stumble a few steps from the tent to explode diarrhea. Now soaked through from the rain as well as sweat, I climbed back into the sleeping bag without a thought of the maroon SUV parked next to the tent or the possibility of driving south.

When my energy levels permitted I flipped open my bible, *Argentine Trout Fishing*. A paperback fishing guide I had picked up after I returned stateside from Chile. Written by the Montana State University professor and self-proclaimed Patagonia junkie Bill Leitch, I read it the first time as if I'd found the Holy Grail, the key to Patagonian trout. The author detailed the major Northern Patagonia river systems with information invaluable to the neophyte wanderer. The information convinced me to make a second attempt at fishing the Southern Hemisphere.

Laying weak with illness in the tent, I flipped open the front cover to reread the end of Leitch's introduction, "We need the knowledge that somewhere far off lies that perfect river with perfect fish that we will deceive some perfect summer evening with our perfect cast and our perfect fly. It's down there alright. Somewhere in Argentina."

As another gust lashed a sheet of rain into the tent,
the noise flared with violence as the world braced.

I reread the last line, "Somewhere in Argentina," and stopped. I'd returned to Patagonia because of words like this from a Bozeman man, a man familiar with Montana fishing, a man who traveled to Patagonia because he didn't believe his perfect moment would happen on the great rivers out his back door, but thousands of miles away in Patagonia.

After reading the words again I looked at the copyright date: 1991. Leitch fished Patagonia twenty years before I pitched my tent on this tributary listed in his Northern Patagonia rivers section. I'd already found glaring factual discrepancies in the book; recommended hotels did not exist, regulations altered, public access turned private. These are inevitable changes with time, but perhaps they reflected a greater underlying change— a change in the fisheries themselves. Where Leitch recounted afternoons of multi-pound fish, I landed infrequent minnows.

It's impossible for a new visitor to a changing landscape to know how much current fishing is a function of transient conditions or long-term trends. Spring runoff played a negative role, as did my inexperience on each new waterway. How much other unseen factors influenced the catch I could only guess. In twenty years since Leitch's writing, how much had fishing pressure increased? In my Montana home I've seen the depressing speed with which a river succumbs to heightened pressure. Then, there are the environmental concerns of water quality and habitat protection. A few days' snapshot of a fishery reveals little about its long-term health.

I found it easy to convince myself of the worst. Illness aside, in my first month in Patagonia I encountered continuous challenges. The SUV and cataraft I shipped from the States met a two-week delay. An uncharacteristically wet spring created flood conditions throughout Northern Patagonia. The two friends who accompanied me on the first leg of the journey returned home. Fish refused to rise. Like my experience in Chile, the fish were all I had—and it's hard to be fulfilled by six-inch-long fish. I felt defeated by the endless landscape of brown ringed by distant, white-capped mountains. The vast networks of rivers were an enigma with no key, no code, no legend. My secret weapon,

Argentine Trout Fishing, did little more than lead me further than prudent from civilization. Had I come too late for the heyday of Patagonian fishing?

A month prior I'd walked down the C-concourse of the Sea-Tac Airport in Washington state to board my international flight. I stepped on each of the bronze inlaid trout that led to my boarding gate. I settled into my window seat with my copy of *Argentine Trout Fishing* and good omens from the inlaid school of bronze trout. A year of planning and stress fell away as the plane gained altitude. Somewhere below on the high seas of the Atlantic a twenty-foot cargo container holding my Nissan Pathfinder and fishing cataraft should have been nearing the port of Buenos Aires.

I planned my arrival in Argentina the first week of November to coincide with the opening of the freshwater fishing season. I was to meet the container at the shipping yards on the Buenos Aires waterfront, pass through customs, and drive like mad through the hours of flat pampas grassland until I saw the tips of the Andes start to poke out into the vibrant blue Patagonian sky. Once in the land of rivers and fish I'd start in the north, working the smaller tributaries—the Ñorquincó, and others that suffered less from spring runoff. With my own car and boat I pictured Patagonia as a playground of freedom. No more worrying about whether or not the company bicycle was available or pleading for raft time.

As the weather warmed into summer, water levels would fall and I would fish the major rivers of the north. Rivers named Malleo, Chimehuín, Aluminé, and Limay, places renown for big fish. I also knew that south of these famous rivers lay a land less scoured by fishermen. In the southern province of Chubut, towns of no consequence dot an otherwise bleak landscape. A place where wind and water carve red stones into crazy shapes, and beneath nature's sculptures lie clear waters with unsought fish. To the west toward the Chilean *frontera*, where green owns the landscape and water rests in productive pothole lakes. Out there I knew I'd find my perfect fish.

That was a month ago, riding the high of new adventure and the euphoria of hope. That was before the rain, and the puke bucket, and the thirteen-inch rainbow that took home best fish honors three days ago. Now I lie in a sweat-soaked sleeping bag and contemplate abandoning the trip.

I turned back to Leitch's book and flipped through the introduction, pages on culture, geography, and history. They were never read, pages I considered filler before the descriptions of rivers, fish, and flies that I devoured as the sole value of the book. What did I care about the range of the native guanaco? But as I flipped through the pages and scanned the pictures I stopped at the boldface heading, "How the fish got there," and read.

Trout themselves are only a recent transplant to the Patagonian landscape. Where we now associate trout with worldwide inhabitance, their origins have a limited scope. Brown trout developed from the primordial sludge in the mountains of an ancient Europe, rainbows in the cascading waters of the Western United States, and brookies in the streams of the East.

Today's environmental consciousness, backed by hundreds of years of trial and error and a few decades of science, warns us about the dangers of non-native species. At this point in our environmental awareness, even the U.S. State Department documents the dangers of introduced rainbow trout: hybridization, native species predation, and habitat displacement, to name a few. These realizations are only part of the recent conversation.

Standard thinking throughout the colonization period of Western history was to propagate the plants and animals considered useful to the far corners of the world. These can range from Lombardy Poplars, a tree planted on farms and ranches worldwide as wind blocks, to Scotch broom, a flowering shrub used as an ornamental garden plant that has spread across the landscape in Argentina, Chile, and dozens of other countries, choking out important native species. While we are now hyperaware of the dangers of these introduced species, the explorers and settlers who introduced them were looking for little more than a way to make life on the frontier of civilization more bearable or familiar.

The cultivation of fish began in the mid-1700s in France. By the 1800s simple ice boxes allowed the transportation of fish eggs across large distances leading to an explosion of aquaculture, as species like trout were regarded as both a foodstuff and a source of recreation. The ever-expanding travel networks of the colonization period, coupled with the technological innovation of the Industrial Revolution, made the transport of species across the globe a reality. Introduced trout were finding their way to Australia, New Zealand, and Tasmania, as early as the 1860s.

That trout found their way to the distant waterways of Argentina in particular remains a miracle. But for a bleep of prosperity at the beginning of the twentieth century and the lush grass of the Argentine pampas, trout may never have made it.

During the late 1800s Argentina experienced an immigration boom similar to that of the United States. Attracted by cheap land and the prospects of a new start, droves of immigrants from Italy, Spain, and Germany set up new homes in Argentina. They brought an energy and will that transformed the Argentine landscape to one of agrarian prosperity. The country led the world in corn exportation and held major shares of the wool, beef, and wheat markets. A subway system traversed the capital city of Buenos Aires, and railroad lines shot out in webs across the country. The burgeoning economy funded public works, infrastructure improvements, cultural undertakings, and recreational enterprises. In Buenos Aires, where two-thirds of the residents were immigrants, they sought to transform the new country into a modern civilization comparable to their Old World homes.

At the peak of the boom, former Argentine Minister of Agriculture and then Ambassador to the United States, Martín García Mérou, negotiated a contract to bring one of the United States' leading fisheries biologists, John W. Titcomb, to Argentina. After expeditions by French and Italian biologists found Argentina an unsuitable location for exotic fish species, Mérou sent Titcomb on a traverse of Northern Patagonia to study for himself the opportunities to increase populations of native fish or introduce exotic species of commercial value.

Titcomb recorded his trials in letters home that are now lost, but enough information remains to appreciate the difficulty of his undertaking. The Patagonia that Titcomb traveled was a remote and wild country with a history of violence.

Only thirty years before Titcomb, Argentine explorer Francisco Moreno traveled the same landscape seeing it for the first time through Western eyes. Moreno's expedition took him through a land inhabited by Argentina's indigenous tribes. Moreno expected hostility due to the area's history of violence against intruders. In Northern Patagonia, he found validation for his fears after falling prisoner to a hostile band of Tehuelche natives. The tribe sentenced the intruder to death and Moreno only managed to escape the day before his scheduled execution.

Moreno escaped to Buenos Aires where his expedition reports triggered a full-scale war against the native populations of Argentina. Known as the Campaña del Desierto, the Conquest of the Desert, Argentine army units employed similar tactics used during the American Indian wars. In an attempt to exterminate native populations, army units attacked villages across the frontier. The native populations, overpowered by cavalry and modern weaponry, fell in bloody, devastating massacres. By 1884 the last of the native populations of Patagonia were defeated along the banks of the Río Limay east of Bariloche.

The brutal Conquest of the Desert occurred less than two decades before Titcomb arrived. And while the Argentine government had long since quashed any native resistance, the new government had yet to subdue Mother Nature. Taking a train from Buenos Aires, Titcomb arrived on the barren steppe in the Neuquén province. It was the summer of 1903 and Titcomb planned to study the headwaters of the Limay River on the shores of Lake Nahuel Huapí. From the train station the lake was a 300-mile journey of rough trails. Today a paved highway stretches the length of his route right into the heart of Bariloche's bustling metropolis. The journey by bus takes just over four hours. Titcomb's journey by wagon took him over ill-defined wagon ruts and the open terrain of Patagonia. Nineteen days after leaving

Neuquén he arrived at the Limay. The area was little more than a frontier outpost of distant ranches surrounded by wilderness.

Titcomb spent two and a half months studying the myriad lakes, rivers, and streams around present-day Bariloche. The native fish populations he found consisted of a perch sub-species with the size and behavior of a trout known as a perca and a small baitfish called a pejerrey. Despite what Titcomb considered optimal conditions for fish—clean, clear, cold water—he noted native fish populations well below expectations.

Based on the small populations of native fish he sampled and appropriate environmental conditions for North America's freshwater fish, Titcomb decided to introduce foreign species to the ecosystem. In today's terms, the decision constitutes an environmental catastrophe. In the historical context, the deci-sion was an opportunity to increase the viability of human life in a barren frontier land. The debate over the existence of trout in Patagonia has emerged only in recent years, and even in the current environmental climate the legitimacy of Patagonian trout remains ambiguous. Titcomb, one of the world's leading fisher-ies biologists of his time, considered the introduction of trout to Patagonia as nothing other than a valuable addition to the eco-system and set to his task unassailed by doubt.

The introduction required construction of the nation's first fish hatchery. He chose a small creek with icy flows not far from the current city center of Bariloche. The first hatchery was noth-ing more than a rudimentary building with holding pools built to receive a shipment of fish eggs from the United States.

For all Titcomb's work, his attempts to introduce trout to Argentina may have never succeeded but for the lush grass of the pampas in the distant east. Too far from the rivers of Patagonia to have any effect on trout themselves, the thigh-high grass of the pampas did little more than blow in quiet green waves and feed cattle. Fortunately for the trout, cattle constituted a major export to the European market. Butchered cattle required spe-cial refrigerated shipping containers to make the trans-Atlantic voyage from Buenos Aires to South Hampton, England. These refrigerated containers provided a crucial link to keep fish eggs cool during their long transport from hatcheries in the United States, through England, and then to Argentina.

Eugenio A. Tulian, chief of the section of fish culture, the government bureau that would oversee the fish hatchery program for Argentina, accompanied the first shipment from the United States. Many of the details of the journey survive in his report to the fourth international fishery congress. The first shipment of eggs left New York on January 19, 1904. From New York to England the eggs sat on ice to maintain a constant temperature of four degrees Celsius. The ice only allowed Tulian the time to cross the Atlantic to South Hampton and secure the eggs in a refrigerated beef container heading empty to Argentina. Without the refrigerated containers to support the Argentine beef trade, ice and eggs would never have survived the long journey from New York to Buenos Aires.

The initial shipment arrived in Buenos Aires more than a month after leaving New York. Like Titcomb, the eggs boarded a train and headed across the pampas to the barren steppes of Patagonia. They too made the last portion of the journey over a rough dirt trail. Packed again in ice, an astonishing 90 percent of the eggs survived the journey and arrived at the Nahuel Huapíhatchery on March 4. Eggs included in the shipment were 1 million whitefish, 103,000 brook trout, 53,000 lake trout, and 50,000 salmon. A few months later the first shipment of rainbow trout eggs arrived.

Over the next few years more eggs arrived in Argentina. Other hatcheries were set up, and fish were distributed into a hodgepodge of waterways where they were left to their own reproductive devices. At times oxcarts broke down or ice melted too quickly. To save the eggs, they were dumped in the nearest waterway and left largely unrecorded. The stocking operations thrived for several years. Some species, such as whitefish, didn't adapt to their new surroundings and perished. Others adapted to their new homes and began natural reproductive cycles.

Why one species managed to make it and another didn't, no one had time to research. In a Darwinian stroke the fish survived or perished of their own accord. Atlantic salmon, while widely introduced, managed to create self-sustaining popula-tions in just a handful of waterways. Trout found the greatest success in their new environment. First rainbows and brookies, then finally brown trout, colonized river after river. With trout's ability to occupy the ecosystem, most Patagonia waterways support self-sustaining populations of the fish.

In 1907 a sharp downturn in the Argentine economy led to curtailed spending on public works. Funding for the hatchery pro-gram was cut, and by the middle of 1908 egg shipments stopped. The pursuit of introducing fish largely gave way to greater con-cerns over a foundering economy, and never-ending political struggles. For a brief window Argentina enjoyed the stability of government and finance required to start a project as ambitious as the introduction of trout into the furthest, most undeveloped regions of the country. The ambitious project lasted just four years, but long enough to give trout a firm footing there.

I set *Argentine Trout Fishing* down on the damp floor of the tent to think about the rainbows I'd caught earlier that week. They were not Argentine trout. They were American trout, the descendants of American trout that found themselves in my predicament a hundred years ago: an icy stream at the end of a bone-jarring dirt road, thousands of miles from home. These fish found a niche in the ecosystem. Hell, they took over the ecosystem. I had a four-hour drive from Neuquén while they and John Titcomb bounced along on the back of a horse for nineteen days. America's fishing exports had a history of success in Patagonia, most facing greater difficulties than the stomach flu and slow fishing conditions.

I woke in the morning feeling weak and groggy, but the sky was blue and the wind, calm. While the tent dried in the morning sun I strung my rod and walked over to the lapping banks of the Ñorquincó. I pulled a small Parachute Adams from my box and tied it on the wet leader. A few casts into the morning, a fish rose and slurped. My fly disappeared underwater and I set the hook. The seven-inch fish came to hand without resistance. I picked up the overpowered rainbow and admired the tiny gray marks on its young skin. Instead of finding disappointment at its small size I marveled at the tenacity of its lineage. In my hand sat a descendant of Titcomb's great expedition—a compatriot.

In the afternoon I drove south toward Bariloche, to the site of Titcomb's hatchery and the source of American trout in Argentina. I was filled with a growing confidence in the long history of American success in Patagonia. More importantly, I was no longer alone. My compatriots filled every waterway.

3
BOCA FEVER

_____

The choicest spot on a river is the boca, the first pool just below the lake from which the river runs. "Boca" means mouth, and in the Argentine foothills the place where the water pours out of a lake to form a river is called a boca—Boca Lolog, Boca Chimehuín, and so on. Big fish? The word "lunker" must have been coined by a fellow fresh from a boca.

Joe Brooks, *Joe Brooks on Fishing*

There are two questions asked of every American angler in Bariloche. Do you know Mel Krieger (the most famous American fisherman in Argentina)? And, have you fished the boca? The two questions measure fishing enlightenment. The best answer would be that you took a fifteen-pound brown trout while fishing the boca with Mel Krieger. Short of a perfect answer, it seems to be enough to just say you've been to the boca.

The boca holds a special place in the hearts of the Argentines. Even those who don't fish know the boca and speak of it with spiritual reverence. Fishermen's eyes glaze over with a distant look, as if the mere mention transports them to some prior time, some epic battle—or perhaps a future bout—with their perfect fish. They speak in the tone reserved for the Virgin Mary, a tone that conjures grand thoughts and celestial energy. Then you fish the boca and you feel for yourself.

The mystical power the bocas hold stems from their incredible ability to produce big trout. At the pinnacle of the big fish years, anglers took multiple fish per day in the ten-to-twenty-pound range. Fishing Northern Patagonia bocas in the mid-1950s, Joe Brooks reported that six-pound fish weren't even considered keepers. He went on to say, "A competent angler can be sure of a ten-pounder and, now and again, a twelve-, fifteen-, or maybe twenty-pounder." Joe's words were not just fishing hype peddled to the *Field & Stream* crowd for whom he wrote.

Since Titcomb's days at the turn of the century, Argentina's introduced fish had been left to their own devices. The trout adapted to their new environment, taking advantage of food sources missed by the native fish, as well as preying directly on the native populations themselves. Without natural predators or competition, they grew to enormous sizes by the time the early anglers appeared on the scene.

When anglers finally took note in the fifties, fish were improbably huge and misleadingly plentiful. Photos from the period show browns and rainbows hoisted on sagging rope stringers and lying in still lines on grassy banks. A photo taken at the Hotel Correntoso shows a banquet table stacked thick with fish. Of the twenty fish laid out there, only a few fit within the three-foot width of the table. Another photo shows a huge kype-jawed brown in silhouette, a man's fist entirely lodged in the huge open mouth. Some of the fish remain as stuffed rem-nants of a bygone time on the walls of restaurants, hotels, and fishing clubs. Most trophy fish were likely thrown out after a few

Even those who don't fish know the boca
and speak of it with spiritual reverence.

pictures. There were always more, and perhaps the next would hit the twenty-pound mark.

Having seen enough glazed-over fishermen and oversized stuffed fish, I boarded the laboring number 71 municipal bus at the bus stop in Barlioche's central square. I found a hard plastic seat near the back and set my daypack in my lap. I stowed my rod tube against the wall and trapped it there with the outside of my leg. I settled into the journey by watching the faces get on and off. Tall and small, light and dark, no person looked alike. It's said racism doesn't exist in Argentina for the simple reason that there are no pure races. Bruce Chatwin echoed the sentiment in writing, "The history of Buenos Aires is written in its telephone directory," referring to the hodgepodge of names from all nationalities that fill its pages. It's a country of immigrants, filled with a mixture of old-country and native names with a population that has mixed several times over during generations.

For seventeen kilometers the bus wound through the city then east toward the outskirts, past the defunct train station, and on past the site of Titcomb's first hatchery. The road traced the edge of the lake while the distant peaks under their snowy hats bathed in a golden haze of afternoon light. Past the small hamlet of Dina Huapi the bus continued to the last row of houses and a rough turnout. I gathered my rod and backpack and jumped out onto the wide shoulder of the road. A few hundred meters ahead the highway bridge spanned the river with the provincial police checkpoint and a small fishing access point on the far side.

The vantage from the bus stop revealed the intersection of landscapes that makes the country so diverse, stark, and beautiful. In the west a high pitch of dark mountains reflected the low sun in a row of snowcapped, dagger-point peaks reminiscent of a jagged crown. Tall and cold, they resisted the onset of spring in their white winter cloaks.

Across the lake to the north, the mountains fell away in a steady decline, their spiky cathedral tops giving way to round-shouldered foothills. Long slides of red rock provided witness to the prominent peaks these mountains once formed. A few outcrops still held on in defiant resistance to the inevitability of time and erosion. The odd swale concealed a trace of winter snow, but spring grasses shot green in the fading light of dusk giving proof of winter's lost hold on the intermediate elevations.

As the foothills slid down to the east end of the lake, the mountains failed completely into the broad, flat Limay valley. On the valley floor the signs of spring were well established. The harsh soil of the steppe was filled with an assortment of prickly, thorn-covered plants, all bright green with the exuberance of spring growth. The little branches flexed subtly under pressure and sprang back to their original location with a healthy bounce. The Lombardy Poplars displayed bright yellow sprouts along their vertical limbs. A few early buds unrolled to reveal the stout beginnings of leaves. Even for the steppe, a landscape barren and brown, the scene had a wonderfully alive and hopeful feel.

As cars rush by on the tarred highway I feel the pull of the boca ahead. Through the belched diesel smoke I feel a strange purity like the sun's warmth sensed through thick clouds. Something outside the realm of normal life is happening at the water's edge.

I stop on the bridge to watch the dark water slide quietly beneath. It splits into little white tongues to race around the pillars. In the fall, browns migrate out of the lake to spawn, stopping for a time in the long run cut by the bridge. In the right light a person can look down to find a half-dozen dark outlines of fish biding their time near the bottom. That close to the bridge, they are safe. The ones further up in the current and near the boca make easier targets.

It's the wrong time of year for the browns, but I can already see the silhouettes of several fishermen working the boca. It's early enough in the season for fish to remain in the river's current before moving back into the lake. But fishermen work the boca any time of year. There's always the chance of a big lake fish dropping into the river to feed. Even if there are no fish to be found, there's always someone convinced of the possibility of it. That's part of the magic of the boca. It is one of those rare places so poised with possibility that it can raise the expectant spirits of the most cynical angler.

I rig my six-weight with an intermediate sinking line and attach a huge black bunny leach. I pull my waders and boots on at the small dirt parking lot and trudge off down a worn track. The path loops across a short cutbank and under the bridge where the trail dips to the water. A decrepit old fence of rusting wire and a collection of pipes forms an obstacle course. Above there are several smashed-up cars being taken over by grass. The small junkyard feels at odds with the beauty of the rippled golden surface of the lake ahead.

From the fence the trail follows the edge of the river; this early in spring it's all under a few inches of water. Here, like most everywhere in Patagonia, the bushes push themselves right to the water's edge in a thick wall. Particularly nasty for fisherman, each plant has its own network of spiny branches and thorns adept at grabbing and entwining fly lines. Once a line is entangled, a recovery mission to extricate it poses hazards for hands, eyes, and especially waders while pushing through the sharp labyrinth.

I move past this wall of green and push upstream toward the mouth. I sneak behind a man clad in full fly-fishing regalia working a long Spey rod. He uses an offhand form of the snake roll, forming two quick loops in his downstream line that remind me of the ribbon toss in gymnastics. Then with two more quick thrusts he puts in a D-loop that looks beautiful and mystical in the afternoon light, and his line shoots out in a powerful rush three-quarters of the way across the channel.

I venture a tentative, "¿Hola, hay muchas truchas hoy?"

"No, no hoy," the angler says.

Even though my first question met with an answer, there are other messages conveyed by nonverbal means—annoyance, for one. Still, I want to stand there and ask a million questions. What was that cast called? What flies do you use here? What weight of sink tip are you throwing? Where do you recommend fishing with a single-hander? I don't know how to ask them in Spanish and I doubt he wants to give up his cast-step-cast-step rhythm to explain them to me. I watch him for a short while longer, drowning in my ineptitude and convince myself that he doesn't want to be bothered with incoherent sentences fumbled out in rough Spanish. "*Suerte,*" I say and trudge away before a reply comes.

The water from the boca cuts a wide continuous channel making it very difficult to wade early season. Almost everyone fishes with long traditional Spey rods to deal with the lack of room to back cast and inability to wade. They have an unwritten code among them of slowly working downstream with the bottom man returning to the top, new anglers also rotate in at the top of the pack.

New water always brings a jitter, especially when other fishermen are involved. There's so much emphasis placed on etiquette in our gentlemen's sport that simply discerning where to fit in on a new piece of water poses challenges. I've had my share of days ruined by rude or inappropriate anglers, and I fear giving foreign anglers a bad name by making a misstep. I don't want to jump in too close, or jump in above someone, making them feel obligated to shuffle downstream into less-productive water.

Standing on the bank of one of the most hallowed fishing spots in Patagonia doubles the usual hesitation. The boca of the Limay is one of the three famous bocas that form the heart and soul of Argentine fishing culture.

In the beginning the founders of fly fishing in Patagonia came to the bocas and, in a way, it was the bocas themselves that brought fly fishing to Argentina. In the '50s and '60s the first fly fishermen didn't come for spring creeks like the Río Malleo or the productivity of the Río Chimehuín; these rivers are new bleeps on the fishing radar. They came to fish a few hundred yards of the Chimehuín, the Correntoso, and the Limay. They didn't care much for a day's amble along a small creek tossing hopper patterns to eager little trout. These anglers set up positions like pillbox entrenchments and cast hour after hour into the same small stretch of water. They cast to the first hundred feet of the river where the water sucks down like it's being pulled by a vacuum cleaner. It's here where wind and current push the entire lake's worth of food to a single collection point. The fish move out of the protection of the calm lake into the river to let the current pull the collected food into their waiting mouths. This quantity of food and ease of acquiring it produces fish of incredible size.

I hold my rod at my side and watch to find a pattern in the angler's movements. It looks as if the three who are fishing my side are spread out and hunkered down wherever they'd found a decent-looking spot. I wade into the boca upstream of the snake roll caster as far from any angler as I can get to work back downstream. I begin on the backside of a poplar grove that stands a few feet under water. I wade out far enough to have a short back cast and throw everything I have into a forward cast. My fly travels a quarter of the distance of the angler ahead of me before splatting into a dead-looking pool. After my recent escape from infirmity in an orange tent I find immense satisfaction in my first poor cast. I work all the way back downstream to the bridge, casting with clumsy overweighted steeple casts as far out into the current as possible. A seam line with promising characteristics runs near the middle of the river, but I have so little chance of reaching it with a one-handed rod that I give up and look for any little pocket or riffle within twenty feet.

I half-expect my first run-through to meet with a great boca brown. In my imagination the calendar reads 1950 and the boca holds enormous browns all year long. But it's not 1950, and it's documented that the size and quantity of boca fish has declined since the late '60s. Fish in the twenty-pound range are now a myth, and outside of the fall spawning months, few fish above five pounds are taken. As a newcomer to Argentina I'm aware of this fact. I'm sure the four anglers spaced along the boca are also aware of it. After all, it is they who come night after night. Yet, as I look upstream and out across the golden water to the far side, I see men casting as if the calendar in their head is stuck in the 1950s as well.

Perhaps this is the magic of the boca. Despite the decline in the fish, the sense of spirituality surrounding the boca only grows. Perhaps the fishermen in this Catholic country fill the time between gigantic fish with saying prayers for the next big take. If this were the case, the number of anglers at the boca would have long since made it the holiest place in the country. More likely it's a simple relationship between effort and appreciation. Anglers now work hard for rare trophy fish and cherish those moments of success.

The power of their vigil seeps into mainstream Argentine culture. When someone hooks into a fish, the entire boca pauses, transfixed. Cars and busses stop mid-span on the bridge with people's noses pressed tightly to windows, construction workers forget about turning cement mixers, other anglers' rods droop into inactivity as they fall into a captivated stare to watch the unfolding drama. They call it "boca fever." The landscape, the history, and the fish combine to form an environment that some never escape.

Sitting on a large gray-brown rock at the boca watching local anglers cast sunset lines, I feel the magic that draws them out each night to throw cast upon cast. The twenty-pound trout becomes inconsequential as the sun reaches its lowest rungs before slipping to the other side of the world. The scene reflects across the lake where long Spey casts glide across pools of gold.

Without so much as a bump on the rod, boca fever infects me and spreads through my body. I leave after dark knowing I will return to the boca time and time again. I ride back to Bariloche with the belief that my perfect cast on the perfect night will fool my perfect fish at the breaking point between river and lake, where fifteen-pound brown trout sulk on the bottom, lying in wait for the perfect fly.

After the boca I make my way back to Bariloche with a new sense of confidence. I hadn't caught a fish or even fished hard that evening, yet I enjoyed myself immensely. Instead of focusing on fish as the only determinate of a successful trip I slowed down and felt the infusion of the boca. I took time to appreciate the scene and the importance of the event for those anglers collected on that particular November evening.

There's more to the journey than fishing, and there's more to fishing than fish. I have a new path, a desire to capture this feeling of fly fishing in Argentina. I know without asking that it's the fisherman I passed using the off-hand snake roll and the angler silhouetted in the evening sun farther up at the edge of the boca who know the answer.

4
RICHARD AMEIJEIRAS

If ye know these things,
happy are ye if ye do them.

John 13:17

Early in the morning I drive south from Bariloche along Ruta 40 toward the self-proclaimed hippie commune of El Bolsón. I drive through a long valley holding a series of deep blue lakes and over a mountain pass between towering rock faces. I search the radio, station by station, listening for one of the odd American rock songs that somehow make it onto every Argentine station's playlist. Above my head the heavy cam straps holding the cataraft frame to the roof of my vehicle make loud flap-flap-thuds as they whip in the wind and collide with the car roof.

Uncharacteristic of my previous few weeks I have only a vague notion where I might fish this time. A few blue lines on the highway map sit in the back of my mind, but rumors of locally produced ice cream and beer seem like more pressing matters. Since leaving the Ñorquincó, fishing feels less important. I'm beginning to feel that success in Patagonia will predicate itself on something other than the poundage of large fish. The story of Titcomb and his unlikely project draws me in to the world of

Patagonia fishing. I want more, but I've exhausted the English literature on the subject with Leitch's short chapter. I need to talk to the crusty old angler who ties his own flies from backyard chickens, a man who fishes the map's blue lines without regard for guidebook recommendations.

Halfway through a chorus of a Tom Petty tune the car behind me flashes its headlights in hysterical fashion, on-off-on-off. In Argentina these signals mean anything: "hello," "you can pass," "danger ahead," "this is a great song on the radio," ... "my light switch makes a great drum." I slow to let the car pass. A white-and-gray Astrovan overtakes me, its driver then moving back into my lane. Oh yes, the "I want to pass" headlight signal.

As soon as the van is back in my lane, the right turn signal comes on and the van slows. I follow suit as my mind recalls bad horror movies about stopping on the side of the road in the middle of nowhere. Had any of those films been set in Argentina? The van continues to slow and the hazard lights blink as the wheels roll off the pavement and on to the wide shoulder.

Hazard lights are a language equal in complexity to head-lights. Naïve to their meaning, I assume the driver is in distress and pull over with a growing pit in my stomach. The driver jumps out and strides toward my car. I inch out ahead of my hood to meet him and brace for any number of things, the most probable an awkward conversation of misunderstanding.

"*Hola,*" I say as he walks within earshot.

"*Buenas tardes, sha-blaba-bla-bla,*" comes the reply I cannot translate.

"*Perdón, ¿Cómo?*" I say with feigned confidence as if I might really pick up the foreign words with a second attempt.

"You speak English?" he asks.

"Yeah."

"I see your cooler, it is open. I am a fisherman too, I don't want you to lose your bread," he says.

"Er, what?" I glance back to the car and see that the cooler lid is indeed upright. "Oh, thanks," I say.

The man's voice barks like a Rottweiler at the end of a chain. His statements are short and clipped, his English vocabulary seems fine so I assume he's trying to convey his annoyance. He wears a pair of khaki quick-dry, zip-off cargo pants and a blue long-sleeved chamois shirt. Around his neck hangs a red bandana knotted at the front, cowboy-style. He wears dark aviator sunglasses and an Orvis hat with a large brook trout embroidered on it. He has a dark complexion, partly natural and partly from a great deal of time in the sun.

I'm confused by the harsh tone and the obvious way he's gone out of his way to help. I hope his offer to help is more than an excuse to berate a foreign angler encroaching on his water. My vehicle with its Montana license plates doesn't hide my identity. He wouldn't have too much trouble working up a good deal of angler rage while driving behind me.

"Where are you from?"

"*Los Estados Unidos,*" I say in Spanish, trying to defuse the situation.

"*¿Qué parte?*" he asks.

"*Montana,*" I say in my best Argentine accent, which makes the name sound like "moan-tan-ya."

"And you are fisherman?"

"*Sí,*" I say.

"Where do you fish?" he barks.

Here it comes. Tell a man you're fishing his water and let the floodgates of hatred open. I give him a brief outline of where I'd been the last few weeks and overemphasize my limited success.

"Ah, have you fished the Traful?" he asks with the first smile of the day slipping out.

"Not yet," I say.

"Okay, okay. I must to go. I have a friend waiting for me outside of Cholula." With that he reaches in his pocket and pulls out a worn brown billfold. He flips it open and sticks his fingers into the slot behind the credit cards and hands me a business card. "I am Richard Ameijeiras. I have a fly shop in Bariloche. You look me up when you come back. Maybe I help you."

"*Soy, Cameron Chambers. Mucho gusto,*" I say with a vague sense of recognition dawning in my voice.

"*Okey. Chao, chao.*" With that, he strides back to his car and drives off.

I stand for a long moment looking at his card and his name. Richard Ameijeiras, Richard Ameijeiras, I know the name from somewhere. Back in the Pathfinder I flip open *Argentine Trout Fishing*. I spin the pages past my thumb until I get to the section on Argentine guides.

"Most Argentine fishermen and experienced North American fishermen readily acknowledge that the best known and longest established fly-fishing guides are Ricardo Ameijeiras, Jorge Graziosi, Rual San Martin, and Jorge Trucco...."

Incredible. One of the crusty old anglers I'm thinking I need to meet actually pulls me over and introduces himself. My general impression of fate has been that it presents itself in a more subtle fashion. Continuing toward El Bolsón I can't help but feel a cosmic alignment set in motion.

Two days later I walk into Richard's fly shop on the main drag of downtown Bariloche. The shop occupies two small window fronts of a shopping strip. On either side of the fly shop are a confectionary, a tourist-activities booking agent, a T-shirt shop, and a women's clothing store. Inside, the fly shop is a bizarre combination of boutique, fly shop, and art gallery.

On the front table are stacks of ink fish drawings and boards tacked with intricate hand-tied flies. Further along the table are GAP boxer shorts and a locally knitted sweater. The walls are covered with an array of photos and handbags. A photo of Richard and a former client holding a fifteen-pound brown trout hangs next to a bright red Gucci knockoff purse. The feel inside the shop is of an overcrowded couples' closet, diametrically opposed ideas competing for space. The only compromise between the two comes in the form of earrings tied in the style of long traditional streamer patterns.

Tucked in the back corner of the shop is a small tying desk with the type of vice found in a discount fly-tying kit.

A big swinging-arm light/magnifying glass reaches over the desk. Along the edge of the desk Flashabou and tinsel tying material shimmer in the light. On the corner a brass spittoon holds an assortment of long peacock feathers. Hooks, thread, and furs I don't recognize are scattered on the worn wooden surface. In the vice a muddler-type fly with an orange deer hair head hangs half-finished.

Despite the odd contents of the store and the crowded workspace, Richard produces stunning flies. Small dries crafted from local bird feathers dot the shelves, one careful glance reveals the work of a craftsman. Most are variants dreamed up on his own to match local insects with local materials. While he doesn't say it, he fancies himself an artist; the intricacy of the flies and the collection of artwork on the walls point to his inclination for form over function. As I grow to know Richard, his fishing follows the same artistic zest. In every aspect he seeks a pure form. At times he comes off as a fly-fishing zealot, but at the core it's a harmless combination of pious Catholicism and an appreciation of nature.

For Richard, one of the area's first guides, his relationship with the area came at the young age of fifteen. As a Porteño, a person from Buenos Aires, he received an invitation from a boating club mate to spend the summer in Bariloche. Over the course of the summer he discovered a new way of life. The mountains, rivers, and outdoor recreation he found engulfed his thoughts. Richard says, "At fifteen years old I spent all day fishing." After seven more years in Buenos Aires he finished his studies and completed his mandatory military service. At the age of twenty-two and recently married he picked up and moved to Bariloche for good.

In the early days few people fished and a mere handful used the fly. Richard learned the sport on his own with a nine-foot fiberglass rod by walking the soles off his shoes along the banks of the nearby Limay. Dedicated to the sport with the heart of an artist, he practiced until he cast a picture-perfect line. Even today he prides himself on a board-straight back cast and tight loops. His casts are a thing of beauty and function. On a river where most turn to Spey rods for extra distance, Richard's exquisite technique allows him the same distance with a stout single-hander.

Richard's skill and dedication to the sport earned him a reputation as an angler in the still-small town of Bariloche. With no formal guiding industry, traveling anglers were referred to his doorstep. He took these passersby to his local haunts, where the combination of his professionalism and skill and the fish led to beginnings of a profession. His doorstep eventually became the entrance to Bariloche's first fly shop/outfitter operation. The posters and paraphernalia of that first endeavor still decorate the walls of what now serves as a guest bedroom.

Paying clients weren't just the beginning of a career for Richard, but part of the beginning of professional guiding in Argentina. Only a handful of others offered similar services. They all knew each other by name and most fished together at one time or another. With few exceptions they were fishermen who stumbled upon business—not the other way around. The friends of Richard's wife said he just didn't like to work. While this may have been the case, he also found satisfaction in his new profession. "Guiding is like being Santa Claus. Fly fishing makes people happy, and I get to bring it to them," he tells me.

As guiding became a full-fledged career, Richard embraced it as more than a job. He helped form the local guides association and presided as the first president. As such he helped implement examinations to certify new guides, pushed the province to introduce catch-and-release regulations, and helped develop guiding into a true profession. By the time Richard found me on the road to El Bolsón, more than three hundred guides belonged to the local association. Six fly shops and a dozen or more tackle shops sold to a booming industry. Wives no longer scoffed at husbands working as fishing guides. Instead they drove expensive cars and owned houses on the wealthy side of town. Local kids idolized the new class of outdoor professionals.

Over the course of several hours in the small shop, Richard shared his life story with me. He has a soft demeanor, deftly working fine thread at his tying table, much different than his sharp tone on the barren stretch of highway. He talks quickly, changes stories without pausing, uses his hands for great gestures, and lets his passion for life permeate the room. Any pretense of guiding or a commercial relationship falls away, leaving only a keen interest in my ambitious project to fish Patagonia. From that afternoon onward Richard played the role of friend and confidant. Before leaving the shop he insists we meet soon to fish his favorite local lake.

The following week I pick him up at his home several kilometers west of the Centro Cívico. A huge hedge of mature trees surrounds his property, blocking it from view. Only a thin dirt double track, fenced at the bottom, provides a passage through the thicket. A short driveway leads up a grassy rise to a landing and the house. It's a stately edifice designed in a European chalet style with heavy wood beams supporting thick walls of slate-gray stone. It looks like one of the nicest houses on the block, and it seems guiding was a wise move financially.

When I meet Richard at the door he beams with a great broad smile that shows his large, perfectly set teeth. "How are you, my friend?" he asks and leans in for a customary hug and kiss to the cheek. He's hauling a large black duffel in one hand and a long two-piece maroon rod tube under the same arm. In the other hand he carries a long black thermos. We load his gear into the Pathfinder and head down the driveway and out of town.

We travel an hour south to Lago Gutierrez, where we turn off on a battered dirt one-lane. It's apparent that during the drive, something's bothering Richard. In his shop he had been upbeat and enthusiastic, but now he's pensive to the point of seeming depressed. I prompt him a few times, getting short answers about a decline in business. No surprise there. With the global economic downturn, guides across Argentina are seeing a 30 to 40 percent decrease in business. I get the feeling Richard imagined himself immune to this trend and has only recently resigned himself to share the fate of the tourism industry.

I don't have the heart to tell him the problem may be more dire: the glory days of guiding are behind him. He's almost seventy, but it's not his age that's the problem. It's the passage of years. Thirty years earlier he was one of three names in the only book about fishing in Argentina. Clients sought him out to schedule trips by phone based solely on reputation and references. He didn't just have the market cornered—he *was* the market.

After thirty years the landscape of the industry he helped create changed dramatically. Richard now faces competition from three hundred guides. There are several outfitters and fly shops, all more focused on profit than tying beautiful flies. The new generation markets itself on the Internet and advertises in the North American media. They set up alliances with stateside shops to get clients. The new fly shops are cookie-cutter images of those in Aspen or Bozeman. The plastic boxes are filled with Montana Fly Company flies that look exactly the same as the ones the client found last year in Missoula, Boulder, or Bend. They make foreign anglers comfortable in the familiar humdrum setting of Winston rods and Sage reels. There are no Gucci knockoff purses on the walls of these shops.

In his oddball little fly shop, Richard still relies on the reference in Leitch's book and word of mouth to draw business. Leitch's book is out of print and on its way to becoming an expensive collector's item. Two Americans put out a new guide in 2009, and there is no mention of Richard in it. In an age where people book their airfare, hotel, and guide from a home computer, Richard doesn't even have a website. He doesn't know it, but he's being crushed by the industry he pioneered.

Across the car in the passenger seat, he tries to come to terms with the business slump. By the time we reach the turnoff he's managed to find a positive note and thanks God several times for his blessings. He offers a silent prayer and makes the sign of the cross, a gesture I see frequently in his presence. With the prayer offered, he gives the responsibility over to God. In a half-jest to draw us out of the silence, he notes that with business so slow he can take days off from the store to fish without losing business.

"Must be God wants me to go fishing," he quips in a less dejected tone.

He finds his normal chipper demeanor, then looks over and asks if I know the three kinds of American fishermen in a way that has me expecting a one-liner.

When I tell him no, he launches into his summary judgment of American fishing clients.

The Yuppie: Wealthy and willing, he splurges the five to six thousand dollars a week for an all-inclusive lodge. He shows up for a true pampered vacation. His guide meets him at the airport with a sign that says "Mr. Yuppie." The guide drives him to the lodge where the owners and staff have turned out to give him a warm welcome around a well-supplied cheese and cracker platter. He gets slightly sauced on the limitless supply of wine and retires for a short siesta before coming back down to an *asado* of beef and lamb.

In the morning he rises to a sumptuous breakfast before his guide shows him to his section of private water. He sees no one and fishes to well-regulated fish. Fish that have been monitored to make sure they don't get too smart or too picky. He takes several nice fish before his guide prepares a streamside lunch and they drink another bottle of wine. They fish a few hours in the afternoon, careful not to stay too long and jeopardize the relaxing aura of the vacation. At the lodge he takes his siesta before dinner and stays up later than he should sipping port while listening to the guides' stories of huge fish and famous clients.

The week continues in this relaxed microcosm of fish. The client has accomplished his goal by the end of the week. He's completed the fishing journey to Patagonia that he'll tell stories about for the rest of his life. He feels a part of the lodge going with him and waves back to the guides and staff as if leaving old friends for only a short journey. Likely he won't return. He will find another lodge in another far corner of the world with new adventures and new stories.

The Married Guy: This poor soul has drawn the worst of the three lots. Down to Patagonia on vacation with his wife, they have arrived in the fishing mecca he has dreamed about his whole life.

He has arrived in Patagonia without the slightest hint of fishing equipment. To have brought a rod and waders would have taken a second suitcase, the space in which had already been allocated to the wife's not-so-small shoe collection. Plus, the fishing gear would have been a flagrant breech of their negotiated truce to travel together and enjoy themselves. The rod makes it far too easy to escape into real enjoyment and foil their plan of rebuilding their love, no matter how painful.

He luckily convinces his wife, perhaps with the promise of an art gallery visit, into two days of fishing. They book their trip and meet their guide. Married Guy is excited beyond belief that he will get to fulfill his lifelong dream of catching a Patagonian trout. Sneaking it in to their mutual vacation adds to the glory of the catch. Married Guy's wife looks less excited. She tries, however, to maintain a positive attitude and convince herself that this mutual activity is all part of the rekindling of love.

By midafternoon the three have made their roles known and their agendas clear. Married Guy has forgotten about the existence of his wife and sees only bugs and fish. He tries to fish through lunch, realizing his time is short and precious. The wife has given up all pretense of participation and has found a comfortable enough spot to read her *Cosmo* magazine. She feigns enjoyment while inwardly reminding herself of her bitter resentment that this is what always happens, just like at home. Already the tide of a ruined vacation has started sweeping across her temperament. The husband is still casting and casting, oblivious to this unforeseen demon. The guide sees it all as a regular pattern and while he makes a few courteous attempts to assuage her anger, he knows before starting it's a lost cause and devotes his time to the husband, betting it will be he who wears the pants when tipping time comes.

They will either cancel their second day or Married Guy will show up alone. This won't upset anyone particularly, especially the wife, who will no doubt use the day for a vindictive shopping spree. At the end of the vacation they will likely look back at the second day of fishing, the one they spent apart, with fondness as the best day of the vacation.

The Retiree: He comes bursting through the door of the fly shop waving a copy of Leitch's book and screaming, "I found you, I found you!" He's been dreaming of this moment throughout his business career of suits and meetings for the last thirty years. He's done with that world now and has taken off to do something he's regretted putting aside since graduate school. He has brought with him two suitcases stuffed with state-of-the-art equipment, a new camera, and a half-dozen fly boxes that contain every conceivable fly.

On the river he hangs on the guide's every word and savors every moment as if he's being shown a lost world that might disappear again at any moment. He fishes hard, takes a short lunch, and pushes the guide to fish later than he prefers. He asks a million questions and pulls a jumble of maps from his bag to chart their progress. He uses his camera as much as his rod and snaps several photos of each undersized fish they catch. Whether it's windy or rainy or the sun blasts down like a furnace, it's the best day he's ever had.

He books a solid week and contemplates staying longer. He's got four weeks of fishing lined up and he keeps the same excitement level on day 28 as on day 1. When he gets home he'll put a slide show together and show it during a club meeting. He sends his guide a Christmas card.

Finishing, the topic brings Richard full circle to declining business. He laments that fewer of these retirees are coming through the door.

We hike to the backside of the lake at the foot of steep green cliffs. The wide path was once the highway between El Bolsón and Bariloche. Every few hundred yards, complex rockwork reinforces the road. Signs of age are present: trees encroach over the side barriers and grasses sprout up in the mortar cracks. It looks to be a decade or more since traffic passed over the route. After hiking a few miles we climb onto a rock wall that once formed a guardrail. On the far side a twenty-foot cliff drops down to the deep blue of the lake.

Richard looks over and says, "We are not fishing. We are hunting." I know what he means. Just as he says it, a large silver-sided rainbow plunges down from the surface into the depths. From our high vantage we can stalk the fish like birds of prey.

We start casting from our perches on the rock wall, making high straight-backed steeple casts to avoid the overgrown brush behind us. With flies on the water, fish drift up from the darkness of the lake in one long, slow motion. They come in a soft line to sip at the fly as if they'd moved but a half-inch. Eating is refined business on the calm lake. They have the leisure of time to make the take a stylized endeavor. They pluck the fly with such subtle lips I miss the first two fish. I find I need a two-count pause to slow my hook set to the rhythm of the lake.

"I missed him; he was a monster." Richard's reflexes are too fast as well.

A minute later Richard lets a loud whoop roll across the water. Twenty feet away his rod is doubled over with the tip-top pointed straight down to the water. He is in to a big fish making a run. I look back below me in time to see a line of bright blue drift up to my fly and open his mouth for a delicate inhalation of my Royal Wulff. I count my pause and the fish hooks itself in its turn to safety. I shout to Richard, "Double!" He pumps his fist in the air while line whines off the reel in the opposite hand.

We soon realize we're twenty feet above our fish. A look down reveals a sheer rock wall with small cracks suited more to rock climbers than fishermen. I pick my way along a slab and find a rock platform just above the water, where I release my fish with less difficulty than I imagined from the top.

Richard wrestles with his larger fish without the same descent path down the cliff. I climb back up to help and search for another means of scrambling to his fish. He finds a series of handholds through a clump of young trees. Giving me his rod, he climbs through the bramble, latching on to tiny handholds. I follow his path to a perch on a narrow edge with ten more feet to the water. I take the rod as Richard finds one precarious ledge after another using his feet as eyes below him. Just above the surface of the water he balances on a two-inch ledge with his body contorted and pressed tight against the cliff for support. I hand the rod back and watch him inch the large fish to the cliff. With the fish a few feet away he reaches out, totters, and lofts the fish out of the water in a single open-handed scoop. I snap a photo that will never show how close he came to falling in. He releases the fish in a long, graceful arc that takes it in a silver streak back down into the dark blue water.

Climbing back up the cliff, Richard refuses to let me take his rod. When he reaches the top he beams at his feat and clasps my hand in an embrace that comes to symbolize our angling brotherhood.

Strolling homeward down the old road, we talk in the failing light of the day's fish and my future plans. I have friends from Bozeman coming down for the next couple of weeks so we discuss logistics for several floats. Richard recalls each river and weaves exciting tales of bygone fish. The thought of these rivers, some not fished for years, brings excitement to his voice. Our conversation has trailed off by the time we arrive back at the car in darkness, leaving only the sound of our footsteps. We stand at the edge of the calm lake, content to watch the stars peek through in silence. Stress over recent economic strains has faded away like the recently released trout to the depths of the lake. Perhaps Richard was more right than he knew, maybe God does want him to work less and fish more.

5
GREAT
EXPECTATIONS

Ask no questions,
and you'll be told no lies.

Charles Dickens, *Great Expectations*

I see the two men through the plate-glass security window in the lower level of the Bariloche international airport. They wait in the baggage line for their oversized duffel bags to clear the security checkpoint. They wear baseball caps and button-up fishing shirts. They look like typical middle-aged Americans on a fishing vacation. Watching them through the window I try to fit them into Richard's classification system. John, the older of the two, looks appropriate for the retiree crowd. Jim, younger with thinning but still-dark hair, looks too disheveled to be a member of the yuppie group and, without a wife on his arm, too independent to fall into the married guy classification.

I met them while volunteering on the Big Sky Ski Patrol outside of Bozeman. Jim worked as the head of training and John used the patrol as an excuse to ski for free. John worked a corporate career in Minnesota's Twin Cities before retiring and fulfilling his dream of moving west to embrace the ski-bum lifestyle. Fortunately his business success allowed him to live in a comfortable log home close to the mountain and not in a dilapidated mobile home near the city dump with the rest of the ski bums.

Jim, though you would never guess it hearing him banter with John, is a first-class fish nerd. He'll tell you he's a fish biologist in Bozeman, which is true. But that's only half of it: his full title is Director of Research at the U.S. Fish and Wildlife Service fish lab. If you wanted to know how drugs, pollutants, or disease affect freshwater fish, Jim can tell you. Or you could just read one of the couple of dozen research papers he's coauthored. His most recent work looks at the efficacy of fish sedatives, and I can only assume the research is intended to give him a leg up on John and me. I'm also hoping he'll start tying flies commercially so I can put a big streamer in my box with a name like Jim's Big Fish Sedator.

Their four oversized duffel bags just squeeze in the back of the Pathfinder, which is already crowded with boat parts and fishing gear. Both Jim and John are large Midwesterners and both look distinctly uncomfortable with the car doors squeezed shut. Jim rides shotgun in the front where there's more legroom, but his knees are pulled up tight to keep them from bouncing off the dash as we hit the first speed bump. In the back behind my seat, the mounds of duffel bags are making an attack on John, and he pushes them to places where he hopes they'll remain.

I'm used to traveling alone or with other young people used to traveling on the cheap. Living in hostels, sleeping in tents, cooking simple meals on the fly—these things are inconvenient at times, but it's how to stretch a budget on an international expedition. I knew the Js were looking for a low-budget trip, but I feel nervous about how much they are actually willing to sacrifice. Driving across hundreds of miles of steppe with attacking duffel bags or waking in the middle of the night to a wild hostel party might not fit their visions.

In Bariloche we check into Perico's, a yellow stucco hostel with a quiet atmosphere reminiscent of a bed and breakfast. We secure a private room for three and let the duffel bags explode across every surface of the room. Rod tubes stand against the walls, piles of socks and underwear form stacks on the beds next to rolls of tippet. The Js ply me with a thousand questions about tippet size, flies, and rods, and attempt to extract a year's worth of knowledge every few seconds. No matter how fussy they might turn out to be regarding creature comforts, they lack no enthusiasm for the fishing.

Over steaks and Malbec I lay out our itinerary, tracing a line on the map held in place by half-empty wine glasses. In the morning our adventure launches into the Río Limay; this calm local river makes for an easy day float and introduction to fishing Patagonia. From the Limay, Ruta 40 heads east and north until crossing the Río Collón Curá and winding back west to Junín de los Andes, the self-proclaimed fishing capital of Argentina. Junín, as it's known for short, sits in the middle of three great trout waters. We will head north, using Junín as a base to fish two of Argentina's most famous rivers: the Chimehuín and the Malleo. I trace a long blue line from Junín south through country uninterrupted by black lines indicating roads. I have visions of a two-day float from Junín all the way back to the Collón Curá through vast tracks of uninhabited steppe.

With the map between us, excitement grows. Both Js describe the countless magazines and websites they viewed in preparation. Big fish spin in their heads on an endless media reel. They haven't actually read anything—they just let the pictures fill their visions of Patagonia. I mention realistic expectations and tell them that even after several months in the country I have yet to hook one of those magazine-cover monsters. But I've also got too much heart to deflate their big-fish dreams on their first night. We are too far into anticipation and too deep in the second bottle of wine for the truth to have an effect.

By dark, the excitement of a foreign country faded and the lethargy of jet lag set in. We retired to the hostel early with a round of self-deprecating jokes about not having the energy to chase young girls at the discotheque. Over the short course of the evening I remembered why I invited two men old enough to be my father: They act like high school boys. They run a never-ending series of jokes at each other's expense and tell embarrassing stories of such immaturity that I blush. I try in the upcoming days to find the line of acceptable conversation, but the further I try to rein it in, the more the Js run with it until I concede defeat and am left to appreciate the complete lack of discretion.

In the morning we load the boat and frame on the car and our fishing equipment inside. We stop at the grocery store for lunch staples and split up among the aisles to divide the work. We reconvene ten minutes later. I've found my assigned food, sandwich makings, without trouble. John and Jim arrive from opposite ends of the store at about the same time. Neither has found the desired lunch items, instead both carry three liter-sized bottles of beer. In addition, Jim has a large bag of potato chips tucked under his arm, and John a bag of cookies and a bottle of wine. They look at each other appraisingly, having worked as independent shoppers.

"Ooh, wine, nice one!" says Jim.

"Potato chips, good thinking," replies John.

Both shopped for the group, getting what they assumed was enough booze for the day, but they convince themselves that six bottles of beer are better than three under the assumption that we'll drink it "sooner or later."

We unload the mound of gear into the dirt parking lot at the river. Every boat owner develops his own assembly system. Not novices to the water, the Js concede to my boat rules without a blink and start taking orders as I direct tubes to be inflated and oars to be assembled. The process is slow the first day as they learn the system. In subsequent days no words are needed; everyone gravitates to the next chore and the boat quietly builds itself.

The process slows as the Js work to get their personal gear assembled for the first time. Reels, their extra spools, and other gear floats loose in dark bags after traveling. With this natural disorder of travel, there seems an accompanying mental disorder associated with fishing in a foreign country. Arriving at our home river we look at the weather, feel the temperature, soak up the breeze, and dip our hands in the water. After this little ritual, performed unconsciously after many years, we decide what layers to wear and then we engage the river. These simple measures are forgotten on foreign ground. Jim holds up two pairs of socks from his bag and asks my opinion on the better choice. I see no difference between the two, save the color. I choose blue; it's my favorite color. In my experience fish rarely get hung up on sock colors.

The Limay has a reputation in Patagonia as a big-fish river. Indeed, looking at photos from the river, there's no arguing it. Each year dozens, perhaps hundreds, of browns over ten pounds are taken. Fish to twenty-five pounds are uncommon, but not unheard of. The Patagonia the Js see in their minds is this Limay, the Limay of ten- to twenty-five-pound fish. And on their first day of fishing they feel confident about hooking one of these incredible fish. Why shouldn't they? The Patagonia we know as Americans is the Patagonia of *Fly Fisherman* magazine and *Fifty Places to Fly Fish Before You Die*. These publications show photo upon photo of monster fish held with gaping mouths by triumphant anglers.

We don't see magazine photos of small fish or fishless days. Writers can't sell articles lamenting the poor catch record achieved during their stay. Looking closely at a recent article on Patagonia I found several of the article's accompanying photos didn't even come from the trip the author wrote about. Fleshing this out a bit further, a professional writer and photographer go to Patagonia. For the benefit of free publicity they are invited to a private-water lodge in the heart of big-fish land, Tierra del Fuego. In the course of the week the two could not secure enough photos to complement a four-page article (six photos). Granted, more goes into a magazine-quality photo than catching fish, but the fact is that our professional photographer still failed to take enough publication-worthy pictures for the article over the course of his weeklong stay. That is Patagonia. In reality, that is fishing everywhere.

It's easy to sit in a Montana kitchen and watch the snow pile up on the window fully believing the 1,500-word article on Patagonia's unbelievable fishing. And for most people, there's no reason to soil the resulting daydreams with reality. Many anglers will never have the good fortune to cross the planet to chase their dreams. We leave the pictures of the huge brown splashed across the magazine cover unquestioned to avoid what may turn out to be an inconvenient truth. After all, how much fun is it to daydream about a thirty miles per hour wind and a seven-inch rainbow trout?

Those anglers lucky enough to get a golden ticket to Patagonia must eventually come face-to-face with the hype. Like Jim and John, they come to Patagonia with false notions of twenty-pound browns. They've been sold the pitch that every waterway is chock-full of big, easy-to-catch brutes. There are huge fish in Patagonia, don't get me wrong. Travis Smith, a founder of Patagonia River Guides, based out of Esquel, Argentina, also works North American summers on the Henry's Fork, Idaho, and surrounding water. He told me, "I can go all summer in North America and not have a single client catch a thirty-inch fish. Down here, I put a woman on a thirty-inch brown last week. I'm confident we'll get several fish that big in a season."

Pictures don't lie about this. But these fish inhabit specific waterways and then only during limited times of the year— particularly when their urge to spawn coaxes them out of safety. Echoing Travis's comments, you stand a far greater chance of catching a huge fish in Patagonia than at home. Yet, during the week at the lodge when the woman caught the thirty-incher, seven other clients did not.

This big-fish hype in Patagonia puts a lot of stress on anglers and guides alike. I know that both John and Jim are fish-ermen who enjoy the sport for what it is: a chance to get outside and enjoy Mother Nature. Under that pretext, either of the two can spend a fishless afternoon on the Madison, or take a small trout from a nearby stream, and feel the internal satisfaction of a day well spent. These same men, wide-eyed from Patagonia big-fish photos, make statements like, "I can't come to Patagonia and not catch a hog." As if catching one huge fish will make or break the trip.

Popular media has placed an unrealistic expectation on Patagonia. An expectation that deprives anglers of the simple enjoyment of a day spent fishing or the thrill of throwing a fly in foreign water. For anglers and guides alike, the notion of measuring success in terms of the weight, length, and numbers of fish leaves more unsatisfactory days than not.

Fifty years ago Patagonia lived up to the legends of multiple monster fish days. The trout received little harassment after Titcomb's experiments. At the edge of a great frontier, people had greater concerns than catching large fish. If they did fish, they fished for subsistence, not caring about bragging rights. Without natural predators the trout found the most comfortable spot to live lives of ease and did nothing more than grow large and fat in an environmental niche not well occupied by the native inhabitants.

These fish chose to congregate at the bocas of the great northern rivers. They held in the transition zone between lake and river where the current of the river sucked water and food past waiting fish. Farther into the lake, the fish must swim to find stationary food items. Moving too far downriver, the concentration of food from the lake dispersed, making the job of tracking down morsels in the current too much work. The boca combined the best of both worlds. Food-rich water from the lake moving past hungry mouths of fish. With little effort, these large fish were able to hold near the bottom of the boca, inhaling the constant line of food. And these stationary boca fish made easy targets for the first anglers. It is these three-foot long, seventeen-pound fish that float in John and Jim's minds during their first day on the Limay. Sixty years earlier their visions may have met fish within the first hundred yards of the river.

Just downstream from the put in, the river makes a left-hand turn. The current picks its way through a few large jagged boulders and constricts into a large white tongue through a sluice of black rock. Below the constriction the river widens and deepens. From the boat, the bottom looks thirty feet down.

The water is so clear that each rock stands out, and a person expects to see big fish hanging on the bottom.

Jim and John both have seven-weight rods rigged with sink tips and heavy streamers. The black-and-olive patterns make a passable imitation of a pancora, the native relative to crayfish. On the oars I hold the boat with hard rapid strokes in an eddy below the constriction. The Js cast back upstream to the calm water behind the large black rocks and strip back in short slow pulls that let the fly sink. With fifteen-foot sink tips we're hoping the sight of a slow helpless pancora flushed through the constriction will provide the incentive to move a fish from the bottom. We work the water systematically downstream. Jim lines a cast into a big boil, hoping the downward plunge of the water will suck his fly with it.

Beginning the middle of March this washout below the constriction will have a constant guard of fisherman. Men and boys from Bariloche take up stations on the rocks above and cast high into the top of the run and let the current strip the line out. With well over a hundred yards of line out, they let the line come taut and swing the deep fly back across the current. Fish often take just as the fly moves from the downstream drift to the crosscurrent swing. Outside the fall rush of fish, a few resident fish may hold in the pool; however, our rods don't meet any resistance to confirm their presence.

Below the long pool the Limay takes on its regular demeanor. It is one of Northern Patagonia's largest rivers, and its high-volume flow pushes hard to the banks in one river-wide current. This strong current pushes out to the green willows lining each side of the river. At times large rocks crest the surface to break the flat plane of water. Like all large, fast rivers, the Limay reads like a closed book. Fish are hard to find in the non-descript current.

The willows make the most obvious holding lies. Their branches sweep out into the river and slow the current. When the weather warms and the insects are active, fish hold an inch under the surface in the little eddies behind the branches waiting to eat. But they are difficult to fish to. The branches impede casts above the surface and provide plentiful escape routes below it. Along with the tough casts into the hollows of water without branches, the abrupt current changes along the edge of the trees make long drifts impossible.

Without surface activity John and Jim take turns casting weighted Wooly Buggers to the edges of the trees. Jim throws daring casts under long, outstretching limbs. With each cast he calls a play-by-play, "Oh, bounces off the branch and ricochets into perfect position. Can't plan it like that, folks. Here we go. A little mend for luck, a second for depth, and strip, strip, tug. Let's go, baby, here's the sweet spot. This is where daddy lives. Come on out. Now where are you? I took it in the front door, through the living room, down the hall, searched the master bedroom, and circled past the kitchen. Where are you now?"

We fish the trees hard, losing a large pile of flies in the process. When the trees diminish we look for the midriver boulders or any other obstruction that might give fish protection from the pounding current. There are good sections of braided channels and cliff walls lower down the river that we fish as hard as the willows—with the same poor results.

Jim and John maintain a good attitude throughout the day despite not catching many fish. By the afternoon the comments about expecting more and bigger fish crop up with more regularity. But when a raft trip of high school kids singing their school song passes us, John breaks into the chorus of a ski patrol drinking song and Jim follows along with gusto. After the kids are out of sight, we open the cooler and pass around another liter of beer. With the sun low in the sky, the red cliffs along the river illuminate the canyon with a glow of golden-red light. With a beautiful broad stretch of the Limay laid out in front of us, we take time to appreciate the scenery and the idea that three guys from Montana are drinking cold beer on a river in a different hemisphere.

In terms of numbers and poundage, the first day of fishing flops. We take less than a dozen fish between us, without a single fish longer than eighteen inches. I feel disappointed for the Js. Even though I'd expected a day of slow fishing, I know how much expectation they had for their first day. Expectations in

Patagonia are built around a house of fish-picture playing cards; for most anglers, that house collapses the first day.

The Js take the day's limited success in stride and shrug it off as a warm-up. By the time we're served our steaks at dinner and hit the bottom of the first bottle of wine, they are already looking forward to the coming days, undaunted. They rebuild their card house of huge fish dreams. At least it's Patagonia, where they're more likely to grasp this dream than anywhere else. I just hope they don't ask too many questions about tomorrow's adventure.

6
THE PROPHET

---

*For those who believe,
no proof is necessary.*

Stuart Chase

**Someone has said that the first
soothsayer, the first prophet, was the
first rascal that encountered a fool.**

Voltaire

On a cool spring morning in 1954 a young man strolled down New York City's downtown streets meandering back to his hotel. The young man, a sportsman, was drawn to the picture windows of the Trail and Stream sporting shop filled with shotguns, rifles, and fishing rods. With a casual push on the door, the man entered the shop and forever changed the world's fishing landscape.

The man's name was Jorge Donovan, an Argentine, and one of a handful of men who chased the trophy trout hidden in the remote landscapes of the Patagonian steppe. Donovan and Bebé Anchorena, a wealthy aristocrat, were playboy founders of a small group of Argentines bent on catching the world's largest trout.

At a time when Tierra del Fuego was a windswept plain frequented by miserable sheepherders, the two men took ocean fishing spinning rods to that remote corner of Earth for no other reason than the brown trout that migrated there like salmon. While their techniques were crude, the innovation of their endeavor left a great margin for error.

When not in the far south, they frequented the bocas of Northern Patagonia and preferred to fish the beautiful stretch of water where Lago Huechulaufquen constricts to form the Río Chimehuín. At the time, Jorge and Bebé were the world's foremost experts on Argentine trout.

Inside the New York City sporting shop, Jorge met the store owner and a salesman. Learning his nationality, the two forgot to try to sell him anything, instead peppering him with questions about the land of big fish for more than an hour. No doubt Jorge told wild stories of Patagonia and strings of fish larger than either men had ever seen or dared to believe possible. The two men were enthralled by Jorge's tales and allowed him to leave only after making him promise to return later that evening.

Arriving back at Trail and Stream in the afternoon Jorge found a new face, Joe Brooks. One of the most accomplished fly fishermen of his era, Joe published several books on fly-fishing technique, with his classic, *Trout Fishing*, still regarded as a must-read for contemporary anglers. Brooks also wrote for *Field & Stream*, the leading outdoor publication of the time. By mere happenstance Argentina's leading trophy trout expert and the United States' leading fly-fishing expert ended up engaged in a conversation that left the two men respectively awestruck. The men agreed to meet at Joe's Florida bonefish haunt at the end of the week to continue the conversation.

Fishing the Florida flats with Joe Brooks, Jorge witnessed the possibilities a fly rod presented. For the first time in his life he saw proper fly-fishing technique and advanced skills like the double haul. Joe's distance and accuracy with the fly rod left a distinct impression on Jorge. He wrote, "There was no comparison between Joe's ability and mine or any other average Argentine fly fisherman." Jorge referred to his time in Florida with Joe as his first fishing lesson. Florida became the first of many lessons as the two agreed to meet again, in Argentina.

Joe Brooks arrived in Argentina in January of 1955 and was met at the airport by Jorge and Bebé. The two Argentine hosts took Joe on a whirlwind tour of Patagonia to the best of the big fish locations. After a week in the far south of Tierra del Fuego they returned north to the area around Junín. They focused their efforts on the mouth of the Chimehuín River.

At the river, Jorge asked Joe, "What do you have there, a shaving brush?" With Jorge's tales of huge Patagonian fish in mind, Joe packed a selection of striped bass patterns thinking of the axiom "Big flies for big fish." When Joe tied on a Platinum Blond, a large bucktail pattern, Jorge's eye saw it as a shaving accessory. The story shows how little Argentina's leading trophy chasers knew about fly fishing.

With his shaving-brush fly, Joe landed fish of eighteen and a half, fifteen and a half, and fifteen pounds. To this he added another dozen fish between ten and twelve pounds. The fish of eighteen and a half pounds was the largest fish ever taken with a fly in Argentina.

During their time together Joe started Jorge and Bebé on the path of learning to fly fish. He showed them a variety of casts and introduced them to presentation, skills, and knots. He left the two men with a vision of themselves casting like he had and taking huge fish with a fly rod. He filled the men with a passion for the sport that carried them through their lives and spilled into several succeeding generations of Argentine fly fishermen. Jorge wrote, "In a land where fly fishing had no tradition, Joe came to us like a prophet."

The buzz Joe created in Argentina around fly fishing echoed in the United States. The backroom fly shop whispers about Patagonia's huge fish found confirmation in an unassailable scout. Joe Brooks published the article "Boca Fever" the following May in *Field & Stream* and set the tone for fishing literature about Patagonia. Joe's catch record in Patagonia gave a first glimpse into the region's incredible fishing.

We follow the memories of that shaving accessory more than a half-century later. We check into a two-story bungalow on the outskirts of Junín. The place is part of a sprawling neighborhood of concrete and brick two-story buildings, all with the same industrial cottage look. These bungalows, like the rest of Junín's sprawl, give evidence that we are but a few of the many anglers to join the chase.

The aftermath of Joe Brooks's prolific day entwined itself with the identity of the town. His role as Argentine prophet to the fishermen of the world led so many piscatorial pilgrims to Junín that it became known as the fishing capital of Argentina. For decades they came in droves to fulfill the yearnings that Joe Brooks's words burned into their brains. They, like us, chased the remnants of a fifty-year-old fishing tale, and in doing so, fueled a town on fish-mania and money.

The fish capital of Argentina became a designation valued as much by locals as the international anglers it drew. There are as many fishing shops in Junín as in Bariloche, while Junín is a much smaller town. At the downtown tourist office the tri-fold brochures are for guides and lodges, where in every other Patagonian town they feature eco-tourism, hiking, boat rides, and cultural escapes. The dirt lanes that crisscross the town's strict Roman grid have the standard names seen in every Argentine town. In Junín, however, each street sign has the street name carved into wood inside a large, white-painted trout. Fish are as important here as the political and military history of the country.

In the Centro Cívico we stroll along the streets looking for lunch among the siesta-closed stores. Peeking in the dark windows of fishing shops we see a devotion to spinning gear. In Junín, like most places in Patagonia, the majority of fishermen are spin fishermen. They throw huge Rapala-type lures with barbed triple hooks. Fly fishermen are a small but growing class of fishermen who only warrant a small rack of rods and a bit of wall space for tippet and leader. Most sales go to vacationing Argentines attracted to the machismo of fishing for a huge

Patagonian trout. These people don't have the passion for fishing it takes to spend hours perfecting a fly cast. They are tourists, looking for an afternoon activity.

The large central square of Junín provides a good cross section of the Argentine community. On one side of the square the Banco Patagonia stands with whitewashed walls and a large shade awning. No matter the time of day a queue waits under the awning to enter the small glass door to the ATM. The town's two ATMs are located at the front entrance of the bank with one or the other out of service at all times. Next to the bank runs a row of red-stucco professional offices with black wrought iron over the windows and curtains drawn.

Along the east side of the square the block begins with a defunct YPF gas station. The pumps are still in place, now covered with black plastic. Underneath the station's large roof, the employees play ping-pong on a table set up where cars used to pull in for fuel. In their blue workmen's coveralls, they look as if they still expect to fill the next car's gas tank from the plastic-covered pumps. Next to the defunct gas station is an artisanal ice cream and fudge shop. Most of the treat shops get their goodies from local suppliers.

Farther along the block, people walk in and out of the Internet café/telephone center, where a row of computers is set up in a dimly lit room. The keyboards are dark with grime, and the Internet limps along. Traveling businessmen check in with the corporate office, young university students chat online with their friends, and the local kids play the latest alien-blasting video game. Continuing down the block is a discount clothing store, a kiosko convenience store, and on the corner, a fishing shop.

On the south side of the plaza, restaurants do a brisk afternoon business. There's a pizza joint, an upscale grill with a dark-grained wood façade, a minutas (fast food place), and another Internet café. Had more restaurants existed in the square, the food variety would have changed little. Argentines have a limited diet. That afternoon we faced the same dietary options as every previous day: pizza, pasta, grilled meat, or a deep-fried beefsteak known as milanesa.

We skip our lunch decision for a moment and pop into the tourist office. Inside, several large fishing posters plaster the walls, and a carved wooden sculpture of a hand releasing a huge brown trout rests like a centerpiece in the middle of the room. Two young people in official-looking khaki vests stand behind glass-topped counters.

I ask about a shuttle service in the area to provide logistics for a float. Apparently most Americans don't show up with their own boat because the tourist office personnel simply give me a list of local guides. The list has over twenty names. Unlike the United States, where local fly shops or private businesses centralize shuttle services, Argentines use an individual network of friends and family to run their shuttles. The system works to a degree (the guides' friends and family pick up extra cash), but makes it nightmare for a foreigner to find someone willing and trustworthy enough to run a shuttle.

Giving up on finding a shuttle, we traipse into the pizza joint. An attractive young waitress brings menus with two full pages of pizza options. Every combination of onion, bell pepper, mushroom, tomato, and ham imaginable. Option 22: Bell pepper, onion, ham. Option 23: Bell pepper, ham. We order a large *jamón y morrones*. It comes out with a thick topping of low-grade mozzarella and a pre-made store-bought pizza crust, standard fare at an Argentine specialty pizza shop. It feeds three people for the equivalent of six dollars.

After lunch we finish our tour of the Centro Cívico along the west side of the plaza. On the corner, the Ruca Huney restaurant looks tidy and classy with whitewashed walls and a dark wood trim. Stenciled fish emblazon the glass on the front doors, and the posted menu boasts of local fish to complement the normal fare of *ñoquis* (gnocchi) and steak. I remember the restaurant from fishing accounts of the area in which anglers gathered for Malbec and *bife de chorizo* after long days on the river. On subsequent nights in town a row of drift boats sit on their trailers outside the restaurant, and more than a few customers sport the unmistakable attire of the angler.

Farther up the street we pass a laundry and an adventure tourism office with a row of muddy mountain bikes parked out front. Across the street in the plaza, couples lay on the grass while mothers shepherd children. Old men sit on wooden benches beneath the long, outstretched limbs of weathered trees while street cops patrol by foot paying little attention to the local action.

In the evening we drive out of town to the east past the sprawling military compound and its olive-drab guards with their black machine guns. Just before the highway crosses the Río Chimehuín, a dirt side road cuts north following the river toward its source at Lago Huechulaufquen. The next thirty kilometers are a mishmash of private *estancias* and high-end fishing lodges. There are a few public access points denoted by blue metal signs along the way. At every access point, several cars are pulled off into the dust. The scene looks more like a crowded Montana summer than the Argentina of our imaginations.

Near the lake we pull into the last public access before the boca. The sandy parking area sits on a hill overlooking the boca, the lake, and the snow-capped cone of Lanín volcano at the far end of the lake. In the fading light the Patagonian landscape makes the trip worth the drive—with or without fish. Looking toward the boca there's the outline of the river's first outside bend, Jorge and Bebé's historical haunt. We gear up and descend a steep hill toward the river. Anglers line the banks. Solitude is not a feature of the upper Chimehuín. We work upstream along a thin trail flanked by thorny trees that cut into our exposed skin and catch in our clothing.

At the first break in thorns we find the river and watch several fishermen working the upper end of a long, beautiful run. Despite the river's designation as fly only, all three anglers launch long casts to the far side of the river with spinning rods. Discouraged, we hike farther upstream to find fresh water and distance ourselves from what we consider an affront to fishing decency.

One of the anglers we pass hunches on a rock near the trail re-rigging his gear. He gives a warm welcome and inquires about our success. Not wanting to offend the local, I follow in cheerful suit and he tells me how the old man on the rock above us took two fish. Curious about their equipment, I ask to see what he's using. Three feet from the end of the line he's attached a huge clear bobber, and below the bobber at the end of the line is a large white marabou streamer—fly fishing.

On closer inspection all three anglers use the same bobber-plus-fly setup. The bobber provides the weight to cast the full width of the river to a promising slot on the far side. The bobber also holds the fly at a good depth in the water column. No wonder they catch fish.

The technique begs serious consideration with regard to the letter of a law versus its intent. In most circles, fly fishing means a form of fishing in which the weight of the line creates the momentum that allows the line to achieve distance. In this case the men were spin fishing, simply substituting a fly for a lure, and in this simple way abiding by the letter of the law.

Not wanting to waste the evening in contemplation of the ethics of spin casting a fly, we move upriver to a series of pools and boulders. We fish small streamers casting upstream and letting the fly sink on long downstream drifts before retrieving with slow strips. I am pleased to start catching fish immediately. They are smallish twelve- to fourteen-inch rainbows with an occasional brown. Most satisfying is the notion that we were bending our rods instead of bending the rules.

We continue working upstream toward the boca as evening wears on. With an hour of light left I round a corner and see the road bridge stretched above the river and the boca a few hundred yards above. It's here that Joe Brooks fished with Bebé and Jorge. I see the long riffle under the bridge and a deep, fishy-looking slough between large wet boulders and then remember one of Joe's stories about Bebé.

In his book *Joe Brooks on Fishing*, Joe tells of Bebé's most epic battle on the Chimehuín. Bebé was fishing below the boca, working the river with long casts to the far side. As Bebé's fly passed over one of these small pools and slots, a huge head porpoised and straightened his line and his rod.

The fish rose in anger and splashed across the surface: the erupting veil of whitewater obscuring the huge fish. Bebé didn't know how big, he just knew from the splash it was massive. He recalled later he thought the fish might weigh as much as fourteen or fifteen pounds.

Here the fight got interesting. Joe tells it best.

The fish went rushing downstream, turned and gave a gigantic lunge forward, went down again and didn't move. Bebé was in trouble. That lunge made the reel overspin and the line was tangled badly. He started walking downstream, untangling line as he went, too busy to watch where he was going. He fell to his knees once, got up and kept going, still untangling line. At last he got it all free, reeled it onto the spool and pulled it tight to the fish.

Big browns rarely jump in flashy tail dancing displays. They are smart, business-oriented fish, the German engineers of the fish world. They may make a few head shakes, perhaps one strong steady run into the backing, but as soon as they realize these efforts aren't working they change tactics. They use as little energy as possible in their fight for freedom and take the fight to the angler by hunkering down on the bottom.

And so it went with Bebé's fish. After the initial run the fish sulked on the bottom and dared Bebé to pry him out of his deep hole. Bebé worked on him with his rod applying pressure for so long the moon started to rise in the sky. The fish clung unmoving and Bebé began to wonder if the fish had thrown the hook in the initial run and he had been pulling on a rock for the past hour.

The fish eventually moved and the fight was on. By moonlight Bebé fought the fish, inching line back on to his reel. He got the fish to his feet and pulled him on shore. The fish was bigger than he thought, he guessed as much as twenty pounds.

The fish ended up weighing 24 pounds, the largest brown trout taken on a fly anywhere in the world.

Staring up into the riffle, I watch Bebé's fight play out in my mind. I envision him falling over, his knee banging on a rock, the line wrapping the reel, and a frantic struggle. I look down at the large, cobbled rocks on the bank. Any one of them could have been that rock. This was the spot where a world-record brown battled and fell. I look back to the water, probing hard with the fisherman's eye. I search out the holding water, finding the subtle tells of the current to indicate a trout lie. I see the spots and look to the far side of the river, where fifty years ago the monster fish slowly porpoised and descended. I check my line, giving the fly a strong tug to flex the thick leader. I step into the water ready to follow in Bebé's footsteps.

I work methodically downstream from the bridge starting in the shallow riffles and casting farther and farther till my line reaches the other side near the magic lie. I work the run down to the large boulder and fish around and past it into a deep pool. With each strip, I hold out hope of hooking a monster. A few times my fly bumps underwater rocks and I twitch my rod in a quick hook set. Each time the hook set meets no resistance and my fly continues through the water. With each attempted set, a pulse of adrenaline flushes through my system.

Above me past the bridge I see the traditional boca run where the big fish anglers spend their time. Groups of anglers, spaced close together, cast a solid blanket of flies over the water. The light fades into shadows and charcoal hues as I work downstream. Upstream, the pattern of casting continues unbroken by the bending of a rod or hissing of a hot fish on a reel.

In my absence the Js worked the water downstream hard to catch small rainbows. I detect a resurgence of disappointment countering the hype surrounding the Boca of the Chimehuín. Joe Brooks, Bebé, and Jorge had it easy. They caught enormous trout. In the summer of 1955, they were likely the only fishermen at the boca. The river saw long stretches of loneliness when no souls bothered to drive the dusty miles to throw a fly into the water. Now, as we see, many anglers use every legal means to snag their own monster.

Whatever the piscatorial makeup of the river, in our mind's eye we envision a river of monsters. We expect our lines to meet Bebé's fish. The words of Joe Brooks and the legions of his followers work on our brain. Like so many before us, he is our prophet.

And we believe.

At the sandy parking area we meet the spin-fishing fly fisherman. He tells us about the old man from the rock again, saying he took an eight-pounder from the run the year before. He tells us the local paper put a picture of the old man and his fish on the front page. Along with the river's designation as fly fishing only, it's also catch-and-release. It sounds like a difficult feat to get the picture and keep the fish alive. Trophy fish in Argentina end up in far more pictures and wall mounts than not. I wondered whether the days of the twenty-four-pound fish are gone forever and whether we are fools for our faith.

7
RÍO MALLEO

——

Conservation means development
as much as it does conservation.

Theodore Roosevelt

At our Junín bungalow we wake to a blue-bird sky and drive out of town toward the rising sun. We cross the Chimehuín via a rusted yellow bridge and bank north into the rolling hills of the steppe. The hillsides form layers of dull greens and yellows stacked upon each other until they turn blue on the horizon. Cattle march along a fence line looking content despite the thorny collection of plants to forage. In the day's new light we expect to see imported European red deer grazing along with the cattle, but this morning they are already tucked into their hiding places high in the swales of the hills.

Thirty miles north of Junín the road drops gradually into another valley where a thick belt of verdant green willows belies the presence of water. The road snakes into the bottom of the valley before taking a hard right over a rickety wooden bridge painted bright red. Underneath the bridge flows the Río Malleo.

On the far side of the bridge the road forks in three directions. The right fork is a dirt road and follows the river downstream. If a person takes this track, he enters the Mapuche Indian reservation. The native people were forced onto this land over a hundred years ago at the end of Argentine General Julio Roca's conquest of the desert. The conquest eradicated most of the native tribes and pushed the few survivors onto small tracts of out-of-the-way land. The campaign sought to open the Patagonian frontier to European settlement and looking at the current population, it succeeded. As part of the trade for the vast majority of their homeland the Mapuches charge ten pesos for passage onto their land and fishing access. Despite this history, the elderly woman who ambles out of the ramshackle little hut with the ten peso sign on it seems to always manage a smile and a heartwarming "Gracias," whenever someone stops to pay.

The lower section of the Malleo through the reservation is distinct from the upper river in that it flows through a tight canyon of crimson- and rust-colored rock. It winds in tight bends with deep pools and long slots. Crude turnoffs are bulldozed into the road every few hundred yards to provide easy access.

Houses are sparse through the narrow valley. Large turnoffs serve as parking lots for the little shacks that fight the arid landscape to survive. These small huts are jumbled together from felled willows, corrugated tin, and odd collections of scrap. Sheep blurt from driftwood corrals, and sleek chestnut horses paw the ground. Smoke rises from a rusted chimney, but without the smell of food.

The men dress in the gaucho style. They wear long black boots that rise to the knee. They tuck their baggy pants into the boots and cinch the waists with thick leather belts. More traditional gauchos wear intricately woven sashes as a belt, and everyone tucks a long knife, known as a *facon*, into the back of their pants. Their eyes are dark and furtive under broad-brimmed hats. Blankets are worn poncho-style on the reservation. A subdued feeling penetrates the landscape, and we unconsciously speak a few decibels softer.

The fishing is good and the river is one of the more popular spots for anglers based out of Junín. There are cars at most turnoffs by midmorning, and anglers make a slow rotation to the different sections throughout the day. It's one of the few places in Patagonia where nymphing produces consistent fish. Working a bead-head Prince Nymph below an indicator through the long pools produces good fish. The lower river holds a variety of species. Rainbows are most common, but browns are a close second, with the native perca also giving a little action.

The water toward the reservation looks swollen from runoff so instead of heading east onto the reservation, we turn upriver toward the Chilean border. The road is a major tourist route to the ski and hot springs–laden destination of Pucón in Chile. Despite the lack of anything but sheep, cows, and shrub, the road is paved to accommodate the tourist traffic, and we make good time heading west to the upper reaches of the Río Malleo.

Driving the road upstream, I see that a large tract of the river disappears behind the terrain and barbed-wire fences announce "*propiedad privada*" at any tempting-looking location. These signs hang on the fence for the next twelve miles, leaving a person to salivate over the missed opportunity.

The land belongs to the San Huberto Lodge, Northern Patagonia's oldest and most exclusive. The lodge opened in the 1960s at a time when sport fishers looked at Patagonia in big-fish monovision. Fishermen wanted boca monsters and looked at other area rivers like the Malleo, where large fish measured twenty-four inches, with disdain. So disregarded was the Malleo by the angling community that a fish-canning plant set up operations on the river without meeting the ire of sportsmen.

By the early 1980s two factors had developed that changed the fishing scene across Patagonia. The first was the depletion of big fish. The twenty-five years after Joe Brooks's visit to Patagonia saw swelling numbers of anglers looking for their own trophy. Despite thousands of miles of rivers in Patagonia, fishermen focused on the few hotspots known to produce big fish, the bocas. By 1980 these tiny stretches of river were denuded of trophy fish.

In Junín at the Chimehuín, in Bariloche at the Limay, and especially in La Angostura at the Río Correntoso, hotel owners and guides began to sense the economic ramifications of depressed fish populations. After thirty years of successful fishing reports flowing out of Patagonia, interest had never been higher. Unfortunately for the lucrative industry, Mother Nature was running out of fish—and drastic changes were needed.

With the decline in big fish across Northern Patagonia and the increased interest in the region by foreign anglers, the door opened for the Río Malleo and other less-known rivers. The Malleo was the first river to attract attention and continues to keep anglers enthralled because it has the best and most consistent aquatic insect life of the northern rivers. In a land plagued by sparse, inconsistent hatches, the Malleo provides consistent dry fly fishing to rising trout. A large Malleo brown will run twenty-four inches and push six pounds, but the majority of fish are smaller than this, averaging fourteen to twenty-two inches.

The new angling vision targeted these smaller fish and brought about a tactical revolution in Argentine fly fishing. Since Joe Brooks's huge shaving-brush fly, the vast majority of fly anglers used heavy rods and large streamers. The most common tactic employed by Argentines and foreigners alike was a downstream swing to mimic a wounded baitfish, a tactic likely borrowed from early steelhead anglers. The technique worked well in the deep currents of the bocas, but found little practical application in the smaller, boulder-strewn rivers more common to the region. Instead of casting huge weighted flies, anglers needed light rods and floating lines for the smaller, but still respectable, resident river trout.

The first to see the possibility of changing the fly-fishing paradigm was a young entrepreneur. Jorge Trucco, age twenty-five at the time, was a vice president at one of Argentina's major vegetable oil and grain exporters. At the company headquarters in Buenos Aires he fell in with the tight-knit anglers club led by an aging Jorge Donovan and purchased fly-fishing books by Joe Brooks and Ernie Schwiebert. Jorge watched as the troubled government of the late seventies changed financial policy to devalue the peso. He recognized the economic disaster probable under such a policy and stepped down from his profitable executive position. With ample savings he crossed the country to San

Martín de los Andes and purchased a bed and breakfast close enough to the mountains and rivers to take his newfound passion from the pages of books to the water's edge.

Jorge, with the idea of finding clients for the following season, traveled to the Fly-Fishing Federation's national conclave in Steamboat, Colorado. Jorge took to the water with his American hosts and fished the small, boulder-strewn rivers of Colorado. The fishing differed vastly from his experience in Argentina. In Colorado they used small dry flies cast upstream with delicate precision. He watched anglers study the riverside entomology to perfectly match the size and color of natural insects. None of his companions took fish on large flies with blind downstream drifts. What's more, the anglers caught fish not that different from those in the Malleo. Fish to twenty inches got huge grins and twenty-twos were heralded as monsters.

Back in Argentina, Jorge headed to the Malleo with new eyes. He rigged a lightweight rod and a small Parachute Adams. He fished careful casts upstream under the willows and took large numbers of fish. Without a doubt a different kind of fishing than boca monsters, but one with its own beauty and challenge. Whether or not Argentines would adopt this new type of fly fishing was beside the point; Jorge knew he had a product he could sell abroad.

As late as 1980, rivers now advertised as the gems of Patagonia were still disregarded by local sport anglers. These rivers ran inside huge private estancias that valued their water solely for irrigation. Asking permission to fish a river was met with a laugh from the landowner, who didn't understand why anyone would waste time on a small river like the Malleo. "Of course you can fish," they would say and wave their hand as if shooing a pesky fly. For all intents and purposes the water and access were public. Anyone with the desire to cross a long green pasture might find a waiting pool of eager trout.

As the only location on the Malleo capable of accommodating guests, the San Huberto Lodge attracted Jorge's interest immediately. He contacted the Olsen family, who owned the lodge, and set up an exclusive-use agreement to board fishermen. With so many miles of untouched river, the San Huberto estancia, while large, represented such an insignificant development that little attention was paid to the change in land use.

Even Jorge himself couldn't have seen the monumental change begun with that first contract. Driving along the San Huberto fence line, we see the remnants of that first agreement in the private property signs. And on almost every northern river we fish, we see the legacy it created. Locked gates and "Keep Out" signs provide a contemporary testament to the changed fishing landscape. Argentine rivers are increasingly more private than public.

We continue along the highway to a long, straight stretch of pavement at the upper end of the Malleo Valley. To the right the valley stretches out flat in a tangle of pasture and dense swamp thickets. On a tip from a local, we pull over at a lone araucaria tree, the only one for miles in any direction. The tree looks like a cross between a pine tree and a dinosaur, with armored leaves like prehistoric scales. It's easy to see how it got its nickname as the monkey-puzzle tree. A three-strand barbed wire cattle fence is stapled to the tree and continues as far as the eye can see in both directions. The fence looks foreboding, and no blue public access marker with the cartoonish white fish denotes the spot. The local, a young Argentine, said the area used to be public, but he wasn't sure if it was these days. "I still fish there," he said.

We climb through, pulling apart the wires of the fence and being careful that it stays well away from our Gore-Tex waders. Before trudging off through the cattle pasture in search of our prime Malleo water, I look up and down the highway. There is a smooth, dark ribbon of asphalt that quickly gives way to a green valley of big, black cattle overshadowed by the much larger triangle of the snow-capped Lanín volcano.

On the far side of the fence we find a half dozen of Argentina's prized cattle. We skirt the outside of the field through a shoulder-high maze of cow trails punched through the wild rose. The rose thorns seem only slightly less treacherous than the barbed wire, making it a slow trip away from the lone araucaria.

The upper Malleo is known as the spring creek section. While technically not a spring creek it possesses all the right characteristics. The water flows with absolute clarity in a single, winding ribbon. The light brown sand on the bottom holds large pods of flowing green vegetation. At most points a person can ford the river without wetting the waders above the waist. The icy water freezes the appendages the whole way across; standing midstream to fish takes a few minutes of acclimation to accomplish comfortably.

The whole section induces a frenzied sense of possibility. A long run abuts an undercut bank, after which the current pushes hard into the branches of a submerged tree before emerging into a deep, cliff-backed corner where, even with the clear water, the bottom becomes obscured. It takes forever to fish as a person casts several times from each position—every cast finding a prime pocket—before taking a small step to begin again.

The three of us work downstream, leapfrogging each other and looking back every so often to a bent rod and a white splash erupting from the river. The fish are small rainbows eager to dart out and take any passing morsel. We use a collection of big yellow hoppers, black crickets, and cone head muddlers. All the patterns work, and we sense that any fly will have the same success.

The coveting of big fish is lost in the continuous action. We land fish for each other and stop to sit on logs and stare at especially good-looking holes. At times all three ply the same water, casting almost shoulder to shoulder and not affecting the catch in the least. At times we abandon a hot pool, achieving some arbitrary level of success before the fish are played out; other times we linger too long at a likely run where nothing stirs. The river invites us to keep walking and exploring, tempting us to discover the secret around each new bend.

Working past Jim on a little elbow of river, the bottom becomes a brown blanket of sand. The run between corners stretches forty feet. At the head of the run a large boulder swirls the current into two white tongues; deep troughs are gouged out of the soft sand at the base of the boulder. Below the rock the river narrows with a gradual slope to a shallow gravel bar.

I walk the bank with slow steps while scanning the river. I don't expect to see fish in the exposed water, but sneak along hoping to sight the first big fish of the day. Nearing the end of the pool I quit watching the water and giving up on the short piece of water, I take two quick steps. It's then I see the fish in the corner of my eye. She's perched just above the gravel bar in the broken water two feet from shore. The twenty-two-inch brown opens her mouth to inhale a passing morsel.

I stop to watch the trout open wide once again, grabbing a midmorning snack. Just ten feet from the fish, I have no escape into streamside brush or behind a rock. In shallow water any bankside movement will likely send the fish off in a rush. I attempt to shuffle slowly back upstream, crouching to shorten my profile. I take two tiny steps, but that's enough to send the fish bolting upstream.

Without proper caution, sight fishing ends before it starts. The shallow run and clear water left my chances with the best brown of the day looking glum. I stick around as J and J move further downstream. I scan each inch of water. The brown hues of the fish camouflage well in the sandy, dimpled soil. Even in the clear water a wave of a tail, a dark shadow, or a white mouth might be the only tells of the fish's whereabouts. And when a slight shadow reveals a fish's location the whole image takes time to develop like a magic visual puzzle.

I search the water to the head of the pool near the large boulder. The deeper water behind the rock offers more protection than the rest of the run and it's here I expect to find the fish. I work the pool with my eyes, find nothing, and work it again. On the second pass a faint shadow emerges a few feet below the rock. Staring long enough through moving water, a sixth sense develops. Shadows eventually fall into two categories: fish, not fish. This shadow is a fish.

With the fish sighted, my thoughts shift to fishing. Sight fishing is the most exacting, challenging, and frustrating type of fishing. When the fish can see you better than you see it, the playing field tips in the fish's favor. A botched cast, the shadow of a casting rod, the light plunk of a nymph on the surface are but a few of the subtleties that send fish into deep, dark corners. At times it doesn't even take a careless movement to blow the gig. I've watched a fish for half an hour from a concealed position without making a move. As I come up with a plan but before any physical execution, my quarry zooms off, spooked. Fish too have a sixth sense.

The large brown trout hangs behind the rock and waits patiently as I formulate my plan. I hold little hope for the adventure. Sight fishing a spooked fish has less statistical success than a lottery ticket. Still, convincing anyone with a fishing pole to abandon the best fish of the day has even less statistical success. And so I cast far upstream and eye my little gold beadhead as it sinks and bounces along the bottom. I adjust each cast to get the right depth and drift of the line with the hope that one cast might hit the fish square on the nose. For me, the nose shot calls it: if the fish doesn't take it, he won't take anything. I can't think of a more effective way to test territorial tendencies.

On one of the first dozen casts the fly passes a few feet to the inside of the fish and it moves to get downstream of the fly. With my fly a few inches off her nose, I wait for the quick strike. Then, without warning she tails back upstream to her original position by the rock. The snub is almost disdainful, as if to say, "You called me over for this?" The first thought in the angler's brain is "new fly."

After I try every small fly in my box the fish has drifted back to the shallow lie where we first met. Several flies pass within inches of her face without inducing her to strike or spook. She still feeds on tiny insects caught midcurrent. She knows my game and no longer allows my buffoonery to interrupt her lunch. I understand why these brown trout are regarded as the smartest of the trout species.

It pains me to give up on such a beautiful fish. Leaving a large, actively feeding brown feels like a slight on my ability as a fisherman. I've seen people in the same situation stick their rod tip into the water and give the fish a good poke. The poke does a fine job of scaring the fish into the deepest recess of the river; the angler can then abandon the cause secure in the knowledge

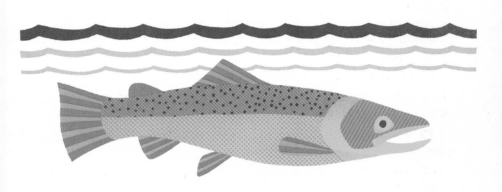

The snub is almost disdainful, as if to say,
"You called me over for this?"

that the fish will remain in hiding for the rest of the day. I won't stoop to harassment to appease my pride, so "farewell brown trout and thank you for the lesson in humility."

I meet back up with J and J downstream. I half expect to find the two engaged in a water fight, but they are working the river as if each cast might hook a six-pounder. The afternoon is getting on by this time, and the sun bakes down on our shoulders. Our water bottles retain a mist of warm condensation while our stomachs ache for the sandwiches left in the car hours ago. Hiking back through the cow pastures and bramble bushes, we find the highway much closer than we expect.

The Malleo we fished flows as it had for decades. It winds past the same cliff faces, the same thick lines of red-rooted willow, and underneath the same snow-coned Lanín. Yet, the river we fish is not the same river Jorge Trucco fished right after his trip to Steamboat.

Thinking about the change, I feel cheated. Twenty years prior I'd have been able to stroll across a cow pasture to any spot I liked and cast a light caddis pattern to a row of nosy risers. Now, propiedad privada signs along the highway and the brown that snubbed my best attempts are evidence of the changes. I picture a day of sunshine, unlimited access, and large fish pulling hard into a tangle of tree roots to escape a new, unknown predator. I imagine a virgin Malleo.

The person responsible for destroying my vision was Jorge Trucco. The private property signs and the educated, picky trout are manifestations of Jorge's business endeavor. I imagine Jorge sitting in his office in San Martin brokering deals for new ranches and the creation of the next private fishing lodge. Out here on the river, the Js and I fish around the deals from twenty years ago. We don't get to fish the same river Jorge built his bank account around. Somewhere downstream in the heart of the San Huberto Lodge, too far of a hike from public access, a few sections might still harbor the magic feel of the virgin Malleo, but with twenty years of fishing guests, even this seems doubtful.

It's hard to fathom how one man's vision so wholly altered a fishing landscape. The only other person to have as much influence on Patagonian fishing has been John Titcomb with his introduction of trout in the first place. For better and worse, both men have left their mark on Patagonia by fundamentally altering the way we humans engage its rivers. Titcomb by creating a leisure activity where none existed, and Trucco by expanding that leisure activity to the far corners and crannies of the region and privatizing it. In stark terms, my experience on the Malleo and Jorge's twenty years prior are significantly different as a direct result of the actions he took.

These accusations make Jorge Trucco an easy villain. Yet, despite the fact that I never engaged that nice brown in battle, I am perhaps the first to jump in Jorge's cheering section. As Titcomb brought trout to Patagonia, Jorge brought the fishermen to the trout. Before Jorge, fishing in Argentina meant the bocas in the spring and fall and a few months of wind in Tierra del Fuego. Even before Jorge, the popularity of the bocas had already doomed them. In fact, most of the bocas had already begun their slide from the glory days of the 1960s before Jorge even thought to fish a dry on the Malleo. Jorge opened the eyes of the world to more possibilities. The hundreds of rivers crisscrossing the country that didn't hold twenty-five pounders still held seven pounders and fun smaller fish.

While Jorge's first private-water venture closed a small section of one river, it also opened the rest of the country's rivers. No laws changed, but the consciousness about where and how to fish changed from a few limited fisheries to a vast expanse of trout water. That today's anglers can float a river without seeing another person, or stake out a piece of personal water on a major river, is a function of Jorge. Anglers all over the country are exploring the no-name rivers and hard-to-get-to waterways because one time this guy named Jorge commercialized this amazing river called the Malleo and changed how we think about Patagonia fishing.

Rivers locked behind private property signs are one of the world's great tragedies. They represent happiness closed off by economics, and yet I can't help feeling reluctantly glad that Jorge brought fishermen to San Huberto. When it comes down to choosing between my hour-long attempt to catch the brown or not ever experiencing the Malleo, the answer is easy. Was it better twenty years ago? Yes. Do I know why and who caused the decline? Yes. But I, and thousands of other anglers who have enjoyed the fishing on the Malleo, owe it to Jorge for putting the place on the map. It's fishing's most diabolical catch-22. If you share a great place, you'll only make it not as great; if you want to keep it a secret, no one will ever share in the greatness.

8
REDEMPTION
ON THE RÍO ALUMINÉ

There's always some little rivulet
no one else wants: a brushy bend,
a pond back from the road under
wild apple trees. Go there.

Thomas McGuane, *The Longest Silence*

The following day we take the same Ruta 23 out of town to the north. When we cross the Malleo on the clunky red four by twelve boards, we don't turn west toward Chile and the lone araucaria or southeast onto the Mapuche reservation, but continue straight on a dirt track winding into the tawny hills. We ride high over the upper plateau across barren gaucho land strung with cattle fences. The only structure we pass is a small one-walled awning with a bench and a bus stop. With no houses anywhere in sight out over the vast high plain, it seems an odd place for the lonely shelter.

After several miles and an equally long dust trail lingering in the rearview mirror, the road turns east and we descend to a valley cut deep with time and showing its age through long-rounded hills. In the bottom, the Río Aluminé reflects the bright morning sky in a long trail of pastel brilliance.

Hanging on the edge of Patagonia's famous trout waters, the Aluminé finds itself neglected like a little brother at a birthday party. With the Malleo, Chimehuín, and Collón Curá a closer drive from Junín, the Aluminé receives little angling pressure.

The highway hugs the river for miles, providing easy access. There's not enough interest to warrant landowner's fussing about propiedad privada, so any pullout works as an access point. There's also nothing but huge slabs of dark gray rock between the road and the river, so no reason for a cattle fence. It makes for a fun way to fish: cruise the dirt road at ten miles per hour until a good piece of water comes along, then pull into the shade of a big willow and slide the rods out the back window. It feels like cheating, like someone's going to come along any moment to scold our trespass.

The hillsides above the river look worn with time, rounded and grassed over. The river bottom looks the opposite, with jagged slabs of rock scattered along its banks and throughout the river itself. The character of the river is young, with sluicing currents barreling into rock and rising in angry white boils. After millennia the force of this water will leave a smooth channel of rounded pebbles, but these sharp rocks are still infants in the geologic calendar. The force of the interplay between stone and water makes the river feel alive with energy. It's a feeling at odds with the serenity of the hills above, like a pot of boiling water that might explode over its calm sides.

We fish good spots along the river working upstream through a series of long, deep runouts. We catch a few fish. I lose a nice rainbow a few feet from the bank. We find a long rock bar with a pool above and a long, riffled run below. Hauling the cooler down to the river, we make salami-and-cheese sandwiches and sprawl underneath the shade of a few young willows to escape the 103-degree day. I rest my head on a basketball-sized boulder and let the sandwich and sun lull me into lethargy. I hear Jim get up and grab his rod. From his footsteps I know he's off to the head of the run below a big pool. I'm glad; it's not the best water. With luck I'll get a quick nap and still have first shot at the water lower in the tailout where it runs itself into a long cliff face.

I'm interrupted before my eyelids have time to stop fluttering. "Wahoooo!" I look up expecting to see Jim overhyping a small fish to shame me into fishing instead of napping. His doubled-over rod and straining posture are no joke. I jump up and bound across the cobbled rock to the head of the run.

"Is he big?" I ask.

"Yeah, it's a monster. Huge, I think," Jim says.

"Where'd he take?"

"Right where the current breaks over into the run," he says.

"Solid strike?" I ask.

"Like a frickin' freight train! Ohweee!" he howls.

I think back a few days to Jim's words, "If I only take one monster, I'll be happy."

I'm always more stressed when other people have a fish on the line. I want to make sure they land it. Trick is, there's not much you can do to land a fish if you don't have the rod or a net in your hand—and on this particular afternoon I had neither.

Short of a net, good advice takes a distant second. There's little of this to be had in the heat of the moment. The three pieces of advice I know of to land a fish are these: keep the rod tip up, don't horse the fish, and adjust your drag (could be up or down). This takes five seconds to summarize. In a longer fight it leaves a lot of leftover time. Fortunately most people forget about their rod tip, so that one can be repeated several times. The "don't horse the fish" bit gets obnoxious after a couple of rounds, so I try to save it for a critical moment. There's also the danger of saying it simultaneously with a break off, in which case you both look like assholes. The advice on drag is a one-time deal with fish under ten pounds.

It's hard to fill the leftover space once the advice is gone. I've had people quietly stand behind me while I fought a big fish—it's uncomfortable. I know I have a big fish on and am trying to concentrate on landing it; the situation's important and stressful. With a silent gallery you're left to wonder how you're doing. Are they back there judging you? Whispering, "That's not how I'd have done it." Because frankly, if there's a better way of doing it, the time to speak up is *before* I botch the whole endeavor. The silent gallery feels like you're putting on some sort of show, a man-versus-nature deal with cheap seats.

I sometimes fall into the trap of working up the fish. "Oh man, he's a brute. That thing will go six pounds. What a great fish!" These are nice comments until the fish busts off and your buddy starts crying because what started a nice fish broke off as the once-in-a-lifetime, cover-shot fish you have just spent the twenty-minute fight creating.

So I stick with praise instead. I point out the things the angler's doing well. Little stuff that probably goes in one ear and out the other. Stuff that if they were really listening to they'd turn around and say, "Are you for real?" then dismiss me completely. Mindless things like "good stance" or "rock downstream left." I know it wouldn't help me land a fish but at least it fills the empty space and lets the person know I'm paying attention to what's going on.

And when they turn around and say, "Shut up," I do.

Jim plays the fish well. He works it from the strong current at the head of the run around a few midstream rocks. Fighting big fish is a fatigue game. At the beginning, a big fish has the strength and will to break a strong leader. A good angler doesn't provoke the fish too much in the early stages to assuage the risk of a furious run to sharp rocks or submerged tree roots. At the start, keep the fish uncomfortable, but not angry. When the fish moves in behind a rock, Jim gently draws him back out into the current. When the fish sulks on the bottom, he pulls him gently sideways forcing the fish to fight back to its natural center of gravity.

Sometimes fish get mad and run. I'll let them go and even strip line out to make their journey easier. It's a physical way to say, "You win, pal. You're the boss, you make the decisions." Then when the run is over, it's back to the same subtle tricks.

Jim plays the coy fisherman to perfection. He draws the fish out of the current by degrees, letting a few feet of river slip by at a time. After a while the fish has neither the security of the powerful current or the rock garden. He manages the fish to the tail of the run where the water runs deep and calm. In this secure position, Jim uses the rod and reel to dictate to the fish. Now fatigued and without a quick escape route, the fish fights against the force of the rod pulling ever nearer the bank.

We see the fish a few times in a golden flash or a white-bellied roll. This is Jim's monster fish. He works it close into a shallow pool and slides its side onto the algae-covered rock. She's a hen thick with spots on the shoulders that taper out toward the tail in alternating red and black. Her belly and fins look as gold as the afternoon sun. Jim can't quit smiling.

After a quick photo Jim holds the fish in the current to let her regain her strength. After a few seconds she tails hard and slips from Jim's hands upstream into the current. With the afternoon sun reflecting off the dimpled surface of the water she disappears within a few feet. For Jim and me, the best part is the disappearing. After finding the fish, hooking her, and fighting her, the culmination is watching a beautiful, healthy fish swim away to continue growing, spawning, and maybe bringing joy to some future angler.

The Río Aluminé, left on fishing's back burner for two decades, still preserves the essence of frontier fishing: easy access and fish unburdened by fishing pressure to alter their activity. Jim took his fish at one in the afternoon on a crystal-clear, sunny day in nine inches of water. It was a spot no self-preserving fish would dare find itself. Not because it was a bad place for a fish, but because it was a place too easy for a fisherman. Yet there she was, a deep-bellied, mature fish, unaware of the consequences of her precarious lie, just a short walk from a well-traveled road.

Filled with a new sense of possibility, I grab my rod and head to the lower end of the run, where I expect the best fish to reside. I work slowly, pulling streamers across the water column waiting for the next big carnivorous brown to inhale the fly.

My efforts are not rewarded; an hour later we are packing up the lunch cooler and heading for the Pathfinder. Even without a big fish of my own, I'm feeling happy. I love seeing the effort of several days of hard fishing pay off in a fish that Jim's been dreaming about for the past few months.

To celebrate Jim's monster we take dinner at Ruca Hueney. The upscale eatery sits on a corner of the main part of Junín's central square. Ample windows pour light out into the street and give a glimpse of the crowded restaurant inside. The Ruca has been a fishermen's haunt for decades and it's still the default for guided parties with its decidedly fishy theme. The walls are a tasteful mix of trout prints, dry flies in charcoal, and sweeping landscapes. Chandeliers of interlaced red deer antlers shower the dining area with a warm, inviting light. The solid wood chairs and linen-covered tables give the final touch that balances the class of fine dining with the ruggedness of the landscape.

Like any *parilla* (grill) restaurant in Argentina, the smell of slowly cooking meat hits the nostrils at the door. Around the back of the dining room there's likely to be a wall-long grill with a dedicated grill master, the *asador*. In a culture emphatic about the quality and taste of its meat, the asador reigns supreme in the kitchen. The meal and the menu revolve around meat. To this end, most parilla menus are á la carte affairs that allow a slab of beef, lamb, or fish to show up on a plate of its own immediately after it comes off the grill. In American restaurants it's not uncommon for a steak to wait under a hot lamp while rice pilaf or carrots finish heating; the same practice in Argentina amounts to a cardinal sin.

We are shown to our table in the middle of the restaurant and introduced to our waiter, who greets us in English. The familiar language brings a smile to Jim and John's faces; they've had difficulty with the language barrier during the trip. The two approach the same impediment in different ways. Jim pretends that everyone speaks English. Fortunately, most Argentines in the tourist industry do. But the few people we've encountered who don't speak English don't deter Jim from talking to them as if they did. He's a big guy with an amiable disposition, so he gets away with it better than most. It's funny to watch him gabbing away at some poor Argentine fellow who clearly does not understand. Through his tone, hand gestures, or some universal human connection he usually gets what he's after. The baffled Argentine gets what he's after too: Jim to leave.

John relies on a strategy he calls "Sí and smile." Whatever someone says to him in Spanish, he replies with "Sí" and follows with a smile. When this isn't sufficient, he rambles a few words that he believes sound Spanish. He admits that they have no meaning. After discussing it with him I'm convinced he thinks about what he wants to say, then imagines what he thinks it should sound like in Spanish. When this goes south—and it's surprising to see how long the polite and completely confused locals will carry on a conversation in this incoherent fashion— John reverts to his "Sí and smile" strategy. His results are less effective than Jim's. At dinner the previous night, Jim and I had delicious pasta meals, whereas John used his combination of gibberish and "Sí" to procure a grilled cheese sandwich from the kids menu. I would have intervened, but had absolutely no idea what John and the waiter were talking about. Though, on second thought, neither did they.

At Ruca Hueney we order a bottle of Malbec wine from the Mendoza region and celebrate in true fashion with bife de chorizo steaks all around. The cut is roughly equivalent to a rib eye in the States, but the raising and butchering processes are so different in Argentina that they don't really resemble each other. With the arrival of our steaks we are not disappointed. We each have a massive slab of inch-and-a-half thick beef showing the sear marks of the grill and oozing its own delicious reddish-brown sauce. The first bite is heaven on a fork; a sip of the deep red Malbec mellows and enhances the salty hint of the steak. It's a meal we savor on the lips like the last kisses of a departing lover.

It's an evening palpably close to perfection and one of those rare times in life you realize you can stop looking and just enjoy the moment. The day has all those elements of the quintessential Argentina that we dream up in our Montana kitchens. Lingering at Ruca Hueney after our meal, we soak in the atmosphere as several decades of fishermen before us have done. No doubt Jorge Trucco and his first clients in the early eighties sat in this dining room satiated by the food and wine and their epic day of dry flies on the Río Malleo.

While our memories of the day are not of the Malleo, we found eight-pound proof that there are still spots in Argentina that are the Argentina of thirty years ago. Places too far from roads or too near legendary waters. Maybe I'm a bit like Jorge myself in telling our tale of the Aluminé. Perhaps in five years my words will have scared that hen back to the depths of the cliff face or the safety of the overhanging willows. There's an opportunity with that danger. I'd have never found the Aluminé had I not been drawn to, and in a way disappointed by, the post-Jorge Malleo. Perhaps a disappointing Aluminé will lead a future angler to another undiscovered river and to sit in the warm light of the parilla with friends, full of good food and fresh memories.

9
GUIDES, SHUTTLES, AND GOOD FORTUNE

It is perfectly true that good fishing is not all luck. But it is just as true that there is no good fishing without some luck.

Roderick Haig-Brown, *To Know a River*

I n Northern Patagonia, few rivers draw as much attention as the Río Chimehuín. Its history at the boca, the proximity to Junín, and the fish it continues to produce give it a revered place in the Argentine anglers' consciousness. Helping to keep the river in a state of abundance, and in a sense adding to its allure, is the difficulty in accessing the majority of the river. Once it leaves Junín's city park it departs alone across the steppe meeting humanity a handful of times before disappearing for good into two extensive private estancias. With the banks locked tight against fishermen by fences and distance, the only way to fish it is by overnight float.

Logistics make it a difficult trip. While it's possible to put in at Junín, the only takeout is more than twenty miles downstream and forty road miles from the town of Junín on a completely different river. The takeout is nothing more than a hole in the roadside trees and the broad flat of rounded river rock. Other than Andean condors circling over the dry terrain, there's nothing but bleak vistas in all directions. To complicate matters the local guides and estancia owners run protectionist schemes on the river to keep private parties from experiencing the river without first filling their coffers.

Scrambling around Junín, we gather snippets of information about the float. Few people float the river without a guide, which leaves the bulk of the knowledge base in the hands of a few commercial operators. With our rudimentary map collection from gas stations and tourist offices, we put together a rough trip itinerary. By rough, I mean the only things we know for sure are the put in and takeout locations. We struggle to even find the part that will connect the two—a shuttle.

The need for a shuttle plays a prominent role in trip planning when trying to float Patagonian rivers. In Bariloche I got lucky meeting a guide at a local pub and getting plugged into his shuttle network. With a quick cell phone call I met the guide's brother, Alexander, at seven in the morning outside my hotel and drove south to the Río Manso. Six hours later the river turned a bend and my car and Alexander sat waiting on the bank. I noticed that the odometer read over a hundred kilometers, more than I expected and the gas gauge hung low, but I had a ride back to town. I was satisfied to hand Alexander sixty pesos, put some extra gas in the tank, and enjoy the convenience of a ready-made shuttle.

For the most part, shuttles in Patagonia rarely are arranged for such a low cost in pesos and stress. Most rivers don't begin or end anywhere near a town, so securing a driver becomes practically impossible. Overcoming this handicap often takes considerable creativity, chance, and often, sweat. I took the chance of running the float on the Río Limay before finding a shuttle, and at the end of a cold afternoon I stood with my thumb in the air for seven cars before getting picked up by a writer for a German wine magazine.

Another time, an Argentine friend convinced a local mechanic to give me a ride back to town. I sat with his small child on my lap and made small talk for an hour using every Spanish word I knew. Farther south on a river in the middle of nowhere I put my running shoes in a dry bag and jogged seven miles of dirt road back to my car. The most complex shuttle configuration involved a two-day rental of a too-small bicycle and two forty-kilometer rides. I'm sure the trip provided the aging Trek mountain bike the most memorable if not the only rafting trip of its long life.

The nontraditional shuttle system works. But that's about all I can say about it. If the shuttle is not set up beforehand, the entire float becomes a worry about how to get back to the car. And with the human-powered shuttle; the last thing a person wants after a long day on the water is get more exercise. Alcohol and steak is a far superior post-float activity.

>>>>

The Chimehuín shuttle requires too much distance and coordination for anything but a true shuttle. I know better than to launch the boat unless something with wheels and a motor waits at the other end. The first stop to secure this, the tourist office in Junín, proves a poor start. I take it as a bad sign that the concept of a shuttle had yet to enter the popular jargon of the tourism industry, especially in a town proclaimed as the fishing capital of Argentina. But it was the difference between Montana and Patagonia that brought me here in the first place, so details be damned.

The best that the tourism office could do was hand me the long list of local guides and a look that said, "Good luck with this one." We set off up the street to the nearest address on the list. A few blocks later I find a small sign in a front lawn for the guide service and a portly man watering his flowerbed with a black garden hose. Parked in the driveway is a Toyota truck and a drift boat. The large man with a mostly gray beard shakes my hand and leads me into his home.

The entryway walls are hung with local fishing paraphernalia. On the right, a display of a hundred or more fly patterns hangs in glass in ordered rows with their names in Spanish and English beneath each. I look at the familiar flies and sound out their unfamiliar Spanish names hoping to remember a few of the more common ones. Moscas Seca, reads one label—dry flies. On the left side of the room is a poster-sized fishermen's map of the area. It's printed on heavy paper that shows its age with a yellow-orange tint. I wonder almost out loud about where and when it may have been printed, and where I might find a copy. It's the exact piece of information I need. The area rivers stand out in bold red lines with roads and access points labeled in black. Through the middle of the poster snakes the Río Chimehuín in a long red line without a single access point marring its curves below a place labeled Puente Manzana. I covet the map, pausing in front of it an inordinate amount of time before moving into the sitting room.

The conversation begins with pleasantries about each other's recent fishing exploits. I describe our trips on the Malleo and Aluminé and catch a look of surprise at our success on the Aluminé. He checks his surprise and shakes his head in a knowing manner. "Oh, yes, we are doing so well right now. This is the best time to be on the river."

He tells me his daughter married a fishing guide and fly-shop owner from West Yellowstone, Montana. Probing me with a list of fly-shop owner's names I've never heard of, he appears to settle on the fact that I am no one of consequence. I wish for a moment I'd spent more time in that fishing mecca of the West. The whole process would be a lot easier with a local connection.

After I describe our plan for a two-day float on the Chimehuín, he picks up the conversation with a typical guide's sales pitch regarding the huge fish and beautiful scenery that could easily apply to any river in the world. It wasn't the first time I'd gotten or given one of these "best time you'll ever have" pitches, and I know to read between the lines and take the opportunities to interject questions. When he says the fish are taking well on the surface, I counter with a query about the specific flies I might use. When he says his last clients did well, I find a tactful way to ask how many and how large. We play a cat-and-mouse game of information gathering. As much as I push him to reveal more, he slides away into ambiguity with equal skill.

After a while I realize that he thinks I'm planning to do the trip with his company. I mentioned from the outset that we had our own boat and planned to do a self-guided trip, but like the folks at the tourist office, the notion that foreigners owned their own car and boat is so far-fetched that he must think I misspoke or he translated incorrectly. The misconception makes it clear why I've gotten so much information out of him. My usual experience pumping guides for information was to either be blown off or get a detailed explanation about how everything was too difficult to do without a guide. I find that most Argentine guides will explain to you at great lengths how it is too difficult to paddle a rubber raft across a swimming pool if he thinks there is any chance you will pay him to paddle you across himself.

I feel compelled to clear up the misinterpretation and explain again that I have my own boat and car, and restate my inquiry regarding a shuttle. The second time around I see comprehension dawn on his face and his expression changes to a look of consternation. I know my advantage won't last long and push forward a few specific questions about the float. He changes tack on me as expected, beginning along the well-trodden path of painting fishing in the most difficult light possible. What was in one moment a beautiful float with large, aggressive fish turns quickly into a troublesome river with difficult-to-read braids and strict rules regarding private land. A shuttle? Of course he doesn't know where I might find one.

Even after he knows I'm not hiring him for the trip, I get more out of him than I should. He's spent long enough in jovial, helpful guide mode that I think he feels too hypocritical to end the conversation abruptly and humors me with half-ass, but valuable answers. After a few minutes he conveniently remembers he needs to get ready for an afternoon client and shuffles me out the door with a distinctly different tone than the one used to escort me into the home.

Still without a shuttle, at least I have more information about the river at this point. The fishing sounds decent. I now know it to be a two-day float in two sections of about twelve miles each. He made sure to impress on me the necessity of camping in one specific spot; the only public land on the river. I largely disregard the information as a spook story designed to scare. My experience with river floats in Patagonia is that they are far enough in the middle of nowhere that ranchers don't care where you camp, and if they care they have no way to enforce their will. The law also dictates that thirty meters from the river-bank is public water, so as a last resort I rely on making a camp within the public stretch of riverbank.

My suspicions lead me to expect the same kind of brush-off from the other nineteen guides on the tourist office list. Wanting to start the float the following morning, I'm growing nervous about our shuttle prospects. I could gamble on hitchhiking, but sixty miles is a long walk if that doesn't pan out. I contemplate hiring a taxi, but what taxi driver is going to drive thirty-five miles down the Collón Curá River to find an American who barely speaks Spanish? Besides the reliability of the taxi driver, I doubt my ability to describe the takeout point ... in English. "Uh, yeah, go down the highway till you see a big, wide stretch of river rocks. That's the spot." But we try anyway.

We bypass a siesta that afternoon and head to Junín's downtown area. We navigate the Roman grid and find the little maroon stucco storefront with "Radiotaxi" scrawled in blue letters. The windows are caged in steel fencing with a heavy wooden door closed tight. The place doesn't have the feel of a bustling business; in fact, it's closed. While we diligently pursue our tasks, the rest of the town takes a siesta. I know better than to run errands at three in the afternoon, but hope and desperation often override common sense.

Stymied at the taxi office we decide to try the *Guardafauna*— the park ranger's office. In addition to doling out a list of local guides, the tourist office told us we'd need a free permit to float the river. We find the large mission-style building with "Guardafauna" painted in brown across the front. At least the door here is open.

Two young officers in head-to-toe khaki meet us before we even step inside. Both look a touch older than twenty. Alesandro is short and thin with dark, curly hair and a three-day beard. Martin maintains a more official appearance with close-cropped hair.

"*Hola.*"

"*¿Cómo te va?*" Martin says.

"*Bien, Bien. ¿Y a vos?*"

"*Bien, gracias,*" they reply in unison.

An odd silence then takes over. Neither party knows where to go next. They wonder what a foreigner wants at the Guardafauna office, and I'm wondering how to say "river permit" in Spanish. Permito de río, licencia del río, permiso por el río? As the silence grows more awkward, I decide to launch into whatever confusing explanation I can concoct for our visit.

"*Ah, Quisiera flotar el Chimehuín mañana en la mañana por dos días y pienso, '¿Necesitaremos permiso?'*""

When I don't know quite how or what to say I find myself adding extraneous information to the sentence. That we were leaving in the morning doesn't matter, but that I can let "*mañana en la mañana*" roll off my tongue with ease gives me a little more confidence with the rest of the sentence.

"Do you speak English?" Martin asks with the slightest trace of an accent.

"Uh, yeah."

"What do you need?" he says in a welcoming way.

After I ask about the river permit, he explains that only guides need the permit. Private parties are free to put on the river whenever they like.

The English conversation draws the Js in from the periphery like vultures on a fresh kill. In seconds they wrap Martin and Alesandro in conversation. I see more value in the two park rangers than small talk and keep trying to interject into the conversations to ask questions about the Chimehuín and the float. Jim picks up on what I'm trying to do and joins in by asking how long the float takes the first day.

Martin's father owns the fly shop across the street from the Guardafauna office, and Martin grew up fishing the Chimehuín. He knows the river better than most of the guides in town. It wouldn't surprise me if Martin's weekend job is floating locals with fly rods down the river.

He recommends a few different patterns; green inchworms eat the trees in droves this time of year and he suggests anything bright green and worm-like. "Even a piece of pipe cleaner tied to a hook will work," he says.

He mentions a few general nymph patterns and then says, "... but my favorite is ..." With this remark he glances around and looks over his shoulder down the open hallway of the Guardafauna office. With a lowered voice, he explains how he uses a hopper-dropper system. He hangs a nymph two feet under a hopper pattern and fishes the wet and dry fly simultaneously. The technique has been popular in the States for two decades; both Js and I easily picture the setup in our heads.

All of Argentina follows a one-fly law, meaning you can fish with only one hook at a time. The hopper-dropper setup violates this law.

"Isn't there one-fly law in Argentina?" I ask.

"Yes, technically. It's a bit of a gray area," he says.

I don't pursue the conversation. I want the hopper-dropper to stay in the gray area, and too much conversation with law-type folks has a tendency to get them feeling self-conscious after a while. That the enforcement arm of the fishing regulations is suggesting the tactic is a good enough reason for me to believe we won't go to jail for fishing a two-fly setup.

A curious look passes over Martin's face as the conversation winds down. He looks back to me and asks how we are going to get our car to the takeout.

I explain the ordeal of schmoozing guides and absent taxi drivers and lament that it might come down to hitchhiking.

At the idea of hitchhiking Martin looks disturbed and turns to Alesandro, whose limited English has prevented him from getting too involved in the conversation.

Martin rushes out a few sentences in Spanish under his breath into Alesandro's ear and the two exchange "What do you think?" looks. After a pause, Alesandro nods.

"What day are you going to be done with the float?"

"Saturday about three in the afternoon," I say.

"*Sábado a las tres,*" Martin translates to Alesandro.

Alesandro nods again.

"If you would like, Alesandro can do the shuttle for you."

Incredible. Each time I get backed into a corner, Patagonia delivers a fishing saint to right the situation. First Richard on the road to El Bolsón, now Alesandro and Martin on the Chimehuín. We came to them in need of information, a permit, and a driver, and leave with all three in a higher quality than we ever hoped. We are on for our two-day float of the Río Chimehuín.

10
RÍO CHIMEHUÍN

People who make no mistakes lack
boldness and the spirit of adventure.

Dale Turner

R ising early to a pink sky, we clean out of the two-story bungalow. The parts and pieces of the boat scattered throughout the living room are corralled and stacked in the back of the Pathfinder. Each little space receives an item until the SUV fills to the point that the shocks are laid low by the load. Suitcases and dry bags are stuffed and prodded into a loose conglomeration of imminent disaster. Fortunately the river flows minutes away from the unloading zone, where the gear can once again explode.

The drive to the river takes us a half-mile across town to the riverfront city park. I ignore the "No cars" sign on the road. Like the locals, I've become adept at ignoring most Argentine traffic signs. After months in the country, red lights don't even elicit a tap on the brakes. I don't expect many people to complain at seven in the morning, but I put on the hazard lights anyway. On the main boulevard of any Argentine city there will be two or three cars double-parked in the middle of rush-hour traffic. Traffic cops will stroll by the parked cars satisfied with the legality of the maneuver as long as the yellow hazard lights are blinking.

We find a grassy knoll above the river and let the tight packing job explode out of the car. We all know the routine by now, so the boat goes up in twenty minutes. The boat is a sixteen-foot cataraft with a metal frame that snaps together like a grown man's erector set. Two big banana-shaped tubes get pumped up by a thousand or so strokes to the hand-powered barrel pump. Snapping and clicking the dry bags onto the frame and locking the oars into the pins, we're ready to bid Junín farewell. The last mission is to drop the car off at Martin's father's fly shop so he can keep an eye on it for the couple days we're gone. I walk from the car back to the boat with unbounded hopes for our overnight float.

The beginning of the float takes us along the edge of town. After a lifetime in the western United States and its obsession with riverfront property, it's odd to see the river in a state of abandonment by the town. A crude walking path and a footbridge over the river gives the only hints of its inclusion in the city's acknowledged attributes. I recall city parks in Lewiston, Idaho; Missoula, Montana; and Bend, Oregon; where lush lawns and well-manicured shrubs complemented the peaceful flows of midcity waterways. The Junín park looks like the back forty. Beyond the strip of rough, untended foliage lies the edge of town and the backsides of the poor barrios. Where I would expect the prime riverfront real estate to have been consumed by upscale boutiques and microbreweries, the town turns its back as if hoping the river might disappear if left unnoticed long enough.

The scene strikes me as paradoxical considering the outward show of fishing enthusiasm in town. In a place where fish are carved into the street signs and the tourist office contains as many pamphlets on fishing guides as lodging, they seem to have forgotten the role the river plays in the operation.

A float through town takes us to the all-too-familiar scene of large brick mansions of the upscale suburbs. The homeowners appreciate the river in classic upscale suburban style by clearing the bank of natural vegetation and pushing their perfect green lawns to the edge, so much so that at one house the Kentucky bluegrass falls into the river at a recently eroded cutbank. I'm certain at one estate I could have stolen the patio furniture with a not-so-long cast and strong enough leader.

These are the second, or tenth, homes of wealthy foreigners and create an eerily comforting scene. But the feeling comes tinged with disgust. In their appreciation for the river, they've abandoned any sensitivity to its needs or a consideration for other river users. The river rebels by claiming a portion of the lawn, an occasional fence post, and, once or twice a century, a few houses.

The stretch of the river through town and beyond is thin water. Even without rapids, the oarsman needs keen attention to avoid collisions with the brambles of willow that line the bank. I begin on the oars; at times the Js are unable to cast due to a lack of room between the boat and surrounding overgrowth. When the river widens the fish tuck themselves under the edges of the willows, where food and protection come hand in hand. Casts are necessarily precise, and flies are lost on attempts that fail to achieve perfection.

I spend the morning rowing and watching for fish. After an hour and a mile of river, I've yet to see much fish activity. Despite fishing many likely boulder runs and deep pools, we've yet to catch or even see any sizeable fish. I have a hunch the culprit is our proximity to town.

There's an inherent problem in upholding fishing regulations with people, or a significant portion of the population, that's hungry. When a person has a freezer full of food at home, it's easy to enjoy a day of fishing for its aesthetic qualities. A person may go so far as to cast a fly instead of toss a lure with the idea that the venture is largely for recreation. Fish or no, the activity finds its success in the level of enjoyment. When fishing as an aesthetic pursuit, fishing is the activity, but fish are not necessarily the objective.

Recreational anglers place such esteem in rivers. But we find our dietary sustenance in a building paid for by long hours in front of computer screens. Because of this we turn to the river to fulfill other needs, whether it be primordial urges to breathe fresh air or challenge one of Mother Nature's creatures, we value the river for its essence—not its produce.

When dinner depends on fish, the activity of fishing takes on a much different direction. Aesthetics be damned if a gill net puts food on the table. These differing needs do not play well together, for the meat fisherman can rob the river of its essence, the essential one for recreational fishermen at least, by denuding the river of fish.

In places, fishing regulations attempt to balance these needs with limited catch numbers, but on the Chimehuín the interests of the recreational fishing economy have won; it's a fly-only, catch-and-release river. Despite arguments that a healthy river provides more food for the town as a whole by bringing in a tourist economy, a good argument stands little chance against genuine physical hunger. We see several people slink into the bushes as we approach in the boat or shoot sheepish glances toward us as they try to determine our legal authority.

As we float past the last remnants of human dwellings, a large pipe of inch-thick iron a foot in diameter projects into the river. From the end of the pipe spews a thick brown sludge of raw sewage. We don't see the pipe in time to avoid it and float right over the stream of feces. Ironically, a very large brown trout spooks out of the effluent and darts upstream. Perhaps the only large fish left in that section of river sought its refuge in our waste.

Shortly after the sewage pipe, the river cuts away from the main road and enters the private grounds of a large estancia. Now the fishing picks up; we are more than two miles from town and isolated by private property signs. A substantial change occurs with the decreased pressure. We begin floating over good-sized fish holding in shallow water in the middle of the river. Like fish in the Malleo, fishing pressure dictates their behavior, and these fish show the signs of infrequent abuse.

One problem with floating shallow water is that by the time you see a fish, you're too close and it's a matter of seconds before the boat spooks the fish to cover. This is frustrating for two reasons. First, you spook the fish, making it impossible to catch. And second, you're seeing fish all the time but you can't catch them. This robs you of most of the good excuses for being fishless. The converse of this problem is going fishless while wade fishing, something that makes you wonder if there are even fish in the river. Both routes are equally frustrating.

We spent the morning in the first state of frustration watching fish bolt from under our boat. After enough frustration a person has a few choices: go home, drink beer, or learn. Going home isn't a real option during a float, so we drink beer. We open a litter of Imperial and pour it into plastic cups. For a while we abandon the fishing and enjoy our personal booze cruise and scream like whale-watching tourists when fish dart by us.

"There's one! Left-side front. Big."

"Check out underneath the far log! You can barely see it."

"Grab your rod!"

"Shit, spooked."

"Pass the beer."

And so it went until we ran out of beer and we were forced into the third option: learning.

Fish have patterns. If a person can pick up on these patterns, he can predict a fish's location and what it might be eating before seeing it (or in our case, spooking it). At its most basic level this is all we are doing when we're matching a hatch or casting to a tempting-looking spot along a cliff wall: making predictions based on past experience and current observations.

In the United States this isn't that hard on the majority of fisheries. We learn to identify the fishy structures: the drop-off ledge, the cliff wall, the boulder field where we've had past success. We can usually move from river to river and find the same general success fishing these go-to structures. Throw in a few identifiable insects floating around in a foam mat and you're a shoo-in on about any river in the American West.

In Patagonia, fish are crazy. You can spend all day fishing those likely runs or all day fishing the mediocre water and end up with the same result. I can't count the number of honey holes I've come across that gave me the spine-tingling sense of big-fish anticipation only to meet a disappointing end in a six-inch fingerling. At other times an errant cast to some rejected water surprises when the fly starts moving on its own away from the boat at an alarming speed.

On a float of the Río Califon I was forced to give up casting to long, deep, cliff-backed pools, boulder runs, and juicy under-cut banks because it took away time to cast to the ankle-deep water on the shallow bank. For whatever reason the fish gravi-tated to water barely deep enough to conceal their dorsal fins, a fact I discovered while my line floated idly and I searched my fly box to find a fly that might draw a fish from the cliff-backed pools and undercut banks.

On Chile's Río Nirehuao I covered a pathetically small amount of water because of these crazy fish. I couldn't hop honey hole to honey hole because the fish were scattered around the river like they'd been dropped at random by plane and never regained their senses. I cast out to every piece of water with equal parts hope and consternation.

From the boat we have the advantage of seeing the fish's position, and after long enough, we piece together a rough idea of where the Chimehuín's fish like to spend their sunny morn-ings. The favorite spot of the big fish is in the middle of the river in shallow water five feet above a break-over into deeper water. Simple enough, right? Even if this was a rule instead of a half-wild guess concocted while drunk, we still had to identify this type of water far enough in advance to pull the boat over without spooking the fish.

Turning this theory into productive reality never comes together as hoped. It takes all three of us to decide where these fish might be. Once we pull over to shore, we lose the verti-cal advantage of the boat that lets us see into the water, so it becomes a case of the blind leading the blind. We stalk the area with one guy acting the part of the angler and the other two as spotters. On a few attempts we come close, spooking the fish on our approach to "the spot." At least on these occasions we guess correctly. More often, however, we spend twenty minutes stalking a fish that doesn't exist. We never catch one, but we feel good about our tactic. It also keeps us from drinking all of day two's beer before noon on the first day.

In lieu of the fact that we've yet to catch much in the way of large trout, the float progresses in enjoyable fashion on the secluded river in the warm sun. I want to kick back and savor the beer but my mind is plagued by one discomforting idea. Namely, that we are well off-schedule to reach our destination.

While Martin the Guardafauna officer assured me that the float took two days and that we could put in at the town park, I begin to wonder if the two statements were actually connected. I was starting to think that putting in at Junín, the float is actually three days.

On one hand I have Martin, a river official with a long history on the river, whom I consider a good source. My other source is a highway map in which the entirety of the thirty-plus mile float takes up six inches of map space. In general, I recommend avoiding highway maps as the main source of geographical information on overnight excursions of any sort (except of course those that are highway oriented).

Martin's word seems the more valid of the two sources of information, and this keeps my alarm at the discomfort stage. But by late afternoon my fears increase as each river corner fails to uncover the Puente Manzana—the Apple Bridge—that provides the only clear-cut marker on the map. That we haven't seen or heard the highway all day adds to my uneasiness, but the fact we've not yet come upon the bridge proves our dilemma. On the map, the Puente Manzana spans the river a touch less than halfway between the put-in at Junín and the one legal camping area on the lower stretch of river.

At six o'clock we can see the highway in the distance. A few bends later the bridge crosses the river. It has taken seven hours to float eight miles of river. By my crude calculation we have three hours of light and seven miles left to float before reaching camp.

We pull over at the bridge, where another group of anglers is pulling a raft onto a trailer. I want to confirm our location before we plunge farther along our reckless path. The group turns out to be clients from a lodge along the upper reaches of the Chimehuín. Three people make up this group: a younger

Argentine guide, an overweight Arkansan baby boomer client, and a gigantic Okie as broker.

There's a fair amount of secrecy, testosterone, and posturing that accompany these encounters in Argentina—in the States too, but to a lesser degree. In the States there's not that much to be secret about; for every stream there's multiple guidebooks, website fishing reports, and daily mobile device hot fly alarms. In Argentina it's still a big game of who's got the hot fly or the right spot. In truth it has more to do with insecure guides worried their clients will talk to another group and find out in fact the fishing is great, but their guide sucks.

To break through this veil of standoffishness, we attack the weakest link, the client. He has no idea what he's supposed to say or not say, so he's usually a good source.

"Hey buddy, how was the fishing today?"

"I don't know, caught a lot of 'em, but they're all such small things."

"Yeah, I know what you mean. Same story for us." It's best to play along with the client, get him comfortable so he keeps feeding information. Play this game right, and he'll divulge everything the guide doesn't want you to hear.

"First time to Argentina?" I ask.

"Yep."

"How do you like it?"

"It's alright. We sure catch a lot of fish. But like I said, they're small and they don't let us keep a damn one. Got to throw 'em all back. What's the point in that?"

Living so long in the heart of catch-and-release fish country, Montana, I'd forgotten that the United States still produces people like this. In Montana it's now so rare for people to keep trout—even though it's completely legal and ecologically sustainable—that to show up at a boat ramp with a stringer of dead fish guarantees sneers, glares, and backhanded comments and risks starting a fight.

"What sort of flies did they have you on?"

With this magic question the head of the broker pops up and he tries without success to casually enter the conversation.

"Used some hoppers, went down with some nymphs, tried a streamer or two," he says.

In other words they tried a vague collection of everything possible. I think I know why the broker interjected into the conversation so quickly.

"Did you guys try any hopper-dropper stuff where you tied a nymph on below the hopper?" I ask the client in a disingenuous tone.

"Yeah, we did quite a bit of that," the client answers. I see the broker go pale. Gotcha!

I don't give two cents whether or not they've been using a two-fly setup. We used it too on the advice of the Guardafauna. I just like the idea of the broker stewing at the thought that we might have something on them. Even though the law is gray on the subject, few guides or brokers care to deal with the hassle or reputation of the practice becoming publicized.

The big Okie broker isn't one to be bullied and he senses the track I'm on. He stands about six feet five inches and weighs over 250 pounds. Looking at him, I think I recognize an old lineman for some state university back in the day who ate raw steak for dinner. He tries to turn the tables on us by hinting that I am guiding illegally. I probably am, so his comments don't surprise me too much. He uses my same tactic and addresses his questions to Jim and John. I let him pursue his track, knowing neither of the Js can say anything that will give us a problem down the road.

I take the opportunity to slide out of the conversation and instead pepper the guide with questions. I'm not sure if he's like the one I approached in Junín to ask about shuttle options. He's younger, which bodes well. Young guides in Argentina are far less cynical. They don't seem to have spent long enough in the business to get cold toward the rest of the fishing world like their seasoned counterparts.

"*Hola. ¿Cómo te va?*" I ask.

"*Bien. ¿Y a vos?*" he says.

"*Bien. Es un día muy bueno hoy,*" I say.

"*Sí, sí. ¿Tú eres un guía?*" he asks.

"*En los Estados Unidos sí. Pero, en Argenina estoy aquí solo por diversión. Ellos son mis amigos de los Estados Unidos,*" I say pointing to Jim and John.

"You fish well today?" he asks, switching seamlessly to English.

"Okay, not great. Lots of small stuff, but had a hard time hooking into anything big."

"The river is tough right now," he says.

"Seems that way. This is Puente Manzana, right?" I ask.

"Sí," he says.

"Hmm. Do you know how far it is to the camping spot mid-river?" I ask.

"Maybe ten or twelve miles," he says, shrugging.

"Shit. We were planning on camping there tonight. We got some bad information in town. How long would it take to float?"

"We do it in ten hours. Maybe without fishing, you can do it faster. No way tonight," he says. The guide turns out to be one of the truly nice guys in the business. I want to stay and chat with him about the other area rivers and how he got into the guiding business. I get his card and promise to call in the future.

About this time I catch a bit of the other conversation; they're talking about our plan to camp at the island. Having the information I want from the guide I try to break back to the other group.

I step in to hear the lineman say, "It's a full fourteen miles to the campground. It takes us ten hours to float. You'll never make it. Don't even think about trying to camp somewhere else either. Just yesterday the policia from Junín got a guide at the takeout. He'd camped along the way and some of the other guides turned him in." He said this part like he wanted to be one of the guides to turn us in. "The rancher along the way has the whole thing locked up in private property. He runs gauchos along the river to look for people camping."

"So there's only one place to camp on the whole river?" I ask.

"Yep. You know how to find it?" he says looking at me. I register the comment with the full amount of disdain he intends.

"Can't say that I know much more than we're looking for an island," I say.

At this point we must seem so pathetic that something inside his linebacker heart breaks like the Grinch on Christmas. Either that or he realizes that we are entirely too clueless to be a guided group and therefore not a danger to his financial interests in Patagonia.

"Okay. You're going to get down there quite a ways and there will be a long, straight section after a left-hand turn. At the end of the straightaway there's a big triangle rock the size of a Volkswagen that makes a little rapid. The takeout for the camping area is a half-mile below the rock on the left. The camping spot is on an island, but you can't tell it's an island and the pull out is just a small cut in the trees. If you don't know what you're looking for, you'll go right past it," he tells us.

"So left turn, straight away, big triangle rock, half-mile, island on left?" I ask back.

"Yeah, but you'll never make it down there. It gets dark at nine," he says.

I want to reply that with his directions we are as likely to find it in the dark as in daylight. Turn right at the big boulder then go farther till you get to the things you can't see until you have passed them and then you're there. I've gotten lost going to high school keggers with directions that included dogs and lefts at funny-shaped trees that sounded easier to find than the Chimehuín campsite.

With our information secure, I make a point of saying goodbye to the guide and promise again to call him as we push off the shallow rocks. I take the oars and begin rowing at a pace quick enough to belie the panic in my brain.

"*Chao. Hasta luego,*" I call back to the group.

Pulling on the oars, we move off the last of the public land for eleven miles. With three hours of light left in the day, we start the ten-hour float.

11
RÍO CHIMEHUÍN
PART II

To succeed in life you need two things:
ignorance and confidence.

Mark Twain

R owing seven miles in three hours takes most of the fun out of a float. Jim and John initially have their rods in hand rigged and ready. The water below Puente Manzana looks better than anything we floated over earlier in the day. The two men toss casts out to the edge of the water under the bushy willows. I'm rowing hard, working with the current to move us downstream so fast that by the time the flies hit the water, we are pulling them downstream. This results in an ugly form of trolling and after the first few casts, the Js refuse to continue out of pride and futility, and the nasty tendency of fouling the fishing line in the oars.

We relegate ourselves to rowing and speculate on the wonderful trout water we pass up. "Look at that eddy." "Can you imagine what hangs out under that tree?" and so on. It's a shame we're forced to pass up so much water; several times it looks so good that I almost beg the Js to throw a fly.

The three of us take turns rowing. Since I'm the youngest I pull for a half an hour, then each J takes over for fifteen minutes. Jim, who's spent a good deal of time in his brother's drift boat, rows well. With Jim at the oars we don't give up anything in terms of speed and he keeps a good downstream tack. John doesn't have Jim's experience level and therefore tries to compensate with zest. I'm sure we travel at the same speed with John at the oars but we zigzag from bank to bank. When a tricky section of boulders and islands comes up in the middle of John's rotation, I can't bring myself to push him off the oars so instead grip the seat mount with white knuckles and try to muster positive words and energy.

"Just a little more on the left oar," I say as we crunch into a wall of willow branches and begin spinning down the channel. We bounce off a few rocks and trees, but come out farther downstream with intact tubes and rods.

By my second rotation on the oars my stomach realizes it's past dinnertime. We can't stop for a meal at this point, so John digs in the cooler to see if we can put together some sort of snack. He brings out an apple, a sleeve of crackers, and a block of hard cheese. A few minutes later he has a gourmet-quality snack plate sitting on the cooler. While he and Jim start eating, with my hands wrapped on the oars, I can only look at the food as it disappears. Jim looks at me with his mouth full of a cracker, apple, and cheese sandwich and mumbles, "This is good."

He makes another sandwich and holds it out in front of me so that I can grab it with my mouth as I come forward on the oar stroke. They feed me another half-dozen as I row us downriver. At this point in the trip we've broken down any real or imagined barriers between us. As night approaches, we are just three friends doing the inadvisable: trying to race against time.

With our sub-par map we never know quite where we are on the river. After several hours of floating we guess anywhere from five to eight miles into the float. Until we find the straight-away and the big triangle rock that the Okie told us about, we are lost on a one-lane road. If we don't find the rock by dark we'll have other problems. Our backup plan consists of floating till just before dark, pulling off the river on the small strip of public access land within the high-water mark, setting up an out-of-the-way camp, and packing up again at daybreak. I don't think we'd be caught during seven hours of darkness and figure that in a worst-case scenario, our explanation to the lower court would result in our being found innocent by incompetence.

We keep rowing until the sun drops behind the western sky. Dusk shows a cloudless gold with a red-streaked base. I don't see the sunset for its beauty; instead I see the cloudless sky for the ability to milk every last second of light out of the day.

We come upon two boats at a broad plane in the valley. This sign of life gives hope to our dire mission. The boats belong to guides and are identifiable by the numbers stenciled on the vessels. A well-clad, middle-aged man rows the closest boat, and two older, pale-skinned people try their best to cast to the banks. Rowing in close enough to yell, I try not to sound desper-ate. I'm sure I fail. I don't even try to start asking questions in Spanish. As guides they speak English and I fear losing any pre-cious seconds with my broken Spanish.

I ask if they know how far it is to the public camping island. The guide pauses for a moment and answers, four and a half miles. The answer fits within our estimate of five to eight miles covered.

The second boat follows the same rushed pattern. No matter how calm I appear in conversation, the frantic rowing I do on the approach must clue them in to our dire straights.

"Do you know how much further it is to the camping island?" I ask.

"About two miles," the guide yells across the water.

I like the sound of two better than four. This also explains the bad information I got from Martin. Even guides on the river have an error margin of more than 100 percent. I hope for two miles for no other reason than we can make the campsite in two. If it turns out to be four we will be camping illegally.

I push on at the oars, skipping through John's and Jim's turns. I do this in part to save time on the transition and in part, I regret to say, to keep John off the oars. We need every minute of light.

Another half-mile downstream, we pass another drift boat eddied out in a shoulder pool casting dry flies in the final light. They are across the river from us and tough to make out in the fading light. We pass by without a word, just a hurried wave and quick strokes on the oars. A little ways farther we come across a set of 4x4 trucks and trailers ready to pick up the two guide boats. The guides' calm demeanor when we passed was due to the close proximity to their shuttles; they weren't trying to make an uncertain island campsite.

A little farther on we arrive at a large triangular rock, and I'm certain we've found the right spot. We float past the rock to a side channel that cuts off to the right to form the tip of an island. We've made it with light to spare. Jumping out, we pull the boat onto a cobbled shore and investigate. I start by looking for signs of human life. With only one campsite for a whole river, there is bound to be ample evidence of this.

I look hard along the edge of trees at the likely spot for a camp. I find a flattened-out area that looks good for tents, but none of the more destructive human signs like fire rings surrounded by hacked-up trees and the inevitable toilet paper garlands. After covering an acre of riverbank I concede our error and head back to the boat. We need a new triangle rock. My confidence in the Okie's directions slips further.

I push harder against the oars now to make up for our stop. My palms have been red and raw for hours from the friction of rowing. Each stroke takes on a faster rhythm of leaning forward and throwing my arms forward. Each stroke, I take a split-second to set the oars, then follow the rush of movement and a taut bend in the oar shafts. My feet flex off the front crossbar and thighs tighten as my legs outstretch. At the same time I pull my hands in tight to my chest. It's an explosive movement that draws the blade through the water in an even sweep just below the surface. Stroke, stroke, stroke, counts in my head and we continue down the river in a trance of activity.

We pass another triangle rock and again take up a vigilant eye watching for any inlet or beach with traces of man. A cliff face on the left and a broad rock beach on the right don't have the promising look of island or campsite. With the light fading, it's almost time to look for a place to hole up for the night.

Searching the bank with the last bit of light, we hear a loud *clank-clank* from upriver and look up to see the drift boat we'd seen earlier against the bank bouncing through the shallow rocks of the last run. Here are our saviors. This late in the evening they must be planning on camping at the island as well. We can eddy out next to the shore and follow their boat into the camping area.

We wait as they close the gap. Getting within earshot, they wave and yell in English. It's a young couple with American accents. She's wearing a light aquamarine fishing shirt with a baseball cap and looks at home holding the rod at the front of the boat.

"Hello. Do you know where the island is?" I yell.

They laugh and I can barely see a knowing and sympathetic look.

"It's at this next corner ahead. You see the tree across the river there?"

I nod. "Yeah."

"Right past that second tree, you want to pull hard into the left bank. There's a sandy little opening that leads to the campsite but you don't have much time to get out of the current," the man says.

"You guys are lifesavers. We appreciate the info a lot. Mind if we follow you in?" I ask.

They pull ahead and we trail them through the trees into the small sandy cove. Up against the wall again, a friendly face with information emerges from nowhere to put us on track. The sense of relief at having found the campsite produces a state of euphoria and smiles all around.

We take a moment on the beach to meet our saviors. Justin and his wife, Rachael, turn out to be more experienced versions of ourselves. In 2002 they bought backpacks, camping gear, and tickets to Argentina. They ended up in Junín for a month, the first day they checked into a hotel, then started wandering the streets looking for a place to rent for a month.

Unfortunately for their fishing, 2002 was a terrible weather year. Spring rains blew out all the Northern Patagonia rivers, so Justin would catch a taxi or hitch to the boca of the Chimehuín and hunker down for the day on the only section of fishable water in the province. After he had two straight weeks on the water without success, one of the locals approached him and let him know that he would never catch a fish with the equipment he was using. He had been hucking huge flies with a heavy sink tip. The setup was so heavy that his casts never reached the holding water at the far side of the river. The local gave him a handful of small flies and told him to go back to town and get a new shooting line, a lightweight Amnesia line, which would give him the extra distance he needed.

The setup looks novel to an American angler even though it's been the go-to system in Argentina for a couple of decades. Amnesia line is really just a thick monofilament line in bright, gaudy colors. Argentine anglers attach a short section of sink tip to the end, then a thick leader and a small fly. There's not much of a cast, just a couple of quick back-and-forths to get the sink tip in the air before launching it. The system can be unwieldy; the thin diameter and light weight of the Amnesia line doesn't allow for much control. Those who get the hang of it can cast a hundred feet or more. Once in the water, the thin diameter of the Amnesia line cuts through the water letting the sink tip drop much faster than a traditional system. But it does look odd the first time you see a good caster rocket a sink tip across the river with a bright, fluorescent-green running line following like a bullet tracer.

Armed with his Argentine Amnesia, Justin headed back to the boca. In time he made friends with the locals, some of who had fished the boca with Bebé and Jorge. He learned to walk along the dirt road on the far side of the river and look down into the holding lanes to spot fish before even rigging up his rod. On rare days he would peer into the main lie and see a dozen or more leviathans holding on the bottom so big and dark they made the river bottom look black. Some magic mornings he would be transported back in time and land four or five fish weighing more than ten pounds.

It is no surprise that Justin and Rachel came back the following year. On a whim they started looking at property in Junín. A realtor showed them a tiny house across the street from the bus station with a $15,000 price tag. They were interested, but their realtor told them they had to act quickly. They put $2,000 down on the property that afternoon. It was everything they had—the money they had to live and travel on during the rest of the winter. What's more, they had only a month to scrape up the rest of the $13,000.

They are now splitting their time between Argentina and West Yellowstone, where Justin runs a fly shop. They've got two kids; the second one was born in Buenos Aires and this has allowed them to become Argentine citizens and cleared several legal obstacles. Most people balk at the idea of such distant households, but Justin says it's not as challenging as it sounds. Other than the language difference, West Yellowstone and Junín are both just small mountain towns. People care about the same things, share the same values, do the same activities; it's really a pretty easy transition from one place to the other. So here they are floating together in the summer sunset while the temperatures back in that ice-box corner of the world, West Yellowstone, are likely below zero.

With only a silhouette to guide them, the two push off again from the tiny beach and drift downstream toward another camping spot—local knowledge. Maybe ten years down the road we'll know about some secret spots. For now we're just fortunate to have found a place to stop for the night.

Beyond the tiny spit of land a narrow trail leads us up from the river into a tall grove of aging cottonwoods. The dirt is hard packed from use, but other than a burnt-out fire pit, no destructive human traces are present. Whether it's the nervous anticipation we've harbored the last three hours or the campsite itself, we unpack the boat with a sense of peace. Just off the area where the fire ring sits in the middle of a few fallen trees

We are sitting around the campfire about twenty
minutes later with the smell of dinner coming off the
two-burner Coleman stove.

that serve as benches, we see a plain of thigh-high grass. We find several flat spots to pitch our tents.

As with everything, we split up the chores so that nothing takes long. We are sitting around the campfire about twenty minutes later with the smell of dinner coming off the two-burner Coleman stove. The fare for the night is nothing special: packaged ravioli with tomato sauce spiced with some Argentine hamburger. As we wait we break into our bottle of Whitehorse Whiskey and pass it around.

By the time dinner hits our plates, the brilliant stars of the Southern Hemisphere sky shine bright through the cottonwood canopy. There's a feeling of accomplishment as we relax to the warmth of the fire. Even though we didn't get to fish a vast section of the river, we feel that the coming together of luck and help from strangers to find this out-of-the-way campsite is somehow more important than the fish we missed. Maybe we are just relieved that the policia won't be waiting at the takeout to haul us off to prison.

In the morning my hands are calloused in thick white lines across the top of my palms. I know the first strokes on the oars will make them crack with pain and I relegate myself to enduring this through another long day of working the oars. Six more miles of river lie ahead of us before we meet our four o'clock pick up.

The valley widens and the river straightens downstream from camp. It's a flatter, more docile river than in the upper reaches. Willow thickets continue to provide ample cover for the trout. Snugging up tight to the trees, it takes a skilled cast to bring the fly down on the little pillow of current off the side of the tree that pushes the fly into the fish's nose and elicits the hoped-for strike.

I soon forget about my hands as they meld back to the shape of the oars and instead concentrate on getting Jim and John into good positions. When fish are rising there's so much that goes into putting people on fish that the mechanics of moving the boat around the river become automatic. The hands and arms maneuver the boat on remote control while the brain focuses on the fishing.

In a second, the front angler can have a fish on and you're moving the boat subtly out into the current to help pull the fish from the safety of the trees. Meanwhile you're keeping an eye on both banks to look for the next riser to put the rear angler on. Then there's the wind to take into account so he doesn't end up casting over you or across the boat. You move your mouth to get out some encouraging word or piece of advice to the front man and still manage to squeeze in a thought about how early is too early for beer.

It's for this reason the rowing seat provides as much pleasure as angling itself. Most anglers who find themselves on the oars have spent enough time in the front and back of the boat to become proficient in the subtle steps it takes to get a fish to the boat. Rowing others with less skill, they know from experience all the moves that need to take place, but don't have the direct motor authority to make it happen. It's like fishing on a sub-zero day where every body part is numb and stiff. The brain tells the arm to move and cast a certain way, and it responds as best it can in a haphazard, ineffective manner. Bad fishermen are like frozen appendages: you can't quite get them to do exactly what you want. This creates extreme frustration when good fish are rising.

The frustration is fitting considering the normal evolution of an angler. Fly fishing has an age-old tradition of making the endeavor as difficult as possible. We have some need to take a system that works, say 4X tippet, and give ourselves even less chance of success by using 6X tippet. This is really how we end up with so many categories of snob in fly fishing. The dry-fly snob, the steelhead swing snob, the bamboo rod snob, all just anglers who have decided in one way or another to limit the amount of technological help they will use.

As Robert Traver wrote in *Trout Madness*, "In the watery and spectral half-world inhabited by trout fisherman there dwell many fanatic sects, each with its own stout band of followers, and each claiming exclusive possession of the one true ladder to heaven." Somewhere out there is a guy who only fishes tiny dry flies with a cane rod and horsehair leader that he makes himself. He probably doesn't catch that many fish and they are all heaped in a mound of pain-in-the-ass, but each one makes him feel superior to his counterparts who use modern technology. In this vein it's only appropriate there are fish bums like me out there who take pleasure in fishing through a less-skilled vessel. Coaxing the frozen appendage into a workable cast or directing a new angler to a rising fish are just another means of making the sport more difficult.

But the reward for those helping the less capable makes the hassle worth it. Coaching the neophyte into a workable if sloppy semblance of technique that fools a waiting trout is a feeling next to greatness. It's a way to share in that magic feeling of something incredible happening that most of us lost a few hundred or thousand fish ago. It's a very real and personal reminder of why we got hooked on the sport and got good enough to start down the snob path in one form or another.

Rowing for the Js, the situation is quite a bit different. As good casters and rowers, and friends, we form a team. The roles overlap depending on the situation and revolve around helping one another to catch fish. You can go from a spotter to a netter to a caster and back to a spotter in the course of a few moments. When John hooks into a fish and Jim's on the oars, I reel in to keep my line from fouling the fish. I set my rod out of the way and get the net to pass up front. I keep an eye out downriver for hazards as Jim is busy getting the net ready. I adjust the oars so they're out of the way and get John's line off a snag on the boat frame. As the fish comes close I pull out a camera and snap photos. When John pulls his fish out of the net it has become a group fish, and the boat's a better place for the shared experience.

The river carries us along in this happy camaraderie past carved-out sandstone formations and millions of rounded stones in an assortment of grays and browns. Whether the fishing is slow or not, I count on Jim and John's banter to keep spirits high. I feel myself playing the role of responsible parent to two high school kids. I hope they take my periods of quiet for a reluctance to debase myself with crass humor instead of the real reason—I'm not quick-witted enough to keep up with their stinging one-liners.

"Hey, Cam, you gettin' tired on the oars?" Jim asks.

"Thanks, Jim, I'm doing alright," I say.

"Okay, I was just wondering because I had to sleep pretty close to John last night and I think he might have had some bad frijoles. If you want we can just strap him to the back of the frame and we'll be jet propelled," Jim says.

"I wish I had some bad beans so I could fart on your head," John chimes in.

"Right there's close enough, buddy," Jim says.

"There's no way you could even hear an elephant fart over your snoring," John retorts.

"Well, once I was overtaken by the smell I wasn't actually asleep then. I felt I was suffocating. I was scared for my life," Jim replies.

"Tomorrow I'll have beans with hot sauce so I can melt you into your tent like shrink wrap," John says.

"Hey, John, I think you have a fish on." I almost don't want to chime in.

"Who me? Shit!" John wildly sets the hook and misses.

"Couldn't catch herpes from a two-dollar hooker. Only bring him along to make me look good," Jim says.

"I guess you don't remember who caught the last fish?" John brags.

"If we're counting that little thing as a fish we may as well have stayed home and fished your goldfish tank," Jim says.

"Well that's one goldfish for me. And it looks like you just missed a fish," John says.

"Me? Shit!" Jim says yanking his rod up to set the hook and missing the fish.

Toward early afternoon, we meet the Collón Curá River. It flows out of Lago Aluminé on the northern edge of trout country and gathers water to become a huge expanse like Montana's Missouri. Like the Missouri, it flows wide and slow with a depth that hides many of the fishy spots. This doesn't matter much since the Collón Curá valley brings with it a brutal north wind. The gusts are hitting us at up to forty miles per hour, so we give up on fishing and concentrate on keeping the boat off the rock walls on the lee side of the river.

We push hard downstream until we come in sight of the highway, then round a bend and see the big rock bar of the take-out. We are a bit early; the place is deserted.

We pull off where a two-track through the rocks comes to a stop and tug the boat out of the water. We disassemble the boat and sit in the sun drinking our last beer while lounging on a pile of rubber and metal pipes. We'd managed our two-day Chimehuín float. With all the uncertainty we faced, we recap our good fortune and the lucky breaks we got just in the nick of time. We may have just as easily gotten ourselves robbed as anything else. Then, as the talking dies out and we settle into a quiet appreciation, a horn explodes from the trees and Alesandro waves wildly from the driver's side window as he pulls up in the Pathfinder.

12
STREAMS, RIVERS, AND CONSERVATION

---

*Use your instinct to catch a trout
and use your intelligence to decide
what to do with her.*

motto, La Fundación Salmónidos de Angostura

F rom Junín we set off toward San Martín de los Andes into mountains that form the spine of the continent. Past the quaint ski town of San Martin the road turns south, cutting through mountain valleys thick with vegetation and views. The seven lakes route, as it's known, hopscotches from one pristine blue lake to the next. The lakes sit in the arms of the mountains that rise from dense coihue forests to jagged peaks of snow and rock. Through gaps in the trees, long waterfalls gush in great streams of white mist and crash down among the trees at lower elevations. The road is one of Argentina's most popular tourist drives and is crowded and slows with each traffic jam. The regular stops give us a welcome chance to look deeper at the panorama.

Midway through the drive the road crosses the Arroyo Pichi Traful, a small river of clear water and a wide, rocky bank. After several hot hours in the cramped car we pull under the shade of a five-hundred-year-old coihue tree along the bank. The Pichi Traful doesn't look like other big-fish waters in Northern Patagonia. Without hearing rumors of leviathans hidden within its diminutive run I may have left the stream thinking it was just a happy respite from summer sun.

Fishy rumors are hard to pin down. Even if you can remember who told you the rumor in the first place, they are rarely the originator, just the carrier of a reclusive truth. Remembering these rumors must be a fisherman's curse. I'll remember the most obscure fishery in the world, a place in Siberia, if someone, anyone, tells me there's big fish there that no one knows about. Patagonia's horrible for this. Vast expanses of land sliced by rivers so new to the fishing radar, and even the easy places are hard to get to. Every rumor has high probability of panning out. There's never enough time in Patagonia to track down every lead. Besides this, a trip to fish one secret hideout yields three more potential spots, creating a list that grows like snakes on Medusa's head.

The government is in the process of paving the seven lakes route to appease the thousands of tourist who suck pounds of dust into their lungs to appreciate the vistas. At the Pichi Traful, rebar formations stand in the river like colossal columns to a post-modern Parthenon, naked metal waiting for a concrete coating and a new bridge. Up and down the road are the signs of construction. Sloppy pyramids of gravel, a stack of cinder blocks, mounds of dirt scattered about waiting for future use. The workers take lunch around the bend at a hosteria before siesta. Even after they rouse again in the afternoon, they don't seem to move any of the piles of this or that. Government jobs are slow.

We park under a tree next to a rusted-out fifty-five-gallon drum painted yellow and serving as a garbage can. It gives hope in this landscape of beauty that man will do his part to preserve it. Then experience kicks in and I have to laugh at the futility of this lone repository. More poignant than its chipping yellow paint is an image from the rocky beach in metropolitan Bariloche that starts to play back in my mind.

As I sat enjoying the whitecaps splashing in to shore with rhythmic regularity I watched a young mother with her two children. They play and laugh on the bustling public beach where couples lounge together taking inspiration from the clouds scattering behind distant mountains. With the sun drifting toward the horizon, the mother packs up her children. She drops their toys into the void of a large tote bag and the blanket receives a shake and a folding. With the bag hung off her shoulder and a child in each hand, the young family steps along the uneven rocks back to the parking lot. In their place sit the remnants of their afternoon: a liter water bottle, two foil ice cream wrappers, two ice cream sticks, a wax paper sandwich wrapper, and a soda can. Like the derelict owners of hundreds of garbage-filled plastic sacks tied in trees seen at every populated and desolate place across the country, the mother leaves assuming that someone else will come by to clean up. No one ever comes.

Back at the yellow garbage drum we pull the rods from the tailgate. With a plan formulated to meet back in a few hours, we split up to search out our own beats. The afternoon is hot so I opt for shorts and wading socks inside my boots. I take a light 4-weight for the small river thinking I'd rather fight small fish with a small rod all afternoon and chance a battle with something big than miss out on the pleasure of tangling with little fish by using a heavier rod.

I always start fishing by walking. The locals hit the road sections too hard wherever you are—it's a universal law. At the Pichi Traful, a faint trail dies out quickly into a mess of wild rose then opens up again to a well-spaced, old-growth forest that's cool under its broad canopy and provides easy walking among the aged trunks.

The river is twenty feet wide and shallow. I walk close to the edge to look into the water in hopes of spotting a big fish. I'm guilty of walking too close and too fast on new water. Only half-believing rumors of big fish, I like to satisfy my curiosity by spooking something first. Then I focus on fishing. But I've blown a shot at my only big fish of the day more than once like this. The recent outing on the Malleo comes to mind.

I walk a long way before a first cast. There's as much pleasure for me in the exploration as the catching. I think it's this curiosity that's kept most fishermen out past curfew. I can't think of a single time I've been held up fighting a fish for two hours. On the other hand, nearly every time I fish I'm late getting back because curiosity pulls me around the next bend, and then the next. Even on rivers I know, I invent an excuse to continue. Maybe there's a pod of sippers or a hatch of caddis, and with these thoughts of possibility, my feet take me further and further away from timeliness.

A mile upstream I find a few long pools with potential and fish them carefully with a high-floating Royal Wulff. A slender rainbow rises to my fly from the heart of the hole; I know right off a big fish doesn't live there. Or at the least he's on vacation. Big fish don't let little fish live in their spots and eat their food. That's not how they become big fish. Generosity is not a virtue in the aquatic world.

Despite the absence of a big fish, trout themselves are a good sign anywhere. One trout means many trout. Many trout mean a viable ecosystem. And even one trout in a viable ecosystem is enough to fuel a big-fish myth. This is the transitive property of big fish. It takes a true philosopher to appreciate it and a dreamer to design a life around it.

I work upstream and see a flash in the water. I recognize the sight as the silver flash of a feeding fish digging in the streambed rocks to knock aquatic insects loose. I crouch low and watch to find the spot again. I spool line into a pile at my feet and load the rod with three quick false casts. My fourth cast shoots out ahead of the streak and settles upside down a few feet in front of the silver flash. It drifts past the fish, unnoticed. I try again with the same result. With a half-dozen more casts come the same results. I'm surprised to see the fish stay put in such shallow water with my fly drifting over.

I creep closer to the silver flash. It rises up and down off the bottom in a slow rhythm. The fish is not feeding. I watch the white belly bob in the current, trapped a few inches off the bottom. I wade out to investigate, employing a time-tested detective tactic: I poke the tail with a long stick. I poke the stiff corpse of a dead fish.

I can't figure out how the fish stays in place. Dead fish float, drifting free in the surface current. Wading all the way to the fish, I lift it with my boot. With it balanced out of the water on the end of my boot, I find thick fishing line coming from the mouth leading to a lead weight the size of a golf ball and more line. I pull everything with me back to shore. Regaining the bank, I set the fish down and continue pulling line. The line is heavy, deep-lake trolling line. As much line as I pull in, I wonder if someone lost a rod. For a moment I picture the corpse of a heart attack victim trapped upstream, rod handle in a death grip. Arriving at the end of the line I find it wrapped several times around a piece of heavy driftwood.

The story develops in my mind. I know why a small, slender rainbow came to greet my fly and I know that no big fish wait for me. Inside the fish, a hook clings to bloody flesh. At one point the hook had bait, a worm dug up during roadside work. Up the line a hunk of lead kept the worm on the bottom, where fish were apt to find the morsel. Farther up the twenty-pound line the driftwood stake waited on the bank for the person who set it to return. The Pichi Traful is a catch-and-release stream.

The beauty of the system is that the poacher doesn't even need to wait around the river for his fish where there's a chance he may get caught. He can slip in before daylight or after dark to set up the trap and return under similar conditions to find his waiting meal. The fish looked like it had been dead for a while; eyes glossed over in a white film and a belly bloated by decomposition. No one bothered to return. A waste.

Illegal harvests are common where laborers work along watersheds. They have no stake in a healthy trout population or a healthy river in general. They are visitors to the ecosystem with their only interest an easy meal. They are many small rivers like the Pichi Traful that can provide little without sustaining great damage. This is why biologists designate these streams as catch-and-release in the first place.

South of Esquel in the Chubut province, a small group of outfitters took clients to a river not much larger than a spring creek called the Nantes Fall. They practiced catch-and-release by choice and took care not to put too much pressure on the water. For their caution, the river rewarded them with marvelous fish. Days taking twenty-six-inch fish with small terrestrial patterns were not uncommon. The place was one of the rumors.

In the fall of 2007 a group of loggers arrived at the river and spent the cool fall days into the winter felling timber along its banks. At lunch and dinner the loggers pulled fish from the stream with ease. The river was closed for the season, but the meals were cheap and easy. Warm fish off a cast iron skillet tasted good in the howling June winds.

When the guides returned in the spring to fish the Nantes Fall, they caught no fish. The loggers left a stream as barren as the stump-covered hillsides.

I slid the bloated rainbow back into the river, where at least his body might fertilize a future generation of fish. I snipped off my fly and reeled my line in to the last bits of leader. I crunched along the rocky beach back toward the car. Had I seen a fifteen-pound brown, I'd have been able to do little more than watch in appreciation and leave the fish with a prayer for survival. The seven lakes road has a long time to completion, which means a still-longer battle for the fish of the Pichi Traful. They don't need another fly passed over their heads anymore than they need another staked-out hook with a worm.

Back at the car I find it comical to see a few pieces of trash sitting in the yellow garbage can. The proverbial drop in the bucket compared to the greater conservation battles in Argentina. The problem is cultural as much as anything. The mother with her children, the loggers on the Nantes Fall, the man "fly fishing" on the Chimehuín with the bobber and his trophy that made the paper, the overwhelming majority of Argentines believe in the unending supply of Mother Nature. In Parque Nacional

Nahuel Huapi, I met Silvia, a khaki-clad ranger from the national park system. She was in a frantic rush to pick up trash and educate weekend families on environmental protection. "They just don't get it," she said, sounding defeated.

Their attitudes are similar to those held by Americans during the development of the western United States. Salmon, steelhead, trees, and rivers themselves were disregarded as unending commodities. We now see the ramifications of such logic. Barren hillsides cascading debris into waterways, rivers devoid of anadromous inhabitants, and a natural world ruined for the foreseeable future. Most Argentines don't see how this can happen, but in places it already has.

Continuing south along the seven lakes route, we reach the small, trendy tourist villa of La Angostura. For over a hundred years this hamlet on the banks of the 330-yard-long Río Correntoso has served Patagonian tourists. One of the shortest rivers in the world, the short stretch of water connects Lago Correntoso with the much-larger Lago Nahuel Huapi.

The hub of early La Angostura was the Hotel Correntoso, built by early Patagonian entrepreneur Primo Capraro after he arrived in the area in 1903. The hotel, still in place today, sits perched above the river looking down on the outlet into Lago Nahuel Huapi and across one of Northern Patagonia's largest and most dynamic vistas. As early as 1930, guests braved the long route from Buenos Aires to relax and adventure along the lake. They partook in boat trips, ski adventures, and naturalist activities in the undeveloped Andes.

While his guests engaged in outdoor pursuits, Primo developed a hobby of his own. As part of the hotel's early waste-disposal system, a pipe connected the kitchen to the river below. All day, food scraps flushed down the pipe into a wire cage in the river where pancora crabs, the crayfish of Patagonia, flocked to the easy meal. In turn, enormous fish came out of the lake to take advantage of their own easy meal of engorged pancoras. Noticing the fish, Primo installed a cable car across the river above the kitchen grate. On sunny afternoons he wheeled himself over the river in the little metal cart and tossed food to the trout below. In Pavlovian style, the fish grew accustomed to Primo's easy meal and came to the sight of the man in the metal cart.

No clear evidence exists when Primo's pet fish became the object of anglers' passions. In all likelihood the earliest guests fished to some degree, but by the late 1940s the Hotel Correntoso was the center of Argentine fishing. Anglers from across the country came to the Correntoso to cast to overgrown, undereducated trout. During the day they fished, and at night they communed in the hotel bar where they carved their catch records into the wooden rafters. One picture shows the carving, "E. Javertavni - 8.00, Valento - 8.00" then fish of 11.0, 9.25, 8.3, 9.0, 9.5. The weights are in kilograms.

Fishermen lined up in queues to take their turn and didn't wait long for a record. Pictures from that period show banquet tables lined with huge trout over three feet long. Men posed with their kills in triumphant gestures. Pictures with multiple fish hoisted high on a stringer are common. In one image a man's large brown trout is laid lengthwise on a table with the gentleman's formidable fist shoved in the fish's open mouth to show its large size. A few fish found their way to taxidermists and some still hang on whitewashed walls. In the basement of the Asociación de Pesca y Caza (the Association of Fishing and Hunting) along the lake in Bariloche are a dozen of these ancient, mottled relics. On a wall of its own hangs Luis Peirano's fish of 11.55 kilograms.

In 1949 Nahuel Huapi Fishing and Hunting Club organized the first National Trout Festival on the shores of the Río Correntoso. Fly and spin fishermen arrived to compete in the one-day derby. As legend has it, the majority of fishermen abandoned their spots to take lunch in the hotel bar. On his way to lunch, Luis Peirano, a dedicated spin fisherman, picked up one of the discarded fly rods and flung his first-ever fly cast out to the Correntoso's clear water. With this cast he hooked and landed the tournament winner, the 25.35-pound brown trout that still hangs in the club offices.

By the early 1980s fish populations and fish size in the Correntoso began declining. They became so poor that at one point, the Hotel Correntoso sat on the hill abandoned. So few fishermen came that the hotel was unable to fill its rooms. The historical records carved into the bar were forgotten. Fishermen turned away to find the next great hotspot.

Today local fishermen gather on the banks in early November to wait in queues and cast into the clear water. Every day, anglers take respectable fish in the four- to six-pound range with an occasional fish pushing ten pounds. There's no question among the older anglers, guides, and biologists that today's fishing pales in comparison to that of the '50s and '60s. The catch record from the hotel bar provides confirmation.

There's been no clear demon declared in the decline. Some blame the building of the new highway bridge over the river, pointing to the pollution during construction, or even vibrations that the bridge supports transmit into the river. There's a handful of people who are convinced the big fish are gone because Primo Capraro no longer feeds them. He died in 1932.

These arguments fail to explain the decline of other local rivers such as the Ruca Malén or the Río Bonito, rivers that once harbored healthy populations of fish to ten pounds and are now devoid of larger specimens. To those who have seen the catalogs of dead fish pictures, or spoken with the legion of contemporary catch-and-kill anglers, it's clear that the anglers themselves should shoulder the blame. Despite the obvious case of over-harvest, few Argentines trace the decline directly to the fishermen. How could man have such an influence? As Ranger Silvia said, "They just don't get it."

I stop in to the Banana Fly Shop on the main street of Villa Angostura. I meet Banana Martinez, the owner of the shop and a guy who grew up fishing the Correntoso. It's not the right time of year for monsters to be in the river, so we talk about when I should come back and what to expect of the river. He laments the change in the size and number of fish since he was a kid, but tells me about the local momentum building to get things turned around.

He tells me about La Fundación Salmónidos de Angostura, a group he and a handful of other locals founded in 1995. The group, an eclectic bunch of environmentalists, guides, and provincial rangers who recognized the area's growing problem, takes an ambitious and comprehensive approach to fish recovery. The program they developed over the past two decades focuses on fish, but understands it's a problem of ecosystems, cultural norms, and societal values. What began the first year as a donation drive over the local radio to build an artificial spawning facility, has itself spawned into a community-wide organization that is slowly changing the way people think about their role in the natural world around them.

Around La Angostura the work of the foundation focuses on four goals: artificial spawning to increase successful egg fertilization, the sanctity of genetic diversity and wild fish, scientific information gathering, and education. To meet the first two goals, volunteers take to area rivers during the spring spawning run to capture and artificially spawn returning fish. Fertilized eggs are taken to a hatchery on the Río Bonito, where they are allowed to grow. They don't use food pellets or otherwise interfere with the rearing process, leaving the growing fry to learn natural feeding habits and find natural food sources in the Río Bonito. In March and April, fingerlings are returned to their home rivers to complete their life cycle. The program allows fertilization rates in the high 90th percentile, which the Fundación hopes will bring more fish back to area rivers.

In regard to recent debates around the world on the efficacy of hatcheries, invasive species, and genetic diversity, the actions of the Fundación Salmónidos is a quagmire of ethical and biological questions. The trout themselves are a hatchery product only one hundred years removed, an invasive species in blunt terms. The National Park System in Argentina has addressed the issue by discontinuing the stocking of nonnative species into its rivers. A decision made fairly easily considering these rivers harbor self-sustaining trout populations that don't require stocking to maintain sportfishing populations. It's worth noting that that system also protects these same trout through catch-and-release regulations.

The hatchery system used by Fundación Salmónidos isolates the different strains of fish by river and artificially spawns hundreds of fish to reduce the effects of hybridization and maintain genetic diversity. This might be ridiculous considering the trout all trace their origins to hatcheries in United States. What's not ridiculous—regardless of the issue of the legitimacy of an invasive species in the ecosystem or the efficacy of hatchery trout—is the desire of a community to pull together to save a shared culture and economic asset.

For those who grew up fishing the legendary waters of the Correntoso and wish to pass the experience on to their children, the issue is not that complex. The same goes for the hotel workers, guides, and restaurateurs who rely on fishing tourism for a livelihood: the health of the trout population plays a large role in the well-being of the small community. It's the same invasive healthy fish desire of Great Lakes steelheaders, brown trout lovers the United States over, and not entirely different from diehard Pacific Northwest steelheaders who hope to see pure strains of steelhead proliferate.

Whether one agrees with their means entirely or not, there can be no debate that the Fundación has taken a measured course on the issue of the declining trout population. They have clearly identified their priorities and worked to implement a hatchery system they believe maintains genetic diversity and wild fish. I doubt anyone would argue that the hatchery is the best system. Banana and the rest of the Fundación would love to leave the process to Mother Nature, but unfortunately too many factors beyond Mother Nature have been at work for too long. For the Correntoso, they believe a hatchery is better than nothing.

The goal of the Fundación is a robust, self-sustaining population. They hope the hatchery will be a temporary Band-Aid in their cause for Correntoso trout. To measure their progress they've implemented an aggressive microchip-tagging program and accompanying database. The program is an accomplishment in and of itself in a country where research as basic as fish counts is rare. The Fundación doesn't have enough data to glean significant results regarding the trout population, but the program reveals significant forethought regarding the need to measure their efforts and scientifically monitor fish populations.

The Fundación's most intriguing work, and possibly most long-lasting in terms of self-sustaining trout, is their efforts with local youth. Beginning in kindergarten, Banana and a cadre of local park rangers get children involved in the cause. They present ecosystem lessons and stage plays in which the children wear fish masks and act out the life of the trout. The children are taken to the Fundación's hatchery during the artificial spawning process, where they hear about and see firsthand the life cycle of the fish. The following March the children return to the Fundación, where they help move the fish back to their native rivers. Banana stresses the importance of the connection the children feel with the fish by March. "The kids feel as if they are putting their own kids back in the river," he says. The program continues through the elementary school years with more complex fisheries education as the children get older.

For Banana, he says he can already see the benefits of starting early. "Right off we're seeing these young children go home and start policing their parents, taking the information they learned at school and sharing it at home." Banana says he's had more than one parent come into his fly shop and thank him for the program, not because of what it did for his children, but for how it changed the parents' views and explaining that they no longer kill fish. He sees many of the children he's taught fishing on the local rivers and can't believe the success of the program. He explains, "The new generation is different: kids understand the idea, they don't kill fish." He thinks they see fishing as a game and understand they need a partner in order to play.

Of course the Fundación is a microcosm of Argentine society. It has a total of seventy members. Banana says they need three times as many to reach their goals. They run their programs entirely on donations. They've tried several times for government support, but have encountered the political problem that fish don't get votes. The vast majority of Argentines still don't "get it." For now the Fundación continues to make it; in times of need they've resorted back to public radio donation drives, and Banana beams at the notion that the community always comes through.

He explains, "The new generation is different:
kids understand the idea, they don't kill fish."

I take my rod to the Río Correntoso the next morning before sunrise. I look up to Primo's renovated hotel; its windows are still dark. Under my feet is the huge concrete piling that once formed the base of Primo's cable car. An Argentine youth stands nearby rigging his rod. I ask him if he will catch *una trucha gigante*.

"I am just happy to be here," he says. "If I catch even a little trout I will be so happy." I can only imagine how pleased the statement would make Banana.

Like the Río Correntoso, Argentina's natural resources face great obstacles: political, environmental, and cultural. Under the continued labors of the Fundación Salmónidos, twenty-pound trout may one day return to the Correntoso, but what of countless other rivers like the Nantes Fall? Their only hope lies in future generations. A lucky few are touched by the message of organizations like the foundation, while most learn on a beach at a young age through the poor examples of their parents. Instead of being nearly won, I doubt the conservation battle in Argentina has yet to begin. I hope the Fundación's motto continues to spread for the sake of the fish: "Use your instinct to catch a trout and use your intelligence to decide what to do with her."

13
BACK TO CHILE

I'm afraid that life as we know it in Futaleufú, as of last Friday, will never be the same.

Simon Carn, Volcanologist, University of Maryland

Lack of information forms a major roadblock to the traveling angler in Argentina. Unlike the United States where a dozen guidebooks provide a hand-holding experience on new rivers, there are few if any public resources in Argentina. The guides themselves vary from less-than-helpful to outright liars, the few books that do exist are photo based, generic, or out of date. Websites are proprietary and maps hard to find and lack sufficient detail. For all these difficulties in Argentina, it's a life of ease compared to Chile.

I spend several weeks in Bariloche searching for information and travel partners to pull off a several-thousand-mile loop through Chile and back up through south-central Argentina. I never find more than the names of a few rivers and some bogus tourist maps that let me know the very general location of these rumored rivers. Based on the lack of information, the

Chile itinerary revolves around two ideas. First, the main highway through central and southern Chile, the Carretera Austral, runs north-south in the small sliver of land between the Andes and the sea. Second, the rivers run between the mountains and the sea from the east to the west. By the time I set off for the unknowns of the Chilean wilderness I know from this most rudimentary geography only that my route south is bound to cross every river in the region. Whether or not these waters are fishable or float-able, only a trip down the Carretera Austral will tell.

A week before leaving, I spot two Colorado boys at the *choripán* vendor, with his fire-grilled sausages in the central square of Bariloche's après ski architecture. I recognize the boys as the dirtbag American fishing bums that they are by their Chaco sandals, cargo shorts, and faded blue shirts—one of them with a gigantic Bucking Rainbow logo plastered across the back. As they munch down on five-peso choripán I introduce myself. The taller of the two is Rob; the one in the Bucking Rainbow shirt is Reid. I ask about their fishing and their general experience chasing fish in Patagonia.

After they tell me about some recent fishing exploits, the conversation shifts to their 1982 Renault Doce, a boat of a white sedan with bald tires held together by duct tape and will. The ancient car cost them $4,000 and a week's worth of paperwork, but gave them the freedom of mobility. A few things they didn't know at time of purchase were the mechanical unreliability of 1982 Renault Doces and their lack of security features—the door lock could be picked with an ordinary butter knife—a fact that set them back a rod, two sleeping bags, and a pile of other fishing gear they couldn't afford to lose after the car was broken into while they did the weekly grocery shopping.

In Esquel they pulled out of another grocery store to discover a trail of fuel streaming from their undercarriage. Panicked, they sped around town until they found an old woman walking home and screamed in rapid pigeon Spanish for directions to the nearest mechanic. The woman pointed and they tore around the block finding the open bay doors of a greasy garage.

They bailed out of the Renault in hysteria under the Hollywood impression that they might explode at any moment. The mechanic strolled to the car with a lit cigarette in his mouth and popped the hood above the pooling gasoline. He fished around for a moment before using his cigarette to point to a weathered crack in the fuel line. Taking out a pocketknife from his blue coveralls, he enhanced the issue by slitting the line in two. Horrified, Reid and Rob looked at the mechanic as he continued under the hood, finding another line (the windshield washer fluid line) and cutting it free as well. Then, as if he'd performed the same maneuver a hundred times since 1982, the mechanic spliced the two hoses together and returned the fuel line to operation. Who needs windshield wiper fluid anyway?

As the mechanic put the finishing touches on the fuel-line fix, the guys noticed a second fluid leak. From the center of the car a white drip collected in a small puddle before running along the broken concrete to their feet. The mechanic looked down, stuck his finger in the white fluid, brought two fingers together as if testing the viscosity of oil, smelled the white tip of his finger, and stuck it in his mouth. "Leche," he said. The groceries had tipped in the mad drive to the mechanic and the recent milk purchase was leaking through the thin floor.

Talking with these two guys from Colorado around the smoky, fifty-gallon drum used by the choripán vendor as his barbecue, they say they are as interested in Chile as myself. The reliability of their Renault Doce is not the only thing holding them back. Legal issues are another. Even though they own the vehicle title outright, as foreigners they are not allowed to leave the country with an Argentine-licensed car. I suppose the Argentines don't want the Chileans to get a leg up on their centuries-old feud by getting a run of '82 Renault Doces across the border. In addition to the legal limitation of the Renault, the Coloradans are also short on gear and flies after the grocery store rip-off. What they need is a reliable car, a boat, and a bunch of gear. What I need are travel partners who want to fish.

Over the course of several days we agree to join forces on a three-week run through central Chile. We plan to head south through Los Alerces National Park and trace the Río Grande west till we hit Chile. It will be the same route I took by bus on my way to Futaleufú and my ill-fated Chilean guiding career. Once in Chile we will continue west until we meet the Carretera Austral and head south. We have few expectations about what we'll find going south—except the idea that there are rivers and fish.

As we prepare for Chile, I find myself thinking about returning to Futaleufú. I still hold a hodgepodge of feelings about my departure from Expediciones Chile. It was the first job I ever quit. And while I think that Spelius's use for me was done, I felt guilty about walking out while there were still clients on the calendar.

As we approach the Chilean border I think more than once about dodging through town to avoid running into any of the Expediciones Chile staff. I'm not sure how I feel about Spelius and can't imagine how he feels about me. Pulling up to the border crossing, I haven't quite settled on the next course of action, but I'm leaning toward avoiding the couple blocks of town around the Expediciones Chile headquarters where I'm likely to run into the staff.

Within ten seconds of passing through the Chilean border I see a white van with the blue "Expediciones Chile" logo painted on the door. Chris Spelius's wife, Rosie, hangs out the door of the cab and spots me immediately, as if she's expecting me. It's a déjà vu of my first day in Chile when the company driver, Benjamin, parked in the same spot with the same van waiting for me to arrive on the bus from Esquel.

I park the Pathfinder and cross the road toward Rosie. She meets me in the middle of the road and gives me a strong hug and a huge smile. Whatever anxiety I had floods away with the warmth of her familiar face. We exchange a quick greeting before her clients walk through the border, and I agree to swing by the office later. Fate makes the decision for me: I will face my Expediciones Chile demons.

The town of Futaleufú is physically different from the one I'd left two years prior. In early May 2008, the Chaitén volcano near the port town of Chaitén, fifty miles east of Futaleufú, erupted. For several weeks the volcano poured ash into the

For several weeks the volcano poured ash into the
atmosphere and pushed lava flows over the caldera.

atmosphere and pushed lava flows over the caldera. Within a week, rain combined with the ash to create a concrete-like mudslide that wiped out large portions of the Chaitén. The damage was so extensive it forced the government to abandon the thriving community. In Futaleufú, prevailing winds brought the several-thousand-foot-high plume of ash directly overhead. For a week, heavy ash rained down on the town accumulating on the street in depths over six inches.

Arriving in Futa more than a year after the eruption, I see gray piles of ash hanging everywhere on the landscape. Outside the Expediciones Chile hosteria two sit-on-top kayaks are filled with the gray, concrete-like remnants of volcanic ash and winter rains. Discarded cans and soda bottles sit solidified in place where tourists once paddled.

As a vacationer I see the town for what it is, another frontera town. I'm no longer looking through the rose-colored glasses of an excited first-year guide, nor the gray glasses of a disgruntled employee. The town looks more weathered than ever from the tons of ash settled like a bitter frosting over an underlying decrepitude.

Excluding the ashy coating, Futa looks little changed since my departure. Mildew and algae cover the faded siding and reduce the white trim around windows to a dingy hue. It looks like a town in defeat. These cosmetic blemishes feel like the early signs of a community that is dying, not one energized for the future. The faded and chipped paint indicates a heyday two decades removed. A time when rows of homes prepared for an assault on the future by proclaiming their intentions in vivid hues of red, yellow, and blue.

By the looks of things, the ambitions of these people were short-lived compared to those of Mother Nature. A corner house sits submissive and abandoned. The north wall has caved in; grass encroaches like a slow wave of green infantrymen to occupy the premises. The other houses down the block don't look too far from surrender either.

In contradiction to this slow decline, public works projects are everywhere. Streets are turned up, new sidewalks are laid, and workers are deep in a beautification project for the main street. Given the state of the surrounding homes, it feels like this project is the result of a government grant or foreign money donated from volcano-relief funds, perhaps.

Reid, Rob, and I spend the day crisscrossing town buying groceries and supplies to push south along the Carretera Austral. We know that along the way, we'll encounter a line of villages equally besieged. A year after the volcanic blast the event still holds the community in conversational rapture. Everyone we speak with has their own opinion about the ash. From the military intervention at the beginning to the agricultural ramifications of the ashy soil, we hear the gamut of post-volcano musings.

We purchase fishing licenses at the tourist office. The agent there tells us the fishing in the Futaleufú is fine except for windy days when ash gets picked up and blown into the eyes. While jogging earlier in the day, I completely understood how miserable a day of windblown ash might be as passing cars threw dust into the air during my run. The tourism agent pulls out air filter masks from under his desk and says we might need them as well. He points to a map on the wall with a diagram showing the path of ash from the volcano; it looks like a flashlight beam pointed at Futaleufú. Later we hear accounts of ash piling up three feet deep and the sky looking like a ski-area blizzard.

We camp along the Río Espolón, the same river I'd pedaled up to catch my first Patagonian fish. At that time the river flowed a crystalline blue, looking down from the bridge outside of town, each rock stood out with distinction. The post-volcano river looks like the silt-filled glacial rivers of Alaska. Sunlight reflecting off the suspended ash, the river flows a rich, creamy white obscuring rocks inches below the surface. Locals told us there were no fish left in the Espolón. Looking at the thick water, that was easy to believe.

Other remnants of the volcano litter the valley. In the campground, a bulldozer's blade marks scar the earth where the machine pushed mounds of ash out of the campsites. High overhead, the once-white snowcaps on the rocky peaks wear a sooty topcoat and foretell a future of siltation.

We stop that afternoon into a local fishing guide's office on the north side of the town plaza and look for a fishing report. We find another local anxious to talk volcano. He has the scoop on the local guiding industry and a story that weaves a complex web of competing interests.

According to his account, immediately following the volcano's eruption the organization FutaFriends, a nonprofit dedicated to helping valley locals, began a campaign of sorts claiming that the Futa valley would never be the same and asked the greater world for donations to assist the adversely effected. "People that decided to stay in the valley due to economic or cultural constraints are continuously inhaling the ash particulate and drinking contaminated water that will ultimately degrade their health … the region has suffered a tremendous environmental catastrophe," FutaFriends' executive director Alan Grundy said.

At the same time Expediciones Chile owner Chris Spelius said in his own Internet dispatches that things were not as bad as they looked. He described Chile as a geologically active country where mudslides, earthquakes, and even volcanoes played a role in the natural environment. He referenced government tests that concluded the ash to be an inert particle and of no risk to human health. His message: This is natural; things are fine.

Views of the disaster differed between parties, each seemingly focused on the position most beneficial to their immediate concerns. Few claims found a basis in fact, perhaps because facts were hard to find. While the Chilean government declared the ash noncarcinogenic and nonthreatening, many people disregarded the finding because they saw the statement as a way to keep the government from having to perform a costly evacuation of the Futaleufú valley. These views found support from an Argentine government ten miles away that declared the ash a health hazard. While the tourism office handed out particulate masks, the local fishing guide dismissed any health threat on the logic there were no documented cases of lung problems associated with the ash. Research on the long-term health effects of the fine-particulate matter supported neither opinion; it will take a few decades before such a study can be done—well after it matters.

Whether or not the ash residue coating the Futa valley turns out to be deadly or harmless, its effect is still measurable. Spelius estimated his business to be down 30 percent. Since Spelius has more long-term commitments from his clients, I suspect the other area guides' businesses are down even more. Walking around town mid-February, peak-rafting season, we should see a community full of local and foreign tourists. Instead we hear the echo of dogs barking down long, empty alleyways. *"Hay Lugar"* signs hang on the hosteria doors to announce their vacancies.

All area rafting companies are running operations as normal. The chalky water doesn't affect the rapids except to provide more dynamic pictures. On the fishing side, however, most of the area lodges are shut down indefinitely. At a small restaurant and tea shop I bump into another local fishing guide I'd known from my time in Futa. He worked for the premier fly-fishing lodge on the river, and we'd met waiting to pick up clients at the airport in Chaitén. He was there at the request of the lodge owner to determine the feasibility of future fishing operations on the river.

For the high-end fishing lodge, feasibility encompassed much more than fishability. Regardless of the effect of the volcano on the fishing, there were other logistical concerns to conquer before resuming operations. The volcano and ensuing mudslides destroyed the transportation infrastructure leading to Futa. The same Chaitén airport we'd met at two years prior was buried under hundreds of tons of cemented ash—with no recovery plan. The small grass airstrip outside Futa lacked a control tower or facilities of any kind that would make it suitable for commercial traffic. To the east across the Argentine border, six hours of pavement separated Futa from the nearest commercial airport in Bariloche.

The guide summed up the dilemma: "We're dealing with clients who pay five thousand dollars a week to come down here. These guys charter private helicopters into backcountry New Zealand airstrips. Now with the airport at Chaitén gone, we've got to sell these guys on flying twenty-plus hours into Bariloche, where we'll have a bus waiting for them. They bus to Esquel for lunch, then continue on to the border where, because of customs, they'll have to walk across the border to yet another truck that will pick them up and bring them to the lodge. All this thirty hours after they depart home. Even if we could sell it, it's a logistical nightmare. You need a bus and a driver on the Argentine side ready to make almost-daily trips. You've got the whole border issue to deal with. Maybe for rafting clients, you know, it adds to the adventure and all that, but for high-dollar fishing clients— I just don't know."

The point hits home several hours later when I stop by the Expediciones Chile office. One of the office workers, a skilled cartoonist, has drawn a picture on the oversized whiteboard. It features Paco, the company driver, lounged up against a taxi in a pose that indicates he's been waiting a while. Behind him is a bus station and a terminal sign in block letters, VIA BARILOCHE, the name of Bariloche's main bus line. It appears that Expediciones Chile is already dealing with the transportation fallout from the volcano's eruption. The remote, isolated town of Futa has always been a challenging place to do business. Adding another level of complexity in getting clients to the valley may be enough to convince a few outfitters to get out of the valley completely.

Other than a transportation plan that's several hours longer, it appears life at Expediciones Chile is much the same. I see Rosie at her corner desk plunking at a keyboard and answering questions from the office staff. One of the employees is new, but the others I remember from my time in Futaleufú. Chatting with Rosie I explain why I'm back in Futa and tell her about my life since leaving. She doesn't seem to remember or care about the circumstances of my departure. But, more guides have quit in the past ten years than stuck around, so my actions weren't that extraordinary.

While we catch up on local gossip and the business, some of the new guides and a few of the old ones filter through the office. It seems to be a busy summer afternoon, and I'm well aware that the guides don't get much free time to dally in the office.

The new guides look like the old ones: greasy, unwashed hair, three-day beards, and thread-bare T-shirts. At one point I peek out the back window toward the old guide house. It looks as run-down as it did three years ago. The lifejackets and spray skirts hung out to dry on the rotting wooden fence show me that the guides are still living under the leaky roof. I wonder if these new faces are having the same problems I did. If their outward appearance is any indicator, it looks as if there are a few on the brink of quitting.

The conversation with Rosie eventually comes around to Spelius, and I ask if he's around. She tells me he's back in the States. I feel relief pass through my body, tinged with a sense of regret. Having gathered the will to step back into the Expediciones Chile office, I want to go through with it all the way. I'm ready for the closure conversation, but with Spelius out of town there's not much reason to hang around the office watching a past life.

That night I sit around the campsite with Reid and Rob. A few feet away the chalky Espolón continues to pull volcanic ash out of the mountains. The white-tinged water flowing by provides the most definitive answer regarding the health of the valley's aquatic ecosystem. It's changed—that's as much as anyone can be sure of. As with everything in Chile, information is hard to come by. The true effect of the volcanic ash on the ecosystem will take decades to determine and, lacking scientific evaluation, will consist more of anecdote and opinion than fact. Then, the health of the community likely has a lot less to do with healthy fish populations than with the human health effects of the ash and the new troubles related to getting clients into the remote valley.

14
THE CARRETERA AUSTRAL

---

*"Sal, we gotta go and never stop
going 'till we get there."
"Where we going, man?"
"I don't know but we gotta go."*

Jack Kerouac, *On The Road*

I f such a thing as a decent road map exists to get through Chile, we never found it. In hindsight, a decent road map doesn't get you that much if you don't know where you're going. For us, *there* was just an abstract concept that we might find down the road somewhere. Our tri-fold gas station map did little more than to keep us from getting turned in a circle. In the end, not having our destination marked on the map from the start actually allowed us to get *there* with more speed and efficiency. Without a destination we wandered through the big, green voids on the highway map driving with the idea that we'd know *there*, when we arrived.

In this form of travel there is some uncertainty, especially in today's information era. It takes some amount of effort to wind up out on the boundaries of knowledge, and Patagonian Chile is most definitely one of those places. After going there it's easy to see why we as a world have worked so hard these past few centuries to eliminate the unknown. It's an uncomfortable feeling wondering if there's a gas station on the horizon before the gauge hits the empty mark, or if there's a Class VI rapid with death and disfigurement between you and the takeout. Perhaps even more unsettling is watching your traveling companion empty the contents of the cooler into his mouth and wonder when the next grocery mart might appear. But this is still first-world adventure. We are traveling on roads in a car. We have a cooler and a CD player. Yet, for people who have grown up in a land of roadside rest areas, highway motels, and car navigation, Chile is the boonies.

We find ourselves constantly asking, "Is this a good spot to fish?" And the only way to find an answer is to pull off to the side of the road, rig the fly rod, and spend a half-day or a week hiking and casting. At lunch or in the evening we meet back up from our separate directions and discuss whether or not we were *there*.

At times we were, like when we sat on the bank of the Río Emperador Guillermo on a thousand-year-old driftwood coihue tree, passing a maté gourd around the fire. We sat in a tight valley surrounded by cliffs and wilderness with a blazing sunset filling the sky with warm light. There had been no fish that day, but we all knew we were *there*.

The Carretera Austral is a thick blue line on most road maps leading travelers to believe they will find a paved road that runs the length of the country. The highway project was a pet of General Augusto Pinochet, the Chilean dictator who ruled tyrannically for nearly twenty years. In some locations, expectations of the Carretera Austral meet reality. A smooth ribbon of concrete stretches out through the canopy of trees and mountain vistas to create an aesthetic and efficient mode of travel. These paved sections arrive at random and last for any distance from tens of miles to a few hundred yards. Then, as abruptly as they arrived, the pavement ends with a shock-springing hiccup and the Carretera Austral, the main highway, returns to an unpredictable and rough dirt road.

For a hundred-plus miles, we head south doing our best to match the dirt road we're driving with the blue line on the map. Road signs seem to come with the pavement, so most of the time we are left to just making an educated guess about the direction to La Junta, or Palena, or some other speck of a town where we might find a fresh loaf of bread and a gas station. We keep a watchful eye on the white needle that's forever working its way toward empty. Gas stations here are far apart and unreliable.

More than once we coast under the green-and-yellow Petrobras canopy for the attendant to come out and tell us they have no more gas. "*No hay nafta*," they say with upturned palms. Plans are altered to wait for the gas tanker to come in before leaving town and heading further than prudent from fuel. At times we see a gas tanker pulled off the side of the dirt highway fixing a flat or piled up in the ditch with a crumpled fender or broken axle.

At La Junta we overnight to attend the local rodeo. The rodeo consists of one event in which a team of two mounted gauchos chase a young bull along the edge of a circular arena. One gaucho pins the bull to the fence while the other gets in front to turn him the opposite direction. They turn the bull back and forth a few times before running him out of the arena. It's a timed event where style counts.

Gauchos from up and down the frontier come to show their skills, their horses, and their attire. Most wear intricately woven ponchos and broad, flat-brimmed hats. They wear long leather boots with big, shiny circular spurs that *clink-chink* when they walk across the hard dirt rodeo grounds. Some look like boys who will head back to school on Monday, while others are showing the slight hunch of old age and the relaxation that comes from knowing they have nothing left to prove.

Gauchos from up and down the frontier come
to show their skills, their horses, and their attire.

Behind the rough planks of the arena seats are the women of the La Junta school district and the rotary club selling food and drinks from their little booths. They drop semi-circle empanadas into vats of hot oil and give out cans of beer from a galvanized feeding trough. The little packets of fried dough contain ham and cheese or hamburger and onion. For 5,000 pesos, about ten dollars, we get a heaping plate of hot empanada goodness. The dough, cheese, and meat disappear with a few savory bites.

Pulling cold slugs from a green Crystal beer can, I end up in conversation with two gauchos. I ask them about floating and fishing the Río Rosselot, a midsized river we crossed over just north of town. The first thinks about the question for a moment before telling me it's no problem to float the river and that there should be fish. Without skipping a beat or in any way acknowledging a contradiction, the second gaucho agrees with the first and then tells me that floating the river is very dangerous and that if we try, we will probably die.

The conversation becomes typical of information-gathering in Chile. Fly fishing, and to a greater degree, floating rivers, are so far from the normal life here in the frontier that the locals have no frame of reference to provide information. To be fair, had the gauchos asked me about the difference in two calving procedures, or the finer points of the rodeo event, I'd have been even less informative. This lack of information makes it hard to plan and creates a fair amount of trepidation.

The day after the rodeo we head out of town along the dirt road that follows the Río Rosselot. We head west toward the mountains and cross the river a handful of times in ten miles. Its looks like a calm, meandering waterway at each of the crossings. Continuing west we find a pull off and a dirt trail that leads toward the river. We gear up and take off in the direction of the river, emerging from the forest a half-mile later to find a roaring Class IV rapid. It demonstrates the difficulty of scouting rivers via road. There are a lot of rapids that can hide in the couple of miles of Chilean river between bridges.

The next day we decide to float a lower section of the Río Rosselot. Our decision to float is based on a collective need to spend a day doing something other than bounce along dirt roads in the Pathfinder and not at all about testing the idea that floating the Río Rosselot will not be fatal.

We launch into a smooth, slow river knowing only that seven kilometers down the road there is another bridge. What lies between us and the potential takeout has been shrouded behind trees and hills the entire drive upriver. The only backup plan we have for Class V–plus rapids is to portage the several-hundred-pound boat. Depending on the topography, this may not even be an option. I've floated more than one section on the Futaleufú where portaging was not possible.

I've heard of a technique called ghost boating. You lash everything down tight to the boat except a backpack or two of survival gear that you keep with you. Then you push the boat into the rapid, hope it makes it through with no one in it, and then swim for it downstream of the rapid. Not being a strong swimmer, I hope our float on the Río Rosselot doesn't come to this.

We pay the price for our adventure halfway through the float when the telltale crash of whitewater starts echoing upstream. I row the cataraft to the bank as the white tops of the surging rapids begin to dance on the horizon. From upstream all I can see is a solid line of white across the river. We get out and hike downstream to scout. As we approach the line of rapids, they only look bigger and less forgiving.

The first set of rapids is a classic picket fence in which rocks stick up at regular intervals across the river like slats in a whitewashed fence. Behind the fence another series of irregular rapids lines up in a gruesome formation that affords no clear line to avoid anything looking smaller than a Class IV. You can frequently find a cheater line on the far side of a picket fence, a sluice of water that will flush you right by the danger in the forgiving shoulder water. Both sides here are bad options: the far side is one of the nastiest boulder gardens of pickup truck–sized rocks I can remember seeing, and the near side is too choked with boulders to fit a canoe, let alone a raft, through.

The only possible line forces a slot through the picket fence at the dead center of the river. Once through the fence, the current pushes hard toward the pickup truck boulder field—and the certain death referred to by gaucho number two. It would take a hard pull away from the boulder field and another half-dozen technical moves to avoid getting flipped or hung up midriver.

We sit on the side of the river a long time watching the surge of whitewater over the rocks. I think that if I watch long enough I might see a secret route of safety. Instead, the midriver shoot seems like a worse and worse idea. I decide the risk of running the picket fence isn't worth tempting certain death and announce that we'll be portaging the boat. This means at least a couple hours of breaking the boat down and disassembling into parts, hiking it downstream to safety, and reassembling it.

We sit on the big rock above the rapid while mustering the energy to hike upstream and begin the laborious task when a green cataraft emerges on the upriver horizon. There's a fisherman in the front with an oarsman standing on his midship seat scouting for his line. Without a pause the boat closes the hundred yards to the rapid, enters the center of the picket fence, pulls hard toward the near bank weaving through three boulders, and exits the rapid a hundred yards later. The only acknowledgement of our presence is a quick glance in our direction from the oarsman just before entering the rapid. Within a minute they drift downstream around the corner.

It turns out to be another one of those fortuitous events that seem to mark fishing adventures in Patagonia. Seeing another boat take the line gives me the confidence to try it. I tell Reid and Rob to hike down below the rapid and walk upstream to the boat. I cinch my life jacket tight, take the oars, and pull out to the middle of the river. In about twenty seconds I've flushed through the picket fence, maneuvered around a huge boulder, and caught a tongue right past Reid and Rob into the calm water below the rapid. I pull the boat over into a little cove of boulders and let the two climb back on board. While we're all relieved that I made it through and thankful not to have portaged, we relax only partially, knowing there may be more and worse rapids

The only acknowledgement of our presence is a quick glance in our
direction from the oarsman just before entering the rapid.

downstream. The green cataraft is the only boat we see on the Río Rosselot.

>>>>

Days on the road yield slow progress. What we think should take a few hours of driving always doubles or triples in time. We are slowed by the kidney-pounding of beat-up dirt roads, hailed to a stop by highway flaggers to wait for road graders and dump trucks, detoured for washed-out bridges, and backtracked to avoid backtracking further.

Semitrucks fly by us, taking most of the narrow road, and we are forced onto the soft shoulder or into a ditch at least once a day. We learn to just slow down and pull over when we see a big truck coming in the distance. More often we just see a huge column of dust billowing above the road and know that there are eighteen huge rubber tires rolling toward us.

We fill the windshield wiper fluid tank every couple of days with water to keep the dust and mud at bay. The wipers go nearly nonstop to combat the dusty film that settles on the window. Opening the door after a few hours of driving results in a pillow of dust whooshing down the side of the car. It's best to crack the door, and then wait a few seconds to get out to avoid the dust bomb.

Our personalities emerge after a week of driving. I'm the perpetual planner, setting dates and times, and trying in vain to devise a schedule to nowhere. I get caught up in the getting *there*, only to realize that I'm already *there* by accident.

Reid becomes a solid travel companion. He's a navigator when riding shotgun, eager to get the lunch food laid out when we're fishing, or prepare his lentil soup recipe of lentils and lentils flavored with chicken bouillon at dinner. To joke about our lack of spices or general flavorings, he likes to say he's prepared the dish with extra flavor bursts, meaning extra lentils. He's the best at enjoying the ride for its intrinsic value. After I've given up fishing, he continues to blast casts, refusing to let a place slip from being a *there* without the maximum effort.

Rob becomes a pain in the ass. He likes to sit in the back seat and complain that we aren't *there* while eating the lunch that's rationed for later in the day. He buys candy bars at the gas station and hoards them in his backpack to eat when he's fishing alone. He gets mad when we can't get information from the locals, but refuses to fumble through his Spanish to help.

At Lago Misterioso we discover that Rob's sleeping bag is missing. He blames Reid and me for leaving it at the last campsite. We are high in the Andes near the border with Argentina and expect below-freezing temperatures at night. Both Reid and I have two-man tents and offer to let Rob sleep in them. Instead he chooses to pack his nylon bivy sack with extra clothes and drink the rest of a bottle of White Horse whiskey he's been hiding in his backpack. In the morning he wakes hungover and sleep deprived from shivering all night. The entire landscape, including tents and bivy sack, is coated in a thick layer of frost-ice. While we make oatmeal over the Coleman stove he refuses to talk to us and looks at Reid and me like we ordered the frost from God to make him miserable.

We follow a dirt road off the Carretera Austral to make our way up the Río Nirehuoa. It's a small river and one of the most fishy looking we've seen since entering Chile. It cuts through a broad, high-mountain plateau and meanders slowly before dropping through a steep canyon and dumping into the Río Mañihuales. We stop at a small pull out along the road on a hairpin corner. Reid and I head upstream, where a game trail picks its way through the blades of vertical rock that lead to the river. Below we see deep pools and flats with streaming beds of bright green vegetation. This structure and plant life has been the missing ingredient to Chilean fisheries. The beautiful, high-mountain streams of the past week have been too fast and cold for anything but fingerling trout.

We fish the deep pools by hanging off the cliff faces and roll casting across the narrow waterway. We use sink tips and big flies to lure something from the dark water. We catch nothing, but can't shake the idea that the water looks too prime to be devoid of fish. We are also in the middle of nowhere. We haven't seen so much as a shack for miles.

We end up against an unscalable cliff in the narrow canyon. The vertical walls are designed more for climbers than fishermen so we head back downstream. Reid eyes a small slot of deeper water along the far side of the river and stops to cast. I climb up higher on the cliff to watch as his pale orange line starts working out over the water. Sitting on a ledge, I'm taken with the thought that this spot is on the brink of being *there*. A bent rod or a fish rising on the far side, and this place will embed itself in my memory.

His third cast cuts through the middle of the deep channel before becoming taut and starting to swing back toward the near bank. As the line heads downstream I see Reid's arm jerk high into the air and a line of tiny water droplets fly off his line into a linear mist. At the far end of the line I see a flash of gold where the fish is swimming in the current. He's tight on the fish and the feeling of *there* fills the canyon.

Later in the day we drive out of the canyon onto the high plateau. It's flat enough to see the outline of the river in the distance demarcated by the dark green line of trees that grow along the bank and stick up six times higher than the tall, golden grass of the prairie. There are few roads to the river and fewer houses to stop at to ask permission to fish. We assume we are far enough from society for people not to care much about an occasional fisherman along the river, but we have been in Argentina and the land of propiedad privada long enough not to worry.

After several kilometers we see a small, weathered home with a rusted metal roof and a collection of animals in the yard. We turn down the two-track drive that leads to the house, and a black mutt of a ranch dog sprints up the road to meet us. By the time we arrive at the front of the house, we can see that several sets of eyes are watching us from the windows.

We climb out and start walking toward the front door. The door opens and an old man who looks to be in his seventies steps out with a young boy behind him. The child is making sure to keep between his grandfather and the front door while still trying to get his head far enough around his grandfather's thigh so that he doesn't miss anything. They both wear blue jeans and thick sweaters. They have the dark skin of native Chilenos and give us a cautious look.

Waving and smiling as we approach, we hope to exude friendliness. We introduce ourselves and start a conversation about who we are and where we are from. The first thing most people want to know is how I got the SUV with Montana plates down from the United States, an answer that takes about five minutes of explaining. They turn out to be a ranch-hand family running cattle for a wealthy landowner. By the time the conversation hits its first lull, the yard has filled with a flock of chickens and two little dark-haired girls.

We get around to asking if we can fish the river, and they ask if we need a place to stay while we fish. We tell them we are planning to camp in tents. They point behind the house toward the river and say there is a good, flat place along the river, that we are welcome to make camp there. We thank them for the hospitality, accept their offer, and start unloading the mound of gear from the back of the Pathfinder. The boy, Alejandro, loses all reserve and jumps in to grab our sleeping bags and fly rods, turning them into nice piles on the lawn. I see him run to his grandfather and tug the old man's sweater with life-and-death urgency. The old man bends down and listens to the boy for a second before nodding and moving off toward the house. Alejandro runs back to us to tell us we can use the horses to pack our gear to the river. Initially trying to avoid having these ranchers go out of their way, we quickly see how much it will mean to Alejandro to help and so change our tune by expressing how hard it would be to move the gear on our own.

Half an hour later we walk across the plateau through thigh-high grass with Alejandro and his grandfather on their chestnut horses holding our gear on their laps. Alejando points out everything: here is the place where he found the dead rabbit, across the way is where they have their asado pit. He shows us to a beautiful campsite on a flat, grassy knoll that overlooks the river.

We unload our gear from the horses and our backpacks and set a pot of water going to make maté. As the water warms in the pot we discuss the land and cattle and the local concerns. We are welcomed into the life of these high-plateau cattle hands. We are *there*—and it has nothing to do with fishing. This is one of those rare moments when you get the chance to feel a different life. For a moment on the high prairie we are not American tourists—we feel like long-lost friends from another part of Chile, fellow gauchos who have come for a visit.

After Alejandro and his grandfather ride back to the house for dinner we linger a long time at camp. We sit on the grass and mill around our unstrung rods, not wanting the feeling of welcome to abandon us. As soon as we slide into our waders and march upstream in our quest for fish, the spell will break. What we are experiencing this moment, this feeling, is the true purpose of the trip. The fish are simply the excuse that draws us along the blue line of the Carretera Austral to stumble into this feeling of welcome, this *there*.

15
THE DE FACTO
LODGE

Angling is extremely time consuming. That's sort of the whole point. That is why in our high-speed world, anglers, as a kind of preemptive strike, call themselves bums, addicts, and maniacs. We're actually rather quiet people for the most part but our attitude toward time sets us at odds with our own society.

Thomas McGuane, *The Longest Silence*

There are two bottles of whiskey on the table and the orange glow from the fireplace throws a flickering, warm light to the wood-planked walls. A row of waders hang from the stairway's heavy timber railing. The small pools of water that dripped to the rough floor are nearly dry in the heat of the evening fire. Outside the rain tap-taps against the single-pane windows, and through the gray haze of the downpour and dusk the cataraft frame sits at the end of the gravel drive collecting water. The small potholes in the road are filled to overflowing, and a spider web of trickles carry water to a gushing ditch.

It's mid-February, the peak of summer, but a coastal front has drowned the better part of Chile in torrential rains. To the south the major tourist road is washed out. At the bottom of the hill the Río Simpson has risen three feet and runs a dark chocolate brown. In a few hours the turbulent water will lap at the bottom of the bridge. The outside temperature is goose-bump cold and accompanied by a blanket of dark gray clouds hanging low in the valley.

Beetles the size of golf balls are supposed to be out there, bringing huge browns to the surface. If they're out there, we can't see them through the rain.

This place is a log house outside of town among the trees. It's not a lodge, only a twelve-dollar-a-night hostel, breakfast included. Somehow it's become a beacon to fish bums escaping the onslaught of summer rain. Walking the hallway past the open, dormitory-style rooms, rod tubes and fly boxes are splayed out on threadbare mattresses. For two nights the talk around the communal dinner table is all things trout.

We're a hodgepodge collection of fishermen united by our common passion and meager budgets. In addition to my Colorado cronies and myself, there are two Missoulians, a solo traveler from Gunnison, and a pair from Alaska. The ages range from barely twenty-something to pushing forty. We come together in the evening after wasting the day wandering the small town of Coyhaique zigzagging the short streets looking for a new restaurant in which to kill a few hours. Reid's eyes bug out into a thousand-yard stare and he wonders out loud how long it will take the rivers to flush back to normal. A voice from the corner replies, trance-like, "It has to stop raining first."

The voice belongs to George, an Alaskan guide on year two of his South American odyssey. He sits at a portable fly-tying vice surrounded by spools of thread, baggies of feathers, and small piles of 4X streamer hooks. He works the black thread around the long shaft of the hook in rapid rotations of his wrist, which cause the short marabou feathers to stand up straight off the hook. As he works the thread toward the eye of the hook, the body of the fly materializes into a wide, black profile. He works with a mechanical efficiency, not needing to look down after so many years at the vice. A pile of completed leech patterns sit to one side. With a quick flip of his fingers he creates a loop in the line and tightens it down behind the eye. Repeating the motion two more times in half as many seconds he stretches the thread taught and snips the fly clean. In another few seconds, the completed fly falls into the pile and he clinches another hook in the vice jaws.

George travels with a man in his late twenties named Hill who wears glasses and reads the local paper. The two were out camping for the first part of the storm. They tried to battle the fifty-plus-mile-an-hour winds, but mostly just hunkered down in their small backpacking tents and hoped the thin, quarter-inch diameter aluminum poles wouldn't snap under the strain.

Both fluent in Spanish, they practice immersion fishing. Everything they own fits into their oversized trekking backpacks. They use public transportation to get to jumping-off points, usually a small town where they hear, or guess, good fishing might be found. Once in town they canvass the place for food and information, relying on the good nature of the locals, their language skills, and big smiles to get themselves to fish.

This process takes time. Between the fixed schedules of bus transportation and the luck of acquiring information or a hitchhiked ride, hours and days are eaten up in the traveler's pastime of fruitless waiting. In the past two weeks the two have fished just two locations. Their adventures never play out the same way twice, with local personalities dictating as much that transpires as their personal agendas.

At the Río Paloma they paid a taxi driver 35,000 pesos to take them out of town and drop them off on the banks of a river with instructions to return in four days. As Hill says, "If the fishing sucks we wish we would have said less time; if it's good we wish we would have said eight." It's tough going in blind. They count among their essential equipment a good tent and more importantly—a good book.

While their methods don't make for a hugely diverse fishing experience, they get to see a side of Chile shielded from the typical client, and obscured from us in our foreign car and boat. For Hill and George, independence isn't an option. Unraveling the complex local system of bus schedules, minibuses, and private-access estancias requires the help of local people. And, like me, they find the help of local people often exceeds the expectation of their previously formulated plans.

On the Río Deseado their taxi dropped them on the dusty shoulder of the road with a long, empty field stretching to a blue ribbon in the distance. They hiked to the river and set up camp in a small grove overlooking the river. With rain falling, they gathered driftwood into a pyramid of fire and sat down to appraise the river.

A half-mile away the gaucho who managed the ranch spotted smoke from the anglers' fire. He rode his horse through the wet grass toward the column of smoke. In retrospect Hill and George guessed that the gaucho wanted them to put out the fire before the ranch owner, the wealthy foreigner, looked out his window and saw the wisp of smoke. The gaucho wanted to get to the fire before this happened to avoid any questions about his ability to keep trespassers off the ranch. He would get to the camp, put out the fire first, and then get the trespassers off the property before the owner noticed.

Finding the two gringos around their fire drinking maté, the gaucho was caught off guard when the two smiling fishermen invited him to join their circle. George and Hill are never without a liter thermos full of hot water and a bag of yerba maté leaves. For an hour the gaucho passed the maté gourd around the circle, taking sips of the bitter liquid and trading stories of life and the Chilean landscape.

When the maté ran dry the gaucho stood up and told the two to pack up their camp. Instead of kicking them off the ranch, a bad proposition considering that the taxi wouldn't be back for two days, the gaucho found a wooden rowboat tied along the bank and loaded the two men and their gear into the small craft. The owner of the ranch on the far side of the river was out of the country, and the gaucho decided the two fishermen and his job would be safe fishing from the other side.

The rains increased to the heavy pelting common in temperate coastal zones. The normally opaque blue water of the Deseado was dirty with forty-foot sections of trees rolling down the swollen river. They crossed the river in a boat the size of a small dinner table. Hill, George, the gaucho, and their gear, weighted the boat low enough that the dirty water lapped over the bow and splashed on the floor.

Midway across the river the gaucho asked the two if they could swim. "Of course," they replied. "*Yo no,*" said the gaucho.

Here was a man who came over to kick a couple of gringos off his foreign boss's land, but ended up risking his life to row those same two guys across a flooding river so they could wave little rods in the air and try to catch fish that they will only release after having caught them.

In another instance, George and Hill arrived at the local bus station, where they proceeded to the local tourism office to inquire about fishing opportunities in the area. Needing a ride to get to any place with fish, the tourism agent went next door to the local radio station. In a few minutes the broadcaster put a message out over the airwaves that there were two foreigners at the bus station who needed a ride to go fishing. Within ten minutes the son of a local ranch owner showed up in a pickup truck, loaded the two in the back, and drove them to the private lakes on their land.

These are wonderful stories of relying on the local people to fish. Less romantic are the hours on the concrete floors of bus stations and the fine coating of dust acquired after several hours on the side of dirt roads thumbing for a ride. When they finish their travels, George and Hill will know about much more than the nation's fish. Unlike most foreign anglers, the two will also know the country.

I see the cost of this knowledge firsthand sitting in front of the hostel fire. The front door opens and Hill enters. Unable to hitch a ride back to the hostel, he's soaked from head to toe from the walk home after dinner in town. Relying on generosity and good fortune can make travel as unpredictable as the Chilean weather. The look of misery on the slump-shouldered individual under the soaked-through raincoat, drenched pants, and squishing shoes exemplifies a few of the pitfalls of their style of travel.

Their satisfaction is not confined to the fruits of experiential travel. Their appetites are not satiated by the aesthetics of the rolling steppe or the successful integration in to autobus society. Even a unique and poignant connection with a nonswimming gaucho are just part, a small part, of the game. George and Hill are trout hunters. They have the same goals as me and the guided clients who roll past them on dirt roads with the windows up and air conditioning blasting. With more fortitude, better language skills, and perseverance, they are after the same almighty reward—troutzilla.

They've been successful. They have pictures. When you get to only two destinations in two weeks, you choose your spots carefully and fish them hard. Five-pound brookies and seven-pound browns are all logged in digital format as proof of their methods and their ability to produce more than a cultural experience.

But then, I've never spoken with anyone as possessed by trout fever as George. Around the hostel's wooden table slowly filling with beer cans, he falls into an enchanted state. His eyes grow as big as dinner plates, he lowers his voice and talks quickly as if to make it difficult for those outside our little fish-bum contingent to hear.

He speaks of a place called Lago Tres in Argentina. Then speculates about the opening of Lago Cinco to the north and a litany of reasons it should have huge fish. Then, without a pause, a myth about a new spring creek south of Esquel, private water only. "I saw the pictures on the Internet...." he says. "Huge." The desire that resounds in his voice draws us closer into his world of big-trout hunting.

"Have you heard of Lago Strobel?" he asks. "Some call it Jurassic Lake." Images of its fish appeared in one of the newsstand magazines two months ago. In the photos, anglers beached slabs of silver fish that looked, with their huge size and chrome sides, like gigantic steelhead. George fished the lake on a previous trip a few years prior when the first lodge there was still using tents, and the only permanent structure was the dilapidated shed of a local *campesino*. In true George style he stayed at the dilapidated shed and fished streamers to over-grown rainbows. He claimed they traveled in schools like ocean fish, prowling the flats in marauding packs. Periods of inactivity erupted into action as a posse moved in. He recalled a particularly productive hour in which he landed three trout over ten pounds. To the casual angler who may not appreciate that statement, that's three fish of a lifetime in the course of an hour.

Asked what food chain supports the unparalleled fish size, he describes how the volcanic geography of the area harbors incredibly rich nutrient content. This leads to an abundance of plant life and in turn freshwater shrimp known as scuds. The shrimp bloat the fish to super-sized proportions. At one point in the fishing he waded out to waist deep and scooped up a double handful of material from the bottom of the lake. What he pulled up was half mud and half shrimp. As he says this he reenacts scooping the muck off the bottom and holding it up to his face. The gesture illuminates the face of a crazed addict like a scene from an old Western in which the old-time miner holds his gold booty up to show his prize and simultaneously illuminates the delirium it's caused. "There were so many they'd just flow out of your hands," he says of the scuds. He looks to his hands as if he sees the little creatures evaporating through his fingers.

There are now three lodges on Lago Strobel, and access is limited to those willing to pay one thousand dollars a day to battle with its monsters. You can guess from George's form of travel that even if he were able to pay that kind of money, he's unwilling. Perhaps that's why he's got that crazed look. Instead of dwelling on it, he's trying to find the next hog heaven. With luck he'll find it and have a few years to fish it before a developer realizes what kind of gold is swimming in and around the lake.

Across the table from George, another American sits with his pink baseball cap cocked back on his head and the elongated forehead of premature baldness emerging. The black stitching on the hat reads Crystal Bar. I know without reading the fine lettering underneath that it says Bozeman, Montana. I'd been to that Main Street dive enough times to recognize the design. The balding man and I may have bellied up to the bar at the same time, having conversations about the same rivers with different people. As I discover, Cliff's life and my own have run parallel, passing each other like shadows for the past few months and maybe even years.

Before I meet Cliff in front of the hostel fireplace I recognized his blue minivan in the outside drive. It's the only other car in Patagonia besides mine with an oversized cataraft frame strapped to the roof. I'd seen the van with Chilean plates across from the fly shop in San Martín de los Andes several thousand miles north. When I first saw it months earlier, I considered waiting at the curb for the owner. I saw it again weeks later in Bariloche while sitting with a beer on a patio restaurant. I knew nothing of the driver except that our plans mirrored each other's.

In the small world of South American trout hunters, I came across a handful of names and e-mail addresses. Cliff's address was one of the few leads that produced any worthwhile information. For months we'd bounced river info off each other as we circled in Northern Patagonia. Quick, two-to-three-sentence e-mails were our style: "Fished the Río Chubut Tuesday. Lots of small fish, water still a bit high, rumors of awesome float and big fish south of Esquel. Logistics look like a bitch." The return e-mail reading, "Might try it in a month. Slammed it on the Malleo. Worth drive to come up, though may rain in a week and fuck it up." We always seemed to be at the opposite ends of a province and on different schedules.

Seeing him sitting at the table in his pushed-back pink hat, it didn't take me long to find out that Cliff owned the van and the e-mail address. He was the oldest of the hostel fishermen and had almost two decades of fish bumming under his belt to all the places that crop up in fly-fishing magazines. Argentina, Chile, New Zealand, Alaska, Colorado, Montana, Idaho, Wyoming; Cliff knew the ins and outs of the publicized big rivers and the unknown small streams. Everyone at the hostel knew this because Cliff was both a talker and a one-upper. After Reid told a story about catching a good fish on the Taylor River in Colorado, Cliff jumped in with his own Taylor River story in which the length of the story and the eventual fish were four times as long.

Cliff liked to talk and it was hard to totally escape him. For one, the common area of the hostel was not that large. Second, Cliff always had a cooler full of beer that he doled out as long as you were sitting around the table listening to him talk. Moreover, the man told a pretty good story. Granted, they were all long winded and revolved around a central theme: Cliff catches the biggest fish. But what kept me listening the most to his self-aggrandizing tales was that the man knew his shit when it came to fishing Patagonia.

He'd been down in Chile the year before fishing from Chaitén southward as part of a loose agreement with a prospective lodge owner in La Junta. The guy paid for his gas and food while Cliff pounded every fishable piece of water in the central part of Chile looking for the next great lodge destination. Nothing materialized out of this time on these long, remote stretches of river except the conviction that big fish in Chile were a hell of a lot of work. After fighting his way onto and down these violent rivers, Cliff knew the area better than anyone I'd found in Chile, including lifelong guides.

We stayed up late at night poring over maps of the desolate country and debating the probability of fish in each blue streak. To get more information, Cliff fired up an ancient-looking laptop and we watched the green LED flicker in and out indicating our connection to the local Wi-Fi network. With Google Earth we zoomed in on the Chilean landscape, finding access points and scanning for rapids. Each page took a full beer to load, providing Cliff ample time to spin his tales.

"You have to fish the *medio* section of the Limay. You've been wasting your time fishing higher up by Bariloche. That's all hype from the guides in town. The real fish are in the medio. Just go to the dam and look down and you'll see these huge fish. There's a section just below the dam that you can't fish, but you can see them in there. The local guys wade in just below the line and cast up. Most of them can't cast far enough to reach the fish. The fish know exactly where to hang out to avoid the fishermen.

"I saw this sandbar out toward the middle of the river when I was watching the fish, so I jumped in and swam out to this little spit of sand. It was super hard to stand midriver with the current pushing me, but I was right in on the fish. I hooked three the first afternoon. I came back the next day, and the local guys were standing out there on my sandbar so I had to cast from the bank. I still hooked two because I can cast far. I've got a Sage with this super-slick line. I make my own grease that makes it really shoot. Anyway, I cast far enough to get out to those fish and still catch two. The local guys were pissed. They thought that by standing in my spot, they would keep me from catching fish.

"The medio's the spot to be. Have you even caught a fish on the upper section? You put in right below the damn and float for twelve miles. I know the names of the people to talk to at the put in and takeout. I can probably hook you up with a shuttle too. The guy's name is Miguel something or other. He's got three kids. They're just bait fishermen, but they can run a shuttle for you. I paid like ten pesos. For you it will probably be more 'cause I got to know them so they didn't stick me with the gringo price. Maybe if you told them you knew there was a gringo price, you could guilt them into ten pesos."

The story goes on in the same vein for another fifteen minutes. I zone out thinking about where to head after the rains taper off. Cliff rambles on with his story, and I keep my head in a perpetual nod adding the occasional "uh-huh" where it sounds like the rhythm of the story requires. I get an odd sense that the conversation must be similar to what happens after years of marriage, and I've only just met Cliff. Maybe this explains why he's forty and single. Though being single likely has more to do with the fact that he's bumming around the remote regions of Chile with a four-wheel drive van and a cataraft.

Around midnight we reach the last of the beers bobbing in the lukewarm water in the cooler. Although I'm weary of Cliff's long-winded tales, I still feel admiration for this balding, middle-aged fish bum. I marvel at the contrast between his style of traveling and George and Hill's method. Other than the occasional stop for fuel and groceries, Cliff travels without need of outside help.

In Cliff's tales of the Río Figuroa, or the Limay, I sense an indomitable spirit. A bravado that comes down to "Where there's a will, there's a way." He tells tales of rivers I balked at after failing to gather adequate river beta. The country boils down to the Google Earth images on his computer screen. Objective pictures, the unmasked face of Mother Nature, are all Cliff needs to decide if a river is floatable.

I tell him of the conversation I'd had in La Junta with the man who warned me not to float the Río Rosselot, "No. No. Este río es muy peligroso. Puedes morir."

"Those locals don't know shit," Cliff replies.

His stories are different from the ones George tells. In George's stories the images that linger are the people who come out of nowhere, the rain-drenched gaucho or the radio DJ. After Cliff describes his trip down the Río Malleo, I concentrate to remember the mile marker of the put in, or the layout of the rapid that lies on river left six miles from the takeout. His reports are factual and specific. I don't doubt that he can pin down exact locations using the zoom feature on his portable GPS.

The stories are no less interesting for their content. They are tales of geography and rivers in the genre of the classic man-versus-nature story line that has captivated campfire listeners since the dawn of mankind.

Cliff's stories indicate a different motivation than the desire to hook monster trout. Like the true explorer, his voice sounds out a passion for accomplishment. The mile markers and river beta form the factual manifestations of a successful adventure. From nothing but a blue line on a foreign map, he arrives and conquers. Instead of a golden medal and a slap on the back from the National Geographic Society, his rewards are the knowledge of the float and the satisfaction of self-accomplishment.

The rain still hammers off the metal roof of the hostel at the evening winds down. The Río Simpson continues to rise, and we'll all be stuck inside again tomorrow, coming together in the communal reverie of the weather-caged angler. I find it astounding how dissimilarly the same vacation has played out in a group of fellow countrymen. Yet, I'm sure we all described our journey in the same terms as we left our friends and family in the United States: "I am going fishing in Patagonia."

16
NO-MAN'S-LAND

Good things come in small packages.

Unknown

A dirt road leads east from the town of Coyhaique. Without a good map you'll be lost in a couple of hours on the labyrinth of dirt ranch roads that cross the rolling green hills in every direction. Using the persistence of a private investigator and more cash than prudent, we track down a topographic military map of Chile. Our destination is a thin squiggle of blue on the map that trails out into nothing as it heads toward Argentina.

Four hours of jarring dirt road later we arrive at an *aduanas*, a customs, checkpoint that leads travelers out of Chile, across a barren stretch of no-man's-land, and into Argentina. There's nothing out past the small aduanas station save for cattle and broken-down fences. I see nothing that indicates the presence of big fish. No river, no lake, only the snaking contour of a hillside in the distance that indicates the historic presence of water.

As usual we're here on the coattails of a rumor. This one courtesy of a young Chilean guide named Martin. We'd met him a week prior on the Río Mañihuales, where he stumbled upon us trying every fly in our box to sight fish a twenty-inch rainbow. He stayed with us long enough to try every fly in his box and tell us about the life of a young *Chileno* guide.

After a high school study-abroad program in Nebraska, Martin returned to Chile speaking excellent English and captivated by fly fishing. A year casting poppers to bass got him hooked on fly fishing, and he couldn't wait to try for trout in his native land. With his excellent language skills and sharp mind he found a position as an understudy guide at Estancia del Zorro, one of Chile's most exclusive lodges. We met him at the tail end of his season at the fishing ranch and facing the same challenges as most first-year guides. He was nearly broke, frustrated by a lack of days actually guiding, and bitter at having been the go-to guy for grunt labor. In short, his summer of cleaning waders and watching others guide fell short of his expectations.

Like all guides in Patagonia, Martin keeps a tight lip on area fishing. Our initial inquiries are met with typically nondescript answers.

"What do you recommend at this point in the season?" we ask.

"Here is good. Really anywhere fishes well now," he says.

We know from the past three weeks in Chile that his first statement is suspect and the second outright propaganda. Instead of forcing the issue we continue to cast flies at the stubborn rainbow trout, taking turns casting and spotting for each other. Over the course of an hour we tell Martin fishing tales from rivers that he's heard about, read about, and dreamed about.

Whether he came to see us as fellow fishermen instead of foreign clients, or our conversation of fishing freedom reignited his summer's frustration, I don't know. But what I do know is that walking back to the parking lot, Martin asks if we have a map. I get out the military topography map and spread it out on the hood of the Pathfinder. Martin searches the map for a landmark and settles his finger on the town of Coyhaique.

Looking back at us he says, "Follow this road out of town," and traces one of the red road lines east with his finger. "Follow this road for about four hours. The road is terrible and there's nothing out there, so fill up with gas before you leave. Take your food too."

We nod in unison.

"You will get to the aduanas guard post. You will have to stop and talk to them. You want to go past the guard post into the empty space between Argentina and Chile. I don't know what you call this. You have to give the aduanas your passport. Explain to them you're going fishing, but not going into Argentina. They will keep your passport to make sure you come back."

I exchange quizzical looks with Reid and Rob, trying to read in their eyes if they too think this sounds crazy.

"Go out past the checkpoint another two and a half kilometers. You'll cross a small stream. There are huge fish in this stream. It is the upper end of the stream I guide clients on. Do not get caught fishing there. It's maybe private or public, I don't know. You don't want to find out. If you get caught, do not tell them anything about me."

"How big are the fish?" I ask.

"Eight pounds. Some bigger," he says holding his hands wide apart to show the size.

At the aduanas guard station I walk up to the window, unsure how to explain what we want to do. I'm not convinced Martin divulged anything other than a regurgitated rumor he once heard while guiding. Passport in hand, I see the guard in his green military uniform reach for the paperwork used to exit the country. In my best Spanish I tell him we don't want to leave Chile; we just want to go a couple more miles and fish. He gives me a sidelong glance and tells me this is impossible.

"You cannot pass here unless you are leaving the country," he says.

Something in his tone or the way he looks at me when I mention fishing doesn't feel right. Instead of settling for his official answer, I explain how a local guide instructed us to do this. As I force the issue, the guard looks at me again, this time with a look that says, "I don't know how you found out about this, but I don't like it."

"*Pasaporte*," he says. Then, "*Cerramos a las ocho*"— we close at eight.

As we hurry back to the Pathfinder, the guard lifts the red-and-white-striped barricade and we drive into no-man's-land.

Traveling in between countries without a passport is an eerie, naked feeling, like the security blanket of American citizenship has evaporated. We are breaking the cardinal rule of international travel: Don't part with your passport. And we do it for no other reason than the rumor of fish.

Watching the odometer, we roll past the two-mile mark without a trace of water. We keep driving, growing more skeptical with each tick of the odometer. At 2.8 miles we roll over a smallish culvert with a trickle of water running through it. I'm convinced we've been duped by rumor again as I pull over to investigate. The stream is three inches deep and two feet wide. I can see every inch of the tan sand of the streambed. I don't need a fly rod to tell me there's not an eight-pound trout in this stream; an eight-ounce trout couldn't hide in this meager water flow.

I'm content to take a nap on the side of the road and write off the endeavor. But after four hours in the car, Reid isn't willing to concede defeat and starts collecting his gear.

"Are you really going to fish this? I can see from here there's nothing in it," I say.

"Maybe not. I'm just going to walk a ways and see if it changes," Reid tells me.

"How far are you going?" I ask.

"I don't know, around a corner or two," he says.

Looking out to the western horizon I see a wide, green valley stretching for what seems like a hundred miles to a range of dark mountains. Closer in I can see the zigzag pattern of the stream for fifty yards before it turns behind a tuft of a hill and out of sight. I know from my own experience that "a corner or two" may well turn into a five-mile hike.

"A corner or two," I say and start fishing my rod out the back of the car.

A mile later the creek looks the same. Three inches of water flowing in a current so slow it's only detectable by the small humps it makes when pushing over streambed stones. At one point the stream deepens and widens to five feet across. In the slow current, weeds choke the stream to the banks in a thick, impenetrable mat. We climb a small hill that forms the inside of a tight meander and look westward. As far as I can see there is nothing that belies an end to this pattern of shallow, unfishable water.

On the leeward side of the hill I find a swale of thick grass. I watch Reid work back down to the water and yell to him, "I hope you catch a monster!" Before he's around the next corner I'm asleep with the cool breeze of the steppe skipping over my sheltered mattress.

Sometime later in the half-reality of the dream world I hear the *splash-splash* of footsteps in water. I pry myself from my subconscious river adventure to see Reid walking toward me. Even through the fog of sleep and I can see his defeated posture. I follow his silhouette down to his hand and see the rough ends of a graphite fly rod snapped into ragged shards.

It's the second rod he's broken in the past week. Between the broken rods and the stolen rod in Argentina, he's down to his last fly rod: a crappy introductory rod borrowed last minute as a backup to his backup rod. As he crests the knoll below me I expect the expression on his face to match the slump in his posture. Instead, he looks as if he's just found Atlantis.

Still half out of breath, he chokes out, "I h-a-d h-i-m."

"What are you talking about?" I ask.

"I h-a-d h-i-m," he says again, even slower. He sits and starts to tell me what happened.

"After I left you I just kept walking downstream. I went about a half mile and came to this spot where the stream opened up. It was weird. I don't know how deep it was, maybe like six feet. The middle was open, but there was a ring of weeds all the way around the outside. I cast in the middle where it was open, and this fish came out of nowhere. It was the biggest fish I've ever seen. It came up and just inhaled my fly. It dove into the weeds. I couldn't fight it at all. I had to jump in.

"I was standing waist-deep in the weeds and I started to pull him back out of the weeds. I kept working on him. Oh God, he was enormous. I got him all the way in. I got him right to me and I was trying to lift him with one hand and hold my rod with the other, but I couldn't lift him. He was too big to lift, so I set my rod down on the weeds and tried to grab him. I got him up out of the water, but I couldn't hold on to him. He was so big, there was nothing to grab on to. Before I could stop it, he slipped out of my hands and landed on my rod. I heard it snap. I tried to grab the fish again but he dove back into the weeds. I scrambled to find my line. I threw my rod up on the bank and found the line coming out the tiptop. I just grabbed the line and started pulling.

"There was nothing there. He broke me off on the weeds. That was the biggest fish I've ever seen. I don't know how big it was—ten pounds, twelve?"

"Are you serious?" I ask, but could tell from his stunned expression that it was true. I tried to wrap my mind around the idea of a twelve-pound trout living in a three-inch deep stream.

"I've still got a rod. We can trade off casting. Let's go," I say.

We walk to the spot where Reid lost the fish. I see two holes in the weed bed where his legs were planted during the fight. It's still Reid's fish so I hand him the rod and let him cast out. Neither of us think there's much chance of the fish coming back up, but we have to try. Nothing rises on a dozen casts, so we decide to move downstream.

A quarter mile later we find a similar spot, a deep hole lined by a ring of weeds. The opening in the middle of the weeds is the size of a card table. I still can't imagine a fish living in the tight confines of the weeds. I check my fly, a large beetle pattern, and give a hefty tug on the leader.

My cast splats in the middle of the pool across the weed mat. Nothing. I wait a few seconds. The pool looks like a barren bog. Nothing stirs. I wiggle the tip of my rod. I see the energy transfer into the line and run in a pulse to the end of the line where my beetle sends a tiny ripple across the water.

No sooner did the ripple leave the beetle than I see a flash of brown and gold ten inches wide slash across the pool and attack the fly. The fish came with so much force he missed the fly and turned back into the hole. I recast on instinct and set the hook a second later when the fish again slashes to the surface. I feel the hook set, and a second later feel the line break as the fish pushes deep into the weeds.

I can't believe what I've just seen. I look at Reid, who's wearing an expression that's part "Holy shit!" and part "I told you so." I estimate the fish at ten pounds, but it's hard to tell in the brief glimpse. Outside of salmon, I've never seen a fish that wide. He broke my 1X leader without a pause. I sit down on the bank to replay in my mind the fish surging up to my fly again and again.

We wander downstream far enough that we can see the outline of a large ranch house. Not wanting to test our welcome, we turn around and walk back upstream. In three miles of walking we find only those two deep spots and just the two lone monsters. We can only imagine the fishing down lower where the stream picks up flow and current.

In the evening we drive back to the aduanas to get our passports. The guard asks about the fishing. I give a sheepish grin. "*Muy bien.*" He smiles back and I understand in his eyes that we've seen something special.

Sometime later I sit at an Internet kiosk and search the web for Estancia del Zorro. Entering the ranch's homepage I find their collage of pictures. I see photos of large brown trout. The stream is wider, deeper, and more characteristic of big-fish water. Yet, I don't see any fish as large as the two we hooked that day. Perhaps they lived far enough from the guided beats, out in water no fisherman would imagine they could find a monster— out in no-man's-land.

We study the map again, taking a keen interest in each of the thin blue lines fingering out into the *frontera* foothills. This is the land for would-be explorers. Here on the edge of Chile the streams and lakes enjoy a flatness of terrain to become proper trout fisheries. Vegetation and insects live in the slow, fertile water providing environments capable of growing enormous fish. That a tiny stream or pint-sized pond can hold these fish makes the adventure a challenge. They are easy to bypass as too small or too out of the way. Without the tip from a young Chileno guide and the perseverance of an American trout bum, I'd never be the wiser that tiny streams in middle of nowhere can hold larger trout than I'd ever seen before.

In that vast land of the southern frontera, days separate the blue lines on the map. A lucky outpost station here or there may have a meager selection of food to resupply. Gas stations are as much of a rumor as the fish themselves. More than once we coast into a tiny town on empty with the prayer of fuel.

It's this remoteness and isolation that keeps the fish a secret. There's a sense of possibility standing on a ridge looking out across the hills of the steppe without the square outline of a house or barn or shed to break the natural rhythm. There is no sense of hurry to reach a river before other anglers arrive. They never do. It's here on the plain of green and brown past the edge of society that I come as close as I can to the Montana of the past.

What I find I was looking for is not a fish, a lake, or a river. It's the feeling of unhurried possibility, the idea that the world is out there waiting for me.

17
PATAGONIA
RIVER GUIDES

---

*Then let's meet here; for here are fresh
sheets that smell of lavender,
and I am sure we cannot expect better
meat, or better usage in any place.*

Izaak Walton, *The Compleat Angler*

From the no-man's-land of the border, Reid, Rob, and I worked north through Central Patagonia back to Bariloche and the end of our adventure together. I dropped them off in front of the hostel we had started at almost a month earlier and turned my sights toward an entirely different type of adventure.

I'd heard rumors of a company several hours south run by two Americans from Montana. Given the strict rules against Americans guiding in Argentina and the enormity of setting up such an operation, I thought the two might have some stories of their own. On a prayer I'd sent an e-mail to the general company account telling them who I was and little more than that I'd like to meet them and swap stories. I'm not sure why they responded, perhaps they empathized with my vagabond fish-bum lifestyle, but they had an opening at their lodge outside Esquel, Argentina, and invited me to stay as their guest for a couple days.

>>>>

I stop at the big double gate hung on flagstone pillars. Juan Carlos, a short Chileno with a graying moustache and coke-bottle glasses, swings the gate open and holds it back for me to drive through. He hops on the Pathfinder's running board, hanging off the roof rack with one hand and pointing down a gravel road with the other. We pass by a four-by-six-foot carved wooden sign painted to look like an Argentine flag with a huge trout in the middle of the three stripes. Above and below the fish are the words "Patagonia River Guides."

Juan Carlos directs me through the compound of buildings and roads that form the estate. After passing a half-dozen buildings we pull up to a two-story edifice with honey-stained wooden beams and a dark gray flagstone walkway that matches the front gate.

"Welcome," he says. "This will be your cabin." Before opening the door I can tell this will be a new experience for me.

Inside the stately cabin, Juan Carlos shows me the main floor: kitchen, bar, dining room, and living area with a wall of windows that look out on the river fifty yards away. Juan Carlos excuses himself, leaving me to explore the place. A master bedroom and bath round out the first floor. Upstairs I find two huge bedrooms with their own separate baths and an entertainment room with another set of huge windows that command a view of the entire Río Grande valley. I lie down on one of the beds and sink into the comforter, only to realize it will be hard to get back up.

I've tracked down this lodge on a long road to nowhere because it's owned and operated by two young Americans. With the ban on American guides and the maze of paperwork for everything, I'm curious how in the hell these two have managed to set up shop. They're light-years ahead of fish bumming out of a Nissan Pathfinder, and while I have no intention of ever setting up a business in Patagonia, I have no doubt that however they've done it, there's going to be a good story behind it.

The first opportunity to meet the owners comes at dusk in the bright lights of the lodge's bar and pool hall. Rance Rathie is thirty-something with sandy blond hair and intelligent, but shifty, eyes. He's talking with a client when I walk in, but I can see his eyes constantly scanning the room. He appears to be one of those people who can keep tabs on everything and everyone simultaneously. No doubt he's noticed the client who wandered in solo in need of attention, the level of crackers and cheese on the second snack platter that may need a refill in another five minutes, a half-full beer perched on the edge of the pool table's expensive felt, and of course me, the unknown person lingering by the wall.

The co-owner, Travis Colter Smith, stands about ten feet from Rance with another couple of clients. Between his sun-dark skin, dark brown hair swept across his forehead, and relaxed, carefree demeanor, he reminds me of a California surf bum. He sips his mixed drink and gives the clients a broad smile before launching into another story.

It's the first night with a new group of clients so they're working the bar scene with extra effort to create the easygoing and welcoming atmosphere the clients will look forward to returning to each night, and with luck, each season. Even without being a part of the conversations I can see that they're doing a good job. There's a hum in the air that draws people in. But then, it's the first night for fishermen about to spend the next week casting flies into Patagonian waters, so the energy level is already high.

It's several minutes before Rance finds a way out of his conversation to meet me at the bar and introduce himself. He pours me a beer and offers a few quick comments. As he's talking I can see his eyes darting around the room to check on things that might need his attention. I get the feeling I'm a brief stop on a customer service track with higher priorities. He's gone again before my third sip of beer.

At dinner I get firsthand exposure to the high-end clientele. A table-wide discussion breaks out regarding the best hotels and steak houses in Buenos Aires, then another one on the state of world airlines, and even the novel topic of the week's fishing itinerary. Travis and Rance play the role of the quiet expert. They let the clients dictate the pace and content of the conversation, chipping in only to help out with the name of a particular river, or in the case of this particular discussion, the names of steak houses in Buenos Aires.

From what I understand, the affluent conversation and refined role Rance and Travis play in it seems nearly comical in comparison to the dinners during the early days of the company. The first few years they ran clients through a tiny town two hours south named Río Pico that had barely enough infrastructure to support the local sheep farms, let alone upscale fishing clients. They ate dinners in the dingy back room of Donkey's, the town's run-down bar. The cast of local characters outnumbered the guests at times. I doubt conversations, when in English, included the state of the world's airlines.

Now seven years later Rance and Travis are in button-downs with white linen in their laps playing moderator to upper-crust American conversations. Those back-room dinners allowed them to become successful enough to afford the honey-stained walls, flagstone-floored dining hall, and the comforts that come with a successful business. The comforts are nice and the food superior, but for a couple guys from tiny ranch towns in Montana, I guess that they'd rather be in the back room of the bar at Río Pico.

Around the table much of the banter is beyond my price range, but the personalities turn out to be disarming and jovial. As we work our way through the three-course meal prepared by the professional chef, the few returning clients reminisce about past rivers and fish. Talk of the coming adventure starts galvanizing the individuals into a loose fishing confederation. Whether it's a function of the wine, the setting, or some Jedi mind trick worked by Rance and Travis, the group achieves a pleasant state of summer camp utopia by the time the dessert plates are cleared.

Seizing a lull in the conversation, Rance announces the next day's itinerary with a description of the rivers they'll head to in the morning. The announcement starts another round of enthusiastic discussion until Rance quashes it with the news that breakfast will be at 7:45 a.m. After that, the clients thin out quickly, heading into the night to find their own deluxe cabin accommodations. The kitchen staff swoops in to collect the remaining crystal, cutlery, and linen. They'll be working another hour to get cleaned up before going to bed and rising in the morning to prepare the breakfast buffet.

I expect the two exhausted owners who've spent the day catering to others' needs will now also head home to get some sleep before starting it all over again tomorrow. At the door to the dining hall I meet them to hear what they have in store for me, and the two exhausted faces tell me to join them. They walk over to the bar, pour three drinks, and sit down at a small table in the half-light of the quiet bar. The business edge drops away in a flash and Rance falls into the first relaxed state I've seen.

The story starts for Rance in a way not too dissimilar from the beginnings of my own Patagonia story. Working on an environmental engineering degree at Montana Tech in Butte, Montana, during the winter of 1998, he was facing the prospects of subzero temperatures in a run-down mining town. Looking for a way out, he did a little research and found out he couldn't legally guide in New Zealand. He turned his attention to Chile and Argentina (Americans were still allowed to guide in Argentina at the time) and narrowed his search further after someone told him he'd find hotter women in Argentina. After calling a number of fly-fishing booking agents, he knew how difficult a task it would be to land a winter gig as a Patagonian guide.

As a second-generation guide, he tapped into the Montana guiding network to get a tip about a man named Martin O'Farrell. Martin owned the Trevelin Lodge in Argentina and had plans to attend the annual fly-fishing trade show in Salt Lake City. The tip also included the caution that Rance had better be able to impress the hell out of Martin if he wanted a job in Argentina;

there were likely going to be a couple hundred other guides at the trade show with similar intentions.

With nothing more than a name and the prospect of cold temperatures, Rance took off for Salt Lake. He wandered through the immense showroom, popping in and out of small groups in search of a short, dark-skinned fellow with "Martin" on his name tag. Rance found him and his head guide, John Roberts. He introduced himself and talked his way into a job.

Rance's first year down south played out like those of so many American guides over the years. He lived in a modified shed on the outskirts of the property behind the lodge. The accommodations were dismal and the working conditions similar. Early in the season Rance was up at dawn prepping for the day's trip by getting food together in the kitchen. As he sipped a cup of coffee, Martin came into the room and told him that guides didn't need to drink the coffee. Foreign guides are considered disposable labor in South America; there's always someone looking to escape the snow and take a shot at guiding in South America. Company owners know this and use it to ride their guides into the ground. As Rance says, it wasn't too long before "Foreign guides don't need coffee" turned into "Foreign guides don't need to eat or get paid either."

In addition to the coffee ban, Rance was also forbidden to do any fishing on his own, to fish with clients under any circumstances, or to discuss any other fishing areas except the one they were at that day.

After the first season Rance was ready to throw in the towel on guiding in Argentina; the novelty of South America had drifted away in the tide of a hundred disenchanted days. I suspect he flew home for Montana's summer season feeling maligned, malnourished, and more than a little pissed at Martin.

The next season he got a call from Martin's head guide at Trevelin asking him to come back down. He agreed to return on one condition: his best friend, Travis, would come along as another guide. The gesture speaks volumes about the value the two men placed on each other considering they knew ahead of time what they were getting into. Rance says of the decision, "Once I knew I would have Travis down there, I knew I could do it."

I suspect another reason Rance pulled the trigger on a second season is the same reason I came down again. After a season of tough guiding, you get a glimpse of what Patagonia might offer. You get fifty miles per hour flashes of streams you are not able (or not allowed) to fish while driving clients back to the lodge. You hear stories from other guides and travelers, and convince yourself of the fishing utopia out there past the confines of the lodge. I think anyone who guides in Patagonia knows by the end of their first season they will be haunted by its waters until they experience it on their own terms.

Rance and Travis made it two seasons together working for Martin. At its low point they were the camp boys for the O'Farrell family reunion. At its high point they were two best friends from Montana working the rivers of Patagonia. They don't know how many seasons they might have stuck it out with Martin had he not stiffed them at the end of the second season, but refusing to pay them for an entire season of work drove the final nail into the coffin.

It's hard to crawl out from under the soft down comforter to make it to breakfast the next morning. It's the first real bed I've slept in for four months. Wandering down to catch the end of breakfast I see the part of Rance and Travis's operation that's more important and impressive than the three-course meal or the sprawling grounds. Lined up in front of the dining hall is a row of brand-new Toyota Hilux trucks with top-of-the-line NRS rafts and frames waiting in the beds. The Patagonia River Guides' staff of professional and assistant guides are milling near the trucks. They are all good-looking Argentines clad from head to toe in the latest Simms fishing gear. The scene exudes professionalism and it's the package of gear and guides that keeps the company growing through tough economic times.

The shiny trucks and spiffy guides lined up in front of the regal dining room look as though they are part of a well-established operation, but the truth is that they are a far cry from where the company started just seven years earlier. After getting stiffed for their season of work, Rance decided to go for it on his own and knew that he needed Travis to succeed. He created a trifold pamphlet for their future lodge and slid it across a table to Travis. It took a few days for Travis to buy in, but the next year they were down in Patagonia with two trucks, a couple of boats, and a company name—Patagonia River Guides.

From the outset they approached the game differently than other lodges in Patagonia. Instead of heading north to compete on the most famous water, they headed south.

It's a two-hour journey on a potholed, twisty dirt road over a steep mountain pass from the airport in Esquel to Río Pico. The scenery is spectacular, but dust can fill every crack and crevice over the course of the drive. The town of Río Pico consists of a main road smattered with defunct, or shortly to be so, buildings that look as if they were built in the heyday of economic prosperity eighty years prior. The grocery store, which measures about twenty by twenty, is frequently out of items as basic as sugar and maté. As rough as the travel and infrastructure of the area are, the locals presented a worse problem. They burned down the first and only fishing lodge that outsiders tried to build in the area.

Rance and Travis had just one connection in the community: a brother-in-law who was assigned as the local schoolteacher. He was good for some introductions, but past that they were still out-of-town gringos who spoke elementary Spanish. For the most part they were on their own to prove to the roughneck ranching town that they weren't like all the other guides who'd come through town and left a bad taste in one way or another.

They set up an interesting home base that included sleeping at the local police station and holding business meetings at the bar across the street. The two occasionally came into conflict; the police station had a ten o'clock curfew for its paying guests, but the best business got accomplished in the wee morning hours at the bar, which was required to close at one-thirty in the morning. Fortunately the cops weren't too strict on curfew and the barman had the courtesy to hang blankets over his front window to let the cops pretend he was closed.

Río Pico was just that brand of small town where a strange face could both find a room at the police station and party next door under a blind eye. After all, just one family settled the Río Pico valley and while there are now a thousand or so people, there are only a few more bloodlines.

Breaking into Río Pico took time. Fishermen had a bad history in the area. Locals complained that guides from Esquel and Bariloche would drive down with their clients and all their food and gear for the week. They'd just blow through town on their way to fish, leaving dust trails and little else. They treated the land like they owned it, cutting through fences and trespassing at will. They left their trash and blew through town again on their way back north without even slowing down to wave. Locals felt like second-class citizens without any means to address the issue except by burning down whatever the outsiders tried to make permanent.

In some ways it was better that Rance and Travis were from Montana instead of two hours away in Esquel; they were different enough that the locals gave them a chance to prove that they would act differently as well. They started by doing something no other guides had done: spending time in Río Pico. By day they rallied their trucks out into the mountains looking for new water. They were also careful to find landowners and ask permission before fishing.

On the maze of back roads and cow trails, finding someone was sometimes more of a necessity than a courtesy. On the Río Pico the only way they could get through three miles of washed-out riverbed and cattle fences was to find the local gaucho and make a donation of beer, cigarettes, and friendship. Miguel Solis led them to the river by horseback and showed them one of the fishing spots that's become a staple in their Río Pico itinerary.

Cell phone and Internet service were as far away as the moon when Rance and Travis started. They would get back from a day of scouting water and head across from the police station to Donkey's bar. They'd start drinking and buying drinks and meeting the locals drifting in for a free beer.

Rance and Travis are from Montana ranch towns. They started driving to Butte to get into fights in middle school and spend an evening drinking with weathered cattlemen. They knew the scene, if not the people and the language. They could take part in a mundane conversation about the weather or just sit and be quiet, both necessary skills in a ranch town. With the help of the barman, Donkey, and an ever-growing bar tab, they managed to meet and befriend most of the valley residents, gaining access to the Río Pico in the process.

Rance and Travis rounded up just twelve clients during their first season. As part of their itinerary they brought those clients to Río Pico. They took them to meet gauchos like Miguel Solis and fish places visited by only a handful of fly fishermen. Compared with the experience I see at their lodge now, that initial adventure was rustic, but it was a foot in the door. The twelve clients generated just enough revenue for Rance and Travis to hang on for another season. When one of the clients tried to stiff them, Rance wrote a note: "I have your address. It might not be today. It might not be tomorrow. But I'll show up." A check arrived in three days.

The company started to grow after the first year. The second season, fifty clients came down. Their facilities and programs grew, upgrading gear and accommodations every few years. Six years after starting, 160 clients come through the leased lodge. One of the most telling statements of their success is that of the twelve original clients, each has returned—except the guy who tried to stiff them.

As they continue to grow, their guide staff becomes a bigger and more important part of maintaining the customer service level they've worked to achieve. I find one of their most tenured guides at a table in the hotel bar just after breakfast.

Esteban Oszust is the former president of the Esquel area guides' association, a race car driver in the winter, bilingual, and movie-star handsome. He's hunched over a booklet of carbon copy forms. He looks across the table at a white printout and back to the carbon copy forms, where he inks something onto the forms. The booklet is a stack of blank National Park Fishing Licenses. He grew up in the park on the shores of Lago Futalaufquen. His father was likely the park's first fishing guide, long before the Park Service regulated such things. His mother still works for the Park Service; she's supposed to do the license paperwork, but Esteban saves her the effort with the lodge's clients.

Esteban is a classic example of what Rance and Travis are doing right. Esteban is a born and raised local who started guiding when he was ten. When his father took out clients, Esteban loaded the clients' kids in a boat and guided them around the lake for the day. It wasn't long before he too was guiding adults around the rivers and lakes of Los Alerces National Park. He proved for decades that he could guide on his own, but finds working for Rance and Travis to be a better option. They handle the leases, marketing, bookings, equipment, and government bureaucracy. For Esteban, that means he can just guide and go home to his wife and kids. Rance and Travis make it worthwhile for Esteban and about a dozen others like him to work for Patagonia River Guides. It is the best of both worlds for their clients. The clients get to book with the familiarity and comfort of a mostly American company and then fish with exceptional Argentine guides.

The success of the model has not come without problems. That their operation is American and successful draws a bull's-eye on their back from government agencies and competitors alike.

At its most basic level it requires Rance and Travis to play the bureaucratic paperwork game in all its frustrating complexity. While most Argentine operations get away with lackluster documentation of their workers' compensation, taxes, and insurance, Rance and Travis spend much more time than they'd like at government offices getting paperwork in order. Travis recalls getting fingerprinted seven different times in the course of a season. From lost carbon copies to "new" requirements, the black ink on his fingers barely had time to wear off. For Rance, days off are too often spent getting some sort of government stamp of approval, collecting receipts, or revisiting some government bureaucrat who is three weeks delinquent on paperwork Rance needs.

Rance and Travis get it from more than just the bureaucratic side of the Argentine government. Local competitors think that eliminating Patagonia River Guides from the equation will increase their business. While this is likely a false hope as Rance and Travis's business model brings in clients who would otherwise not be in the area, local guides are fixated on the idea. They've tried to create a second guides' association and written letters to the government urging them to change area rules and remove Rance and Travis's ability to guide in Argentina. While not achieving success, their attempts create more hassles to an already-overloaded schedule of running a business, guiding, and trying to enjoy the experience.

As much as some of the local guides despise the presence of the two Americans, most of the local citizens appreciate the changes Rance and Travis have introduced to the guiding industry. On a drive through Río Pico and out into the country with Travis, it's hard to make it to the river, not because he's lost on the maze of dirt roads, but because we are stopped every fifteen minutes by the town butcher, the local mechanic, a gaucho on a horse, a gaucho herding sheep, and just about everyone in general. Rance and Travis have become a part of the fabric of the community in Río Pico, and even though it's been seven years since their hard-charging days and all-night benders to initially build their business, the relationships they have created live on.

The relationships remain strong in part because of the legacy they helped create in Río Pico. Rance and Travis were the first to explain the value of the land and water as a fishing resource. They backed up their words by paying for fishing access historically abused for free. Turning access into a commodity has had the twofold benefit of protecting the resource from human poaching and overfishing, and creating a consciousness about the importance of natural resource conservation. Locals now make decisions with fish as a consideration. Whether it's overgrazing, irrigation uses, or the placement of a new road, they understand that without fish in their waterways, their income decreases, as does the value of their land.

When asked about Rance and Travis's contribution area, locals usually focus on less subtle changes. Town mayor and mechanic Adrian Gaggo met with me in a grease-stained orange jumpsuit after coming out from underneath a fifties-era tractor. He remembers materials donated to the local hospital and soccer uniforms donated to the youth soccer teams. Francisco Solis, a descendant of the original settlers of the valley who wears his jeans tucked into his cowboy boots and the traditional black *boinas,* the beret, of the gaucho, recalls dental equipment brought down from the States and getting so drunk roasting a lamb behind Donkey's bar that he and Rance did a complete clothing swap as a good-faith gesture.

Rance and Travis have also donated material to the local elementary school to build a greenhouse, and then purchased the produce grown in it to use at their lodge. They frequently keep food staples in their trucks to drop off at homes out on the steppe for those who might be either too poor to buy them or just too far from town to make the trip. On the lonely dirt road from Esquel to Río Pico, Travis pulls over to pick up a ragged gaucho he says once walked three days in the dead of winter to reach Río Pico and avoid starvation. The gaucho doesn't want a ride, only a pack of smokes. Travis digs around in the truck for a minute before pulling out a half-crushed pack of Phillip Morris cigarettes and hands them to the man. The toothless gaucho's big smile says it all.

My last night at the lodge I watch the guests arrive back from their day's adventure. They pile out of the Toyota trucks indecisive about whether they want to cling to their guide or find the nearest set of ears to recount their adventure. They are beaming with smiles and tales of fish and missed opportunities. With each truck that arrives back at the lodge, the volume of praise rises. The two company owners are there to take part in the celebration. I have to think that for all the work they have done, and continue to do, this early-evening hum of contented clients is both a form of payment and instills the confidence that they are doing something right.

I think of the myriad hassles that have assaulted me on my Patagonian adventure and try to translate that from one guy and a car to an entire lodge operation. The enormity of the undertaking for these two young guides from Montana is staggering. Turning twelve guests eating out of the back of Donkey's bar into the professional staff chef busy on tonight's three-course meal in seven years seems almost unfathomable. But what I'm most envious of is not their business success, but the relationships they have created along the way. The enormous respect they get from their staff of guides is obvious, as is the gratitude from the entire valley of Río Pico citizens. They've managed to be successful in a tough market—and share that success with the whole community.

Perhaps the most encouraging thought is that the model they use is slowly spreading across Patagonia. They keep pushing the bar higher on everything from the quality of equipment to the treatment and pay of guides. The result will be a higher quality experiences for anglers, but more importantly a lasting industry with benefits to local communities and incentives to maintain their fisheries.

18
A MODERN-DAY THOREAU

---

*I went to the woods because I wished
to live deliberately, to front only
the essential facts of life, and see
if I could not learn what it had to teach,
and not, when I came to die, discover
I had not lived.*

Henry David Thoreau, *Walden*

The deskman at the backpackers' hostel spots my rod tube and subsequently forgets about his duty to check in wary German tourists and answer beeping phones as we embark on a thirty-minute conversation about fly fishing. Behind the counter is Gonzalo, a lanky, good-natured local who's been fishing the area with his father since he was old enough to hold a fly rod. By the time our conversation wraps up, we've discussed about a dozen Patagonian fisheries, and there's a growing line of cranky customers in the hostel trying to acquire their room keys. In addition to us picking each other's brains about these fisheries, he's invited me to head south for the weekend to fish a remote lake in Nahuel Huapi National Park and meet a family friend who lives on the shore of the lake.

I meet Gonzalo at dawn a few days later in front of his white stucco rental. He slips out the door trying not to wake his young wife or their toddler son. We are on the road before the streetlights have gone dim. We head south out of Bariloche, taking a road that avoids the intricate Bavarian architecture of the upscale downtown district and goes through the working-class neighborhoods of small cinder-block houses that sit on tiny, grass-free lots. Farther out we are surrounded by a sea of shanties, dark but for the occasional streetlight. The earliest rays of sun illuminate the pink-orange peaks that tower above the road. High on the ridge, the rock climbers of the renowned Frey valley are waking to tent walls caked with ice. Farther down the ridge, the gondola terminal of the Cerro Catedral ski area rests waiting for the huge cable wheel to start delivering summer hikers to the breathtaking panorama that awaits on top.

An hour and a half later after wrapping around the shores of Lago Mascardi we arrive at Lago Fonck. A chill hangs in the mountain air and the morning fog clings to the deep recesses of the valley. A wisp of smoke drifts from the chimney of the lone cabin. We park where the road peters out into untrammeled grass and make our way to the front door.

We are greeted by a man in his late fifties with broad shoulders, a bushy moustache, and loose gray hair. Carlos's dark brown eyes look out in a perturbed survey before settling on Gonzalo and changing into a warm glow of welcome. He ushers us in the door, pulling Gonzalo up in a great bear hug. I shuffle into the corner near a coatrack hung with fishing hats and fleece jackets. Gonzalo and Carlos chat in rapid Spanish. They speak of Gonzalo's father, Manolo, who is an old friend of Carlos's. Beyond that I am lost in the pace of the conversation.

The small cabin has its own disarming comfort. All outward appearances show the quaint, unassuming abode of country lifestyle; unhurried and focused on life's true and patient plea-sures. The worn wood plank floor gives a hint about the age of the place, and the red hues of the stain used on the paneled walls and the exposed ceiling beam add warmth.

In the living room, separated from the kitchen by an eight-foot-high wall of book shelves, sits a couch, love seat, and armchair, all made of exposed wood frames with rough cowhide coverings. The upper-left corner of the book shelf is made of crisscrossed wooden lattice that houses an ample wine collec-tion. The spaces in the shelf below the wine are overloaded with books. I can see volumes on Argentine history, politics, poetry, international affairs, and fishing, all stacked and stuffed into every available space. The collection of literature feels discor-dant with the simple nature of the cabin, and I can already see there's more to Carlos than his lifestyle as a hermit fisherman.

The only opening in the wall unit holds a collection of plastic tackle boxes. Inside are compartments of huge Lago Fonck flies. After several minutes of taking in the cabin, Gonzalo introduces me to Carlos. Carlos speaks no English. He has a soft-spoken voice and a gentle demeanor, and with Gonzalo working as trans-lator and Carlos making an obvious effort to slow his speech and use simple words, we get along well with our conversation.

Before long Carlos offers, "¿Tomemos mate?" He disap-pears behind the wall unit to the kitchen area, and I hear the whoosh of the burner igniting. He opens a few cupboards in the back room and returns up front to grab from the wall unit one of several coffee-mug-sized gourds. The one he takes is solid silver with a matching straw poking out. There are others on the top sill of the wall unit. One looks like a hollowed-out cow hoof with hair still attached. One is covered in dark brown leather with the top and bottom cased in bright silver and connected like a drum by stands of silver across the middle.

When Carlos emerges from behind the bookshelf, he carries a small platter of cookies in one hand and a large tin ket-tle in the other. When he returns again with the silver mug and straw, I explain that this is my first drinking of maté outside the informal setting of a gaucho campfire. His face lights up, and over the next few hours I learn the art of maté from a man with a passion. Carlos abides by the customs of Argentina's national drink with stringent vigor. I sense in his earnest voice that he feels a profound sense of pride and kinship across generations in the simple tradition of passing the maté gourd among friends.

He starts with a basic lesson on the main ingredient. Yerba maté is a tree grown in the northern reaches of Argentina. The leaves of the tree contain a caffeine-like chemical known as mateine and a host of vitamins and minerals. The leaves of the tree are harvested and dried over smoky fires to seal in their nutrients. The dried leaves of the plant are then ground up and packaged in paper rectangles.

The yerba maté plant is served in a maté, which is the cup-like container that can be seen everywhere in Patagonia. Traditional matés were made of small pumpkins hollowed out and dried. Today they are also made from wood, metal, or even plastic, although most, like those on Carlos's shelf, are still made from pumpkin rinds. The pumpkin shells are covered by leather or silver to make them more durable, but the shell itself is retained to elicit the proper flavor. In addition to the maté, a *bombilla,* or straw, is necessary. The majority are metal with intricate twists and carvings along the shaft. At the base they have a filter mechanism to keep the leaves from getting sucked up the straw.

With the maté and bombilla in hand, the tradition begins. The *serviente,* or server's, duties are all encompassing and the position is one of honor. The first step is to load the yerba into the maté to three-quarters full. Then the *servidor* cups one palm over the top of the maté to form a tight seal over the opening and vigorously shakes it so the fine dust from the maté collects on the server's palm, which he then blows away so it doesn't get sucked up the straw. The next step is to position the bombilla at the bottom and shift the yerba maté leaves back to level.

Water is heated to just below boiling; if the water is too hot it will burn the yerba leaves and not produce the proper flavor. The temperature is so important that instead of coffeemakers, most Argentines have an instant hot water heater with a selectable knob with settings for both boil and maté.

Pouring the near-boiling water into the maté heats the metal straw to the point that is uncomfortable on the lips. Argentines who have been drinking maté their whole lives are accustomed to the heat. Several times I have to nurse my maté down in short, quick sips to avoid burning my lips. The process takes extra time, and on a few occasions I see the annoyed glances of others in the maté circle waiting their turn. Saying thank you when one receives the maté is the sign that you are finished taking maté, so if you say thank you on the first round you will not receive another.

The maté travels the circle in a clockwise direction, and the server will not stop serving until each person has said thank you to indicate they are done. In a long maté session the leaves may lose their flavor, becoming *lavado*, or washed out. To keep going, the kettle may be refilled and the maté reloaded with fresh yerba several times.

Traditional maté is known as *mate amargo*, or bitter maté, for its taste. Those who don't like this bitter flavor often add sugar to the yerba leaves before the water is added to form *mate dulce*, or sweet maté. A great deal of flavored yerba leaves are sold commercially, and in the summer people will make maté with cold fruit juice instead of hot water.

Because I am a new guest, Carlos honors me with the first pull from the maté by passing me the gourd with the straw facing my direction. I take the maté and stifle my desire to say thank you. The maté feels heavy in my hand, but my palm cups its curvature well and the heat radiating through the metal covering has a relaxing effect. The maté water is filled to just below the brim of the gourd. The little rough-cut particles of yerba sit like yard clippings across the surface.

I take my first sip of the sludgy-looking green liquid. Unsure of the proper custom, I take a small sip and look up with questioning eyes. The hot liquid shocks my tongue and it takes a second for the yerba's flavor to circulate on my palate. It's bitter, tea-like, and oddly appealing like sharp cheddar or bitter chocolate. I swish the yerba in my mouth searching for a suitable flavor association. In the end I'm forced to add a new flavor to my palate—maté.

We pass the maté around more than a dozen times. Sitting in the same spot on the leather couch, I don't notice the boost in energy I'm supposed to get from the matiene. If anything I see the value of maté as a social tool. Whether an American male trait or a more idiosyncratic personal flaw, I have always had trouble sitting down to chat. The conversation dribbles off into awkward silence until I find myself searching for plausible exit excuses.

During a maté session, the purpose is maté. Without an emphasis on communication the pressure to force a conversation falls away and an acceptable silence ensues when a person leans back to take a pull from the bombilla and savor the flavor of the yerba.

The tradition itself facilitates communication. In its unhurried way, the slow route of the maté around the group gives conversation time to develop, to stall, and to continue along new tangents with increased vigor. There's no need to reach out with words to the quiet members of the group; the passing of the maté provides them with a silent physical participation.

By the last round of maté, the three of us need a walk across the lawn to the nearest patch of trees. Gonzalo and I say, "Gracias," in turn, and Carlos sets the maté down on the coffee table. I rise to thank Carlos for the instruction and hospitality, and suddenly feel the energy of the maté rush through me. I wobble and drop my hand to the couch's armrest to steady myself. It's like standing up after too much alcohol and feeling the intoxication slam your body in one unsettling wave of drunkenness.

I learn that first afternoon that maté produces a noticeable jump in my energy level. The yerba maté's matiene stimulant is estimated at about five times the strength of coffee. One morning I have a particularly long maté session before heading out to fish. At the river I feel so jittery that I have trouble crawling among the large rocks to get a good casting position. On top of a rock, I wobble so badly I'm afraid I'm moments away from toppling into the river.

>>>>

When the wind starts ripping across the steppe and the fishing borders on ludicrous, it's common to see Argentines retreat to a haven in the lee of the wind and break out their thermoses.

The first time I saw this was fishing the boca of the Corcovado, a short stretch of water south of Río Pico and known as the windiest spot in Patagonia. Because there is nothing but water between you and the mountains, the wind sweeps across the vast, flat surface of Lago Vintter and slams into whatever waits at the opposite side of the lake. The trees all grow with a permanent slant, having given up the battle for vertical growth.

On this day the wind played its normal role in fouling the fishing. I cast my 7-weight with all the strength a person can push through a quarter-inch-diameter piece of graphite. I kept my cast low to the water to cut through the wind, yet each cast shot straight for twenty feet only to be pried upward by the force of the wind driving underneath it like a snowplow. My line rose, twisted, and fell back in limp, loose piles twenty feet away. I counted each cast that made it past my shoulder a victory.

I saw them amble across the open grass plain at the boca while I maintained the last vestiges of patience with my wind-blown casts. They walked shoulder-to-shoulder with hoods over their heads and rods held at their sides. They passed in route to the RV parked off the road. I remember a sensation of pride coming over me at the notion that I, a foreigner, remained at my station while these locals abandoned the effort. With swelled ego, I pushed a cast out to an astonishing twenty-two feet. Take that, wind!

Still cocksure in my superiority, I kept an eye on their progress to see how long these local ninnies might let themselves be bested by Mother Nature. They pulled out folding camp chairs and huddled around a small fire they had built on the lee side of the RV. The angler on the far left in a blue chair was the serviente. A big, gray steel thermos sat at the leg of his chair, and the maté returned each time to his hand.

I saw the one on the outside left of the group most clearly. When the maté reached him, he cupped it in both hands, undoubtedly stealing a bit of heat to thaw his numb fingers. He bent forward to take two long pulls from the bombilla. His motions looked calculated and precise, as if he possessed a scientific method of imbibing as much heat as possible from the small cup. When finished, he passed the maté back to the server with a slow reluctance.

Ninnies, I thought again, and continued with another cast. The boca of the Corcovado narrows down like a great V, funneling the broad expanse of Lago Vintter down into a smallish river that a person can cross with a good cast on a rare calm day. The river constricts into a rapid at the bottom end of the boca stretch, and overhead runs Ruta 40 on a single-lane concrete bridge.

At this point, I evaluated my strategy. For the better part of two hours I'd failed to throw a cast far enough to reach a fish, nor had luck intervened sufficiently to produce one. The waves rolling down the lake crashed into my legs with enough force to make the act of standing on the cobbled bottom of the river hazardous. The endless wetting and drying process of stripping and casting in the cold wind left my hands in a mild state of paralysis. I blew my lungs' small supply of warm air on my pink fingers and looked back toward the RV.

Clustered around their crackling fire the Argentines had their hoods off, legs sprawled out in front of their chairs. Their hands waved in big gestures of animated conversation that led to frequent laughter. Their looks of misery had been replaced by smiles of joy. Seeing this, I was irked. Fishing is supposed to be the fun part.

Later I'd come to embrace the midfishing break as a staple in the Argentine effort to stay warm and wait out the wind on the barren steppe. The centerpiece of those wind-inspired breaks always became a thermos of hot water and a maté passed between sets of cold hands.

>>>>

After the maté session with Gonzalo and Carlos, we set up our tent in a grassy depression below the cabin and agreed to fish the afternoon. From the cabin, a short run of grass falls away to a timbered cutbank that drops sharply to the lake.

The shore is no more than a two-foot spit of gravel before the lake drops off again to an unseen depth. What little shelf might exist under the surface makes a bed for the lush junco plants. The juncos are a cane, similar to cattails, that can grow to the surface from great depths and rise above the surface by three or four feet during normal water levels. The plants themselves are a deep green and grow in a thick cluster in which each plant rises up within a palm's length of its neighbor. These plants are widely scattered throughout the lakes of both Argentina and Chile and make bank fishing impossible. To wade past them a person would need thirty-foot legs; casting over them is little more than an invitation to lose a fly per cast.

On the positive side, fish love juncos. Juncos provide them with protection and dinner, since both aquatic insect life and small fish are drawn to the protective maze of the juncos. Every fish I've hooked on the edge of a junco bed has made its first mad run as deep into the juncos as it possibly can. For the most part, however, I suspect larger fish cruise the outside of the juncos like prison guards waiting to take down whatever little creature comes too close to the outside fence.

For the afternoon fish, Carlos loans us one of his boats. He has three Carolina flat-bottomed skiffs with gas motors he keeps moored at the foot of the hill below the cabin. We take a twelve-foot boat named *Bruma*, with the notion to fish the junco beds in the adjacent bay.

From the boat, the stifling thickness of the forest canopy falls away and the beauty of the Fonck valley shows itself. To the east, a long ridge of slate-gray cliffs run out till the eye can no longer discern the jagged slots that form the range's tight, rocky ravines. To the east, up the lake, the forest rises in a thick green mat with its own cliff-like steepness. Poking from the uniformity of the forest are a few individual coihue trees, 150 feet tall and likely seven feet around at the base. These trees hang off the banks along the lake, stretching their great mass over the water. A good-sized house could fit under their wide arms.

To the northwest the bright white snow and blue glacial ice of Cerro Tronador contrasts with the green and gray of the valley. Rising to 11,453 feet, Cerro Tronador is the highest peak in the southern region of the lakes district. Looking up at the mountain from Lago Fonck, you see the southeast face of the mountain. In spring, when the weather begins to warm, avalanches of ice and snow plummet off this buttress several times a day, filling the valley with the powerful and unsettling sound of explosions.

As the light fades in the western sky, the mountain holds its bright white light, glowing like a beacon in the dusk. Then, at the last light, it burns a deeper and darker shade of pink as the alpenglow of sunset burns brilliant. I break from fishing after every cast to look back over my shoulder at the developing scene. I don't recall what the fish I caught that evening looked like, but the image of the mountain fading hot pink into the darkness is a permanent etching in my memory.

That evening in the cabin we share a bottle of wine with Carlos; the social lubrication helps my Spanish enough that the need for Gonzalo's translations lessens considerably. Carlos starts talking about the different seasons on the lake and tells us that his favorite is summer, when dragonflies dot the surface. He loves the splash of the big fish that have come up from the depths to smash the big, blue dragonflies.

He brings down the top box from the wall unit of his living room. Spreading the inventory across the coffee table, he shows us a dozen different varieties of dragonflies, some baseball sized and tied bright with Krystal Flash and pearl tinsel sides, others tiny emerald-green bead body nymphs. Many of the flies he tied himself, but some are immaculate and intricately tied; these he admits were gifts.

The trout, which average four to six pounds, come from the
bottom with such reckless force that they have no chance
of slowing down for a casual inhalation of the trapped insect.

He holds up a simple foam-bodied pattern and says this works as well as anything so he feels no compulsion to add tedium to the tying process. He then picks up the most ornately tied of the dragonflies: a white pattern with a CDC underwing and a woven ribbing of metallic flash. He turns the work of art in his hand to let the light dance along the ribbing. He smiles and sets the fly back in the box in its own compartment.

I ask what brought a man out to the end of a rough, often impassable road. He lives far from his nearest neighbors, a guard shack of Argentine infantrymen, and enjoys the full-time companionship of only books and the lowing cattle outside.

Carlos grew up in the hustle and bustle of Buenos Aires city life. He lived a middle-class existence that allowed him to attend university, where he earned a degree as a geologist. He specialized in roadwork and bridges, and went to work on the country's innumerable road improvement projects. He spent his adult life in this profession and accomplished the worldwide dream of marrying and having a child.

While working construction projects in Patagonia he met Gonzalo's father, Manolo, in Bariloche. Manolo had already started down the fly-fishing path and provided Carlos his first rudimentary instruction in the sport. In reality the two were learning together. Fly fishing in Argentina was still in its infancy, practiced by only a few elites like Jorge and Bebé. Those trying to learn were limited to their own devices. Equipment was hard to come by. Rods and reels were purchased in Buenos Aires or ordered from abroad. Everything was expensive. Despite these limitations fly fishing took a firm grasp on Carlos. His old spinning tackle still hangs in the rafters of the little cabin, collecting dust and unused for a decade.

Within a few years Carlos left his position as a geologist to pursue the life of a fishing bum. Free from professional obligations and divorced, he fished a great portion of Northern Patagonia before settling down again.

At the end of the rutted-out dirt road Carlos found Lago Fonck and an abandoned cabin. In the lake he found large, eager trout and in the cabin he found the framework of a new life. He made a deal with the Park Service to renovate the cabin and live onsite at the lake. In return for the Park Service letting Carlos live rent-free on their land, he acts as a de facto park ranger, interpretive guide, campground host, and road engineer. He meets his limited financial needs through guiding and renting the three Carolina skiffs.

He arrives at the cabin the first week of November to coincide with the opening of the fishing season. Some years, snow may still cling to the ground in small patches of dense shade. The road at this time of year is nothing more than a track of mud perforated with swampy bogs and sloshy creek crossings. He spends days hiking in supplies from his red, two-wheel drive Fiat sedan. Gasoline and perishables, wine, and kilos of maté make up most of the loads.

Depending on the weather, clients may or may not arrive in early November. With sunshine, a few diehards will drive down from Bariloche and hike in. The first few weeks of the season are some of the best fishing on the lake. The fish are hungry and aggressive from a winter without much food and take flies wantonly. If paying clients come, Carlos will row them to the prime spots on the lake. A few nondescript bays that hold more fish than others, a few secret creek mouths that congregate fish and conceal themselves under heavy brush, Carlos knows them all and doesn't waste time casting into vacant water. He's become a bit of a snob in his own fishing and holds off pulling his rod from the wall until he hears the splash of rising trout.

By late November the sun stays out long enough to provoke the lake's insect life into activity. Sporadic hatches of caddis, blue-winged olives, and midges hover over the lake and start the spring action, but the fish and Carlos are waiting for the dragonflies before getting excited. Most years, December brings the two- and three-inch dragonflies to life and they buzz around the lake zipping in and out of the junco jungles looking for whatever dragonflies look for.

One of the most captivating encounters on the lake is hearing a trout rise to eat a dragonfly. The trout, which average four to six pounds, come from the bottom with such reckless force that they have no chance of slowing down for a casual inhalation of the trapped insect. Their strike carries them past the insect into the air and they crash back down to the lake with a splash that can be heard and seen at great distance.

The echoing splashes entice Carlos to take his rod down from the wall. With the warm rays of spring sunshine on his shoulders, he takes the boat to one of his favorite bays and lets the wind push him along the shore. He casts a big dragon-fly toward the shore; blue is his favorite color. The bank is heavy with downed trees and junco beds that form a thousand different covers. He casts out to the edges of the obstructions and lets the fly sit for a few seconds. If nothing happens Carlos twitches his rod to impart some subtle action to the fly.

The fly vibrates on the water, sending a shock wave pulsating away. The movement looks like the struggle of a dragonfly trapped in the surface film and if the fish had any reservations about taking the fly, those vanish faster than the fly. The water erupts in a loud, splashy rise and the fish sets the hook on its turn back toward home. After the hook set comes a tense battle to keep the fish out of the trees. The fish hit the fly with such force that they often miss and come back a second or third time to corral their prey. Even if they never connect for hookup, the excitement of the rise overshadows the rest of the battle anyway.

With the dragonflies come clients, and Carlos spends most of December, January, and February on the water. The few days he has off from clients he spends with people like Gonzalo and me, who have come to the lake on our own.

Truth be told, Carlos is often besieged with guests. One spring day I sit reading a book under the large coihue tree that grows on the edge of the cutbank across the grass from the cabin. During the three hours I read, I watched a group of National Park rangers come to the cabin and take maté, then tour the grounds with Carlos discussing a proposal to build three tourism cabins at the lake. While Carlos was out on the site inspection, a family arrived and knocked on the door several times before turning with a dejected air toward the lake. Just as the group of rangers left, a guide from Bariloche and his two clients popped into the cabin to get the latest fishing report. Before this group leaves, two more people arrive to hire Carlos as a guide for the evening.

The steady stream of guests and clients makes Lago Fonck much busier than in the dreary days of early November. The stream of visitors during the high season must grow wearisome. The area cleared of forest is less than an acre, making escape to a secluded spot impossible. Everyone at the lake travels the same ground, with Carlos's cabin perched right in the center of it. Still, I've never seen him greet anyone with anything short of warmth.

In the cooler days of fall, visitors are fewer, providing a little relief and a welcomed return to a wilderness feel. In addition to catching up on his reading, Carlos uses the dry roads of early fall to prepare for next season. His visits to Bariloche gain frequency as he stockpiles dry goods for the coming November. With the Fiat sunk low on its shocks, he drives right to the cabin door and unloads the various sundries into waiting cupboards and cabinets.

The leaves in the valley change from yellow to a deep blood red as the calendar changes to April. The water in the lake cools back down after the summer heat, and the fish become more active as the browns and brookies prepare for their spawn. Morning brings fog and sheets of frost on the cold ground. The fishing day begins after the sun has risen and burned off the traces of the approaching winter from the ground. Most days are still short-sleeve weather, but as the month drags on, the chill fall winds find the valley more frequently. With the beautiful fall colors and increased fish activity, Carlos gets a late-season spike in clients. It's the final push into winter when he'll close up the cabin and leave the grounds at Lago Fonck to misplaced cattle and resilient pumas.

Carlos winters in Villa Mascardi, a small collection of homes forty-five minutes south of Bariloche on the shores of the lake from which the town receives its name. To supplement his income he takes geological work on local highway projects. Several area fisheries stay open into May, or he might take a vacation in the north of Argentina to fish for dorado. Just because he lives six months a year on one of Patagonia's most beautiful and productive lakes doesn't mean he has quenched his thirst for fish. No matter what winter brings, November will find him *squish-squashing* through the mud with a heavy backpack and straining shoulders to open the cabin and kick the mice out of their comfortable winter quarters.

>>>>

The following day Gonzalo, Carlos, and I take the skiff to the far end of the lake and work the bays and inlets all afternoon in a slow meander back toward the cabin. We hear the loud splashes of a few fish across the lake, but overall it's a bit early for dragonflies. We work sink-tip lines with simple black Wooly Buggers and bring several nice fish to the boat. But Carlos seems disappointed we don't have more luck on the surface. He wants to share his unique piece of Earth at its full potential.

Around two in the afternoon and for no apparent reason, Carlos tells Gonzalo and me to reel in our lines. He then lowers the motor into the water and fires it up. We skim across the lake with the bow jumping off whitecaps and water spraying over the bow at each bounce. We make a direct line to a bay on the far side. Approaching the bay Carlos makes a slight adjustment to point straight at a single tree hanging off the bank into the water. A hundred feet out from the tree he cuts the motor, gliding us in and coming to stop a long cast from the last branches.

Of the two rods I have rigged, Carlos instructs me to pick up my 6-weight rigged with the large blue dragonfly he gave me from the box in the wall unit. I'd started with the rod in the morning and abandoned it after an hour of unproductivity. With rod in hand Carlos points to a large branch coming out of the trunk just above the water's surface. The branch and the trunk form a V that cuts down into the water. "*Acá,*" he says.

I strip line off my reel into a pile at my feet. I flip the first length of it out and pick up the rod. I get the line in the air five feet at a time until I have a long trail of line unrolling in each direction. With the full length of line in the air, I sight the V in the tree and let go with a forward snap. As the fly comes to the end of the line I stop it short to pull a left-hand hook into the last four feet of line. The cast runs along the main branch before curling into the V.

The fly sits still on the surface. No fish rise. I look back to Carlos. We wait a few more seconds. No rise. Carlos makes a little twitching motion with his right hand. I make the same twitch with my hand. A vibration shivers through my rod to my line. Out at the full length of my line the blue dragonfly rocks back and forth. A little ripple vibrates out in a circle from my fly. Then the scene erupts. My fly disappears behind a wall of white water rushing into the air. A fish bursts through the white water and makes another larger splash going back into the water.

Setting the hook, I feel the fish on the line. The fish turns down into the V of the tree. I pull back hard on my rod and tighten down the drag in one movement. The fish pulls a few slow rotations out of the reel before turning to swim back toward the boat. I thrust the rod high in the air and reel like mad. I catch up with the fish past the danger of the tree. The fish plunges down into the depths of the lake once, twice, and a third time, which takes my line under the boat. I pull up hard, pumping as if pulling a halibut off the bottom of the ocean.

A big, beautiful brookie comes to the surface. I pull the fish alongside the boat, and Carlos scoops it into his long-handled net. I don't know if this particular tree is a sure-fire fish location or if something called to Carlos from across the lake. We fish dry flies without taking another fish that afternoon. There is magic in the air for a few minutes that day. But then, the sixth sense that good guides develop after spending day-in and day-out on a piece of water seems like a heavy dose of magic to those who aren't in tune to nature's subtle rhythms.

19
TEN-POUND TROUT

*Many men go fishing their entire lives
without knowing that
it is not fish they are after.*

paraphrasing Henry David Thoreau

The alarm on my wristwatch blares to life at a quarter to six in the morning. From my bed I can see the pitch black outside the window. The room is cold. It's hard to throw off the wool blanket and walk across the frigid wooden floor to the bathroom. It's fall; nighttime temperatures drop below freezing. There will be a heavy frost on the still-green grass. I think for a moment about throwing my watch across the room and rolling over for another few hours of sleep. The next thought is of the boca.

I'm back in Bariloche, and the big browns are starting to run into the boca of the Limay. I also know that upstairs, Richard Ameijeiras is slipping into his fleece pants and will be waiting for me at the car in another few minutes.

Getting out of bed, my excitement starts to build. The boca is a different place than when I first saw it in the spring. The budding poplars growing through three feet of spring runoff are now shedding their first yellow leaves and are forty feet from the water's edge. Boulders that sat invisible under the strong spring current are now an easy wade in a gentle current. On the horizon the mountains hold the first traces of the coming winter instead of the last traces of the previous one. Then there are the fish, brown trout the size of king salmon that come from Lago Nahuel Huapi to spawn in the river. Looking down from the bridge you can see the dark torpedo shapes between the current riffles.

I meet Richard on the front porch. We are in our waders and boots already, and both have on winter ski hats with headlamps over the top. We waste little time loading our rod cases into the back of the Pathfinder; we know we must be the first to the boca to have the best chance at one of its monsters. It's over an hour before first light—when it becomes legal to fish. It's a twenty-minute drive from Richard's house to the parking spot next to the bridge. No matter how early we rise, we won't know if it's early enough until we get to the parking lot and see if anyone has beaten us.

The uncertainty makes it a tense drive along the lake into the heart of Bariloche. Nearing the Centro Cívico we see a few small groups of teenagers just getting out from an all-night dance party at the discotheque. Most of them are tourists like me. How different our mornings seem.

Richard is at the wheel, accelerating through town and doing forty-five in a thirty miles per hour zone. His anxiety must be as high as mine. In the passenger seat I can't keep my feet still and keep checking the pale green digital clock on the dash. With each minute that ticks by I feel our chances of getting a boca monster slipping away. I also know that it could be four in the morning and I'd still be acting the same way. It's impossible not to feel the excitement of the boca.

Getting away from the center of town, things start to look like it's still the middle of the night: house windows are dark, closed signs hang in business windows. We pass a gas station, and I inadvertently look to the gas gauge to make sure we don't need to pull over and slow down our morning. No trace of morning light shows in the distance as we drive east toward the river. The stars are still shining overhead in their Southern Hemisphere brilliance. The lack of human activity makes it easier to believe we're the only ones making the boca trip this morning.

Nearing the river, Richard slows down to coast over the bridge. When the river comes into view we look in unison upstream to the boca. The porch lights from nearby houses reflect just enough light off the water to outline the large boulders that form the mouth of the river. We look to the small cluster of rocks where the calm lake breaks into a current and forms the river. We stare hard, looking for the tiny white light of a headlamp.

Thirty yards further we pull into the dirt lot of the hundred-year-old steakhouse once visited by Butch Cassidy and the Sundance Kid. We haven't seen another vehicle parked along the river at this point, but we won't start to relax until we're standing on the boulders of the boca, where we'll wade in and try to land our perfect fish.

We grab our rods and reels and head to the boca without bothering to rig up. Richard takes a footpath behind the restaurant assuring me it's alright, he's known the owner for years. Pushing through the brush we come out onto the rounded rock of the riverbank. We get our bearings from the clump of willows ahead and turn toward the boca. Moving fast over the rocky bank, we near the boca where the rocks are bigger and more jagged. We switch on our headlamps and slow down to keep from tripping on the rough terrain. After crawling over a few boulders, we reach the water's edge. All we find are the small waves of the lake splashing on the rocks.

This morning we are the first fishermen at the boca.

Our anxiety relaxes as we sit on the boulders and pull our rods from their tubes. We assemble our rods one section at a time in the dull light from our headlamps. With the four sections snugged together, we sight down the spine of the rod to make sure the eyelets are aligned. There's another forty-five minutes to wait before we can legally fish so we take our time to make sure our rods are just right. Then we dig out our reels and spin them into the nickel fittings at the butt of the rod.

We'd normally inspect the thin, clear leader at the end of the fly line for wear and weak points, but we'd both put fresh leaders on the night before. Richard won't let you fish with him in the fall on the Limay unless you put a new leader on each day—sometimes he makes you put on a fresh one during the day if he thinks your leader has been weakened by a fish or a rock. At five dollars a pop, it gets a little pricey, but if you've spent a couple thousand dollars on a trip to Patagonia you don't want to lose the fish of a lifetime on a five-dollar leader. We string our fresh leaders through the rods until the only thing left is the fly. We each pull out fly boxes and start the ritual of picking a fly.

I know from experience that Richard will pull out a little muddler-type pattern that he tied himself. At the boca he prefers a small fly of about an inch and a half in length. It's much smaller than most fishermen use—I've seen several fishermen at the boca with six- to eight-inch patterns. There are no right answers when choosing a boca fly. The maxim of big flies for big fish led Joe Brooks to use his shaving brush of a fly, but Richard has been catching boca fish for the last thirty years on his small muddler variant. The one he chooses this morning has a dark spun deer-hair head, a light deer-hair body, and a chartreuse wing. It's one of his favorite flies.

I've been saving a pattern in my fly box for this morning. It's an olive-green leech pattern with an orange bead for a head. It's longer than Richard's fly, but not by much. The thing I like most about it is the articulated hook. Instead of the fly being tied right on the shaft of the hook, the hook hangs off the back of the fly by strong nylon. It's a style of fly that's becoming more popular because it allows the hook to rotate once it's inhaled by the fish. In theory this decreases the chances that you'll torque the hook out of the fish's mouth when you're fighting it. Whether or not it makes a difference, it makes me feel good enough about the fly that I pick it out from a few dozen other flies. I also like the olive-and-orange color combo; this time of year the freshwater crayfish are changing into similar colors.

With flies tied to our leaders we are ready to fish. We can now see the faint outline of distant eastern hills. So far, dawn is only a sliver of light drowning out the stars at the edge of the sky. They're still bright overhead, but we can see that morning will arrive shortly. Richard takes a few steps toward me and puts his hand on my shoulder. "Let us go now," he says.

I hold out my hand in a gesture that suggests I'll wait to follow him.

"No, you are my guest. You go first," he says.

The boca of the Limay is a tricky place to wade. Most spots a few feet from shore are too deep to stand in without the water going over your head. There is one area right at the mouth of the river where a few boulders are strung together tight enough to walk across. They are nearly impossible to see during the day, and at this hour you can find them only by using your feet to feel around in front of you. Richard knows what he's looking for and directs me more to my left. My foot bumps a large boulder, and it takes a big step to get my other foot on top of it. Once I do, I go from waist-deep water to mid-shin. I help Richard up on the rock and we keep moving farther out into the edge of the lake.

A few feet below us the force of water being pushed from the lake smashes into a boulder the size of a pickup truck and swirls away in a white rush. The current below us is strong and fast. If we are swept away it will take half a mile or more before we can reach shore. Swimming with waders and jackets on would be a precarious adventure. We are careful with our steps to stay just inside the boundaries of the lake where the current is slow.

After a couple of boulders I set my foot down on what feels like a concrete sidewalk. I inch my foot forward and then take another step and feel sidewalk again. I've reached the *barra*. The barra, as the locals call it, is a rock shelf about three feet wide that makes a semicircle around the mouth of the river. From where we are, it extends about twenty-five feet until it's too deep to wade. On the far side of the river it's nearly fifty yards long. It's so smooth and flat that the first time I found it, I had to ask Richard if it was man-made. Even with the flat surface we walk carefully, knowing the consequences of a missed step.

There's nothing between us and the fish but a few more minutes of darkness as we stand waist deep in the middle of the boca. We look downstream and see another headlamp making its way toward the boca. We see it pause for a moment, looking toward us, then turn back downstream. The angler did not rise early enough for the boca and is forced to settle on the water just upstream from the bridge. Above the bridge is a good spot, but everyone would rather be where we are standing.

Soon we see a solid streak of white light across the eastern sky, and Richard tells me to start casting. I strip a pile of line off the reel and start working my fly out. It's all by feel since it's still too dark to see the small olive-green speck of my fly sailing around above me. I let my first cast go and it flubs out fifteen feet into the lake with a small splash. Almost immediately it gets sucked into the river, and my line goes taut downstream. I can see I need to cast further into the lake and strip faster to keep up with the current. My next cast lands forty-five degrees out into the lake; I strip it in, just keeping up with the current. Richard peeks over my shoulder and tells me to put another cast in the same spot.

My third cast shoots out a little further than the last. I see it splash down and give one long strip. Starting the next strip, I feel the line go taut and shoot my rod into the air to set the hook. In the next instant the line is slack again. I can't strip line in fast enough to recast.

I may have just missed a twenty-pound brown trout.

The next cast lands a little off the mark but I strip away. Two strips in, I feel the strike again. This time my hook set meets the weight of a fish—and the fight is on. The fish tries to make an initial run into the river but I manage to turn him back into the lake. He makes a long run that screams line off the reel as he plunges into the depth of the lake. The current is too strong to land a fish on the barra, so I start working back toward shore. Richard points out the way back and starts to come with me. I wave him off and tell him to take the barra and hook another. Once it gets too light, the fish drop back down into the lake or head into the river for more safety. I want both of us to get a fish this morning.

Working back toward shore I move slowly, feeling for the rocks with my feet again. My stout, 7/8-weight is doubled over as I adjust the tension and angle to keep the fish from making a run back toward the river. I know it's a big fish, but the surface of the water gives no clues just how large.

Getting back to shore I try not to think about breaking the fish off. I can't see the minefield of sharp boulders just under the surface of the dark water, but I'm certain he'll try to make a run for them as he gets close. As I work him in, he makes another run toward the mouth of the river, right toward the big boulder where the current is deep and swift. I get my rod low to the water and pull as hard as I think the OX leader can withstand. I silently thank Richard for his insistence on using a new leader each day.

I get him turned at the last minute and back him into the shallow, calm water of shore. The last ten feet, his whole weight is on the thin strand of leader. I work him around the boulders poking out of the water. These last few feet always seem to take the longest.

Glancing back out to the boca I see that Richard's rod is bent over. He's starting to work back along the barra. We've got a boca double. This is as close to the Argentina of rumor and myth that we will ever achieve.

I back out of the water and try to pull my fish in to shore. Without a netter, I'll have to land him on one of the tight, smooth-rock beaches. Pulling hard, I bring his head out of the water for a second before he pushes back down with a powerful stroke of his tail. The movement brings the whole silvery side of his body to the surface.

He is a monster.

He looks to be three feet long and a foot wide. My heart skips as he turns and tries to run back to the lake. I check the run after a few feet with a hard rod switch to the other side of my body.

I know I have the edge now. He's tired and cornered in the shallow water. His only hope now will be to break the leader on a rock or through a careless move on my part. I settle into a patient give-and-take of inches. I pull the rod to vertical, moving him closer to shore, then take up line to maintain the position.

After a few cycles he panics in the shallow water and darts back out a few feet. We play this game for several minutes, which feel like an hour.

Richard has made it to the edge of the barra and is stopped as he feels around under the water for the sharp step-off to the bottom of the lake. His fish is running deeper into the lake. He's in good position if he can find the foothold under the dark water. His experience helps; he knows the big boulder should be just underneath his foot.

At this point I'm five feet back from the edge of the water with the fish a few feet out into the lake. I work the rod back and forth low to the water, trying to line his head up with the narrow piece of beach. I manage to pull him back toward the boca, getting everything in the right position, and at the last moment I switch my rod to the other side of my body and pull hard while reeling in line. He slides smoothly onto the small, rounded rocks of shore flapping his tail as he comes out of the water. Holding my rod high to keep the tension, I spring forward and grasp just in front of his tail. His tail fills my whole hand as I slide him away from the water. I lose my grip on the wet, slick flesh and he flaps again.

The morning light illuminates the brilliant colors along his flanks that lead to his big, kyped jaw. He looks like a mammoth version of the Montana browns of my youth. Black and red spots etched into the dark brown back taper to golden-yellow sides and a brilliant white body.

It takes a moment for the adrenaline to flush through my body, and the realization of the moment to set in. This is the moment I set off in search of six months prior when I boarded the plane for South America. I kneel at the water's edge with one hand wrapped around the thick tail and the other slipped gently under the fish just behind the jaw. I rock the huge slab of beautiful fish back and forth in the water watching the massive gill plate flutter in and out. It's a strange feeling to finally live a vision that's played through your head too many times to count. The moment has a strong feeling of déjà vu.

In the half-light of morning with the soft waves of the lake lapping at my waders and a leviathan in my hands, I am in the

It's a strange feeling to finally live a vision that's played
through your head too many times to count.

midst of the Patagonia I set out to find, the Patagonia of legend and rumor.

Six months before, lying in an orange tent puking for days, I had realized there was going to be more to this adventure than fish. From Richard, the fishing legend with the doubled-over rod at my side, to the Chilean gauchos and guides and the various companion Americans (from both North and South), the people have given character to the adventure and enjoyment to the pursuit. The faces, campfire stories, and misadventures will forever occupy a bigger place in my memory than the image of any big trout. I guess that even the memory of this morning will have far more to do with the early-morning anticipation of the boca, and sharing such a fish with Richard, than the fish itself.

EPILOGUE

At the beginning, I said Patagonia was a land of too many rivers to fish in a lifetime. After the better part of a year traversing the country with a fly rod in hand I can reiterate that statement with confidence. My list of places to fish in Patagonia is always growing. There's the land of fire, Tierra del Fuego, as close as a person can get to the ice of Antarctica where brown trout have morphed into seagoing creatures of enormous proportion. There's Lago Strobel—Jurassic Lake—with its steelhead-sized rainbows that circle the shores devouring scuds.

Then there are those places still swaddled in secret, like no-man's-land spring creeks or a handful of other hidden valleys stumbled across by accident. There are the thousands upon thousands of miles of empty terrain where the only guides are hope, rumor, and a piss-poor map.

Add to these unknowns the Chimehuín, the boca of the Limay, and the friends who stalk those epic waters. The places fished once, twice, then once more again. Even if I wanted to fish every river in Patagonia, these familiar favorites would draw me back far too often to make much headway. As a fisherman and human, what unknown destination could pull me from the pre-dawn rocks of the fall boca with Richard at my side and a rod strung and ready?

I know I'll never be done chasing rumor in Patagonia, and with luck, that will lead me to more of what rumor has already helped me find—fish, friends, and unforgettable memories.

For my father, Dwight,
who taught me
ten and two in the backyard.
I'll always remember you
at sunset on the boca.

Cameron Chambers first experienced Patagonia while working as a fishing guide on Chile's Futaleufú River. Cameron's articles have appeared in *Fly Fisherman*, *American Angler*, *Traveling Angler*, and other magazines. When he is not fishing in Patagonia, Cameron is a firefighter in Seattle. He has also served as a smokejumper for the US Forest Service.